AF244210

CHANGE YOUR VIBE

How to lifehack your way to social success!

PATRICIA REILLY PANARA

Published by Beef on Weck Press, Lakeland, Florida.

ISBN: 978-0-9726015-9-7

Cover design & interior formatting:
Mark Thomas / Coverness.com

Author photo:
Kim Carpenter/Kimcarpenterportraits.com, Lakeland, Florida

DEDICATION

For My Sweetie
And for Maple, the most social cat I have ever encountered

TABLE OF CONTENTS

PREFACE

If you've come to this book looking for the latest research on social interactions, set the book down very carefully and back slowly away. This is not a book about research. It's a book about RESULTS and how to get them.

I'm not about ground-breaking research. I'm about inertia-dissolving ideas and life-transforming habits. And although I do have a few degrees floating around if I need to cross diplomas with anyone in an argumentative-type fencing match (which I NEVER recommend due to the potential for paper cuts), for this topic I'm a proud graduate of the prestigious University of Trial & Error. Motto: If you haven't made a lot of mistakes in life, you haven't been trying hard enough!

There are some major differences between what I've written and what is generally out there in terms of self-help books on socializing. One is the level to which I take things to the most basic, nitty gritty level. I will break things down so small you'll imagine I'm floating around in your bloodstream or camping out in your brain. (ooh! Weird image. Well I have a lot of stuff like that.) I'm always sprinting through the forest of ideas, crashing through the branches and grabbing at the leaves.

If we're going to talk about socializing, we should be having a ROLLICKING good time. I like to bring the fun to whatever I'm doing. So there's no way I'm going to write a book on socializing and have it be anything other than fun.

I'm incorrigible as an advice giver. So I throw it around freely like someone tossing candy to a bunch of wild-eyed second graders at a school fall festival. (And if you're starting to suspect I've done that you'd be right.)

Picture me writing a Social Advice column for a newspaper. It would be titled, Your Social Sleuth. Maybe it could single-handedly cause people to start enthusiastically buying newspapers again. (Dream big, people!) My second novel was about a young nun who drives a Camaro and gives relationship advice on the radio. So high-concept. Yo, Hollywood! What actress would NOT want that role?

Anyway we're going to have a great time with this. You'll practically be able to see the light in my eyes as I'm writing it. I'm not pontificating from on high at you. Instead we're having this GREAT conversation.

In this book I'm using a casual language and tone. I'm not so much writing AT you as I'm trying to create this interaction, this connection with you. I want you to feel my vibe as I'm doing this. I need that joie de vivre to bust through the page and land on your lap. So I don't apologize for doing it this way. I also like to dust off the occasional vintage word or phrase. Even if I'm the only one who enjoys that or is amused by it.

I'm literally the sort of person that vibrantly-colored staples are made for. They serve no purpose other than to add joy to the process of doing something thankless like stapling papers. I'm trying to add a ridiculous amount of JOY to the mundane task of slogging through everyday life.

We're going to have some fun together! So read the introduction, or you'll miss a few inside jokes. See you over there!

INTRODUCTION

The topic of this book has been tickling the edges of my brain for several years. I wanted to write something where people could say, "Wow, I read that book, and I've made a big change for the better!" Could there be anything more gratifying than causing people to literally live a better life?

Deep down you're filled with personal preferences, fascinating facts, fervently-held hopes, dreams, history, stories, skills, talents, observations, spirituality and so much more. We have a vital goodness that is yearning to get out and connect with the world.

However lack of key social skills sometimes becomes an almost insurmountable barrier to being able to see and appreciate your own goodness and uniqueness. Your gifts to the world can remain largely hidden. And that's a terrible loss, both for you and for others who could be getting so much joy from interacting with you. Developing and learning to deploy your social skills is not only essential to others' perception of you, it's critical to your OWN perception of yourself!

If the world's reaction to you isn't welcoming, curious or appreciative, you end up feeling ignored, neglected, abandoned, unloveable, un-friendable. You lose sight of your own worth, your own dignity, your own absolutely unique status as a person put on this earth for a purpose. You can't see your value clearly. And neither can anyone else.

That's why it's important to work on transforming not who you are, but how you show who you are to the world. That's the key to changing the world's perception of you, along with your own view of yourself.

And whether you're great at socializing, terrible at it, or somewhere in between, I think I've written something that will help you look at things just a bit differently, and in ways that could help almost anyone.

There's nothing like trying to keep a dozen vital social tips in the forefront of your already overtaxed brain. I can only deal with one, maybe TWO thoughts, max, while trying to wink and chew gum. So dozens of tips are great in theory, but useless when your mind is going blank because some important discussion just foundered onto a conversational sandbar and is stuck there talking about the weather.

I'm fascinated with weather and LOVE to talk about it. I have radar apps on my phone that thrill me to no end, and I'll probably share them with you at a party. I like maps too! I fall for "do you wanna see my globe?" every time! We have a globe. It's cool. We even have a beachball globe. A beachglobe.

Okay, you can see how I'm an acquired taste conversationally. But really, I'm happy to talk about YOUR obsessions too! That's what makes the world go 'round, i.e. "makes the globe spin." Also I have this bad habit of bringing up safety topics all the time, so I'll try to rein that in at least somewhat in this book. That will seem ironic when I mention our recent small house fire.

So really, WHY another book on socializing? I bring something new to the table. I cut through the clutter, slalom around the studies and run roughshod over the research. I have a very definite penchant for trying to break things down in ways that are easy to understand, simple to retain and straightforward to implement. In other words, there's no excuse for not being able to get, remember and do the concepts. I vanquish the complications and unveil the essence.

I don't want to give you a bunch of details that will make your brain glaze over. And there's nothing harder than trying to socialize when you're also trying to juggle a lot of concepts in your head. It's almost the antithesis of socializing well. A lot of my approach depends on the ability to operate from a gut feel, from a vibe, instead of a list. Nobody wants to interact with a list.

They want to interact with YOU. The best you. The most approachable you. They don't want you focusing on the firmness of your handshake, the length of your eye contact or the exact right words to say. They want to meet the REAL YOU. And my book is about breaking down barriers to finding the real you, and releasing that in a fun and positive way. It's about dissolving the force field that exists like an invisible obstacle between you and the world.

Any time there's a big task, I have to break it down into smaller, easier-to-manage pieces. I knock them down however small they need to go, from boulder to rock to pebble, to sub-atomic particle, if need be. There's always someplace smaller you can start from.

In spite of the sheer volume of advice available, there are still plenty of people who feel sad, lonely, unable to communicate well, or who have difficulty connecting with people the way they'd like to. And even if you're a great socializer, you can always be better!

As an author you're supposed to be very specific about who your audience is. "Find your niche!" they tell you. So guess what special niche I picked. I like to guess. Don't ever say that to me as a throwaway line, like 'guess who I just saw.' I will want to guess. I will want at least three guesses. I will need you to tell me if I'm getting warmer or colder. I LOVE guessing.

Before I get to that I have to share this brief anecdote about my dad, who passed away in 2019. He was great at socializing. He could've taught me a lot if I had been paying attention. But he was also super direct.

Occasionally he'd get off the phone, and with a very serious face, he'd say, "Guess who DIED."

Like, omg. Really Dad? Nonetheless, I always had to guess. I'm incurable that way. But still, very wary of this delicate situation.

So I'd start off slowly. "I need a few hints. Is this, um…a RELATIVE?"

"No." (Whew! I mean, surely he wouldn't announce an unexpected family death this way. I think. Well I'm not sure. You just never knew with him!)

"Okay, is this someone that it's going to UPSET me when I hear who it is?"

He shakes his head. (Great. I'm a whole lot more relaxed now. The family, friends and neighbors are apparently in protected territory.)

"All right. Someone you know from work?"

He nods. (Terrific! It probably isn't even someone I know. Maybe just a name he has dropped at dinner one time.)

So I name some ancient former colleague. Wrong guess! Instead it's some other random ancient former colleague. Yay! Sorry to be so celebratory on that score, but I was really worried about the relatives, friends and neighbors at the beginning. I feel confident Dad has made the rounds in heaven and knows everyone's stories by now. That's the kind of guy he was.

Anyway, I picked this amazing Specialized Niche: Humans. Yes, everybody! No, it isn't because I'm lazy. It's because whether you're a beginner, or whether you're a complete expert at socializing, there's STILL something you can do better. And I'm sure at a minimum I mention some conversation starters that never would've occurred to you.

I once applied to be Ann Landers. I did this many years ago. Advice columnist Ann Landers (the twin to Dear Abby) was leaving the *Chicago Sun-Times* newspaper. Probably as a publicity stunt, the paper ran a story about how they were looking for Ann Landers' replacement. So I applied.

However I didn't get the gig. I still remember the name of the guy who got the job. (I just looked him up online, only to discover he died in a car accident in 2012!) So whatever goals you've got in life, get going on that! Don't wait until it's too late to make those major improvements and life changes! Sorry for the exclamation points but I just startled myself with that internet search.

So instead of replacing Ann Landers I continued working my job, which was as a public relations professional for a General Motors automotive parts manufacturer in Ohio. (Packard Electric Division of GM.) They made "power and signal distribution systems." Which is basically the wiring that runs your car. My boyfriend at the time was part of an engineering team that invented that doohickey with the buttons that lets you control things from your steering wheel.

I was also the "company photographer" and ran the darkroom back when cameras were manual. We once had former presidential candidate (and founder of Electronic Data Systems Co.) Ross Perot speak at one of our fancy events. So a lot of people asked me to take their picture with Ross Perot. Well guess who doesn't have a picture of herself with Ross Perot? ME. Because I was the company photographer. (Yes that would've been the perfect historical moment in which to invent the 'selfie.' Alas.) But whatever. I'm just amused that the best I can do for name-dropping is a somewhat obscure former presidential candidate.

I have a long history as an advice-giver. I'm the oldest in a family of six siblings, so I just expect to be asked my opinion on things. When my brothers started getting married and buying houses, I was all like, "WHAT? You didn't ask me whether you should pop the question? Or buy that house? Or take that job?" So I had to really get over the fact that they no longer needed my opinion. And they've done fine on their own, I must say! So has my sister.

When I leave this planet I want to be able to say I wrote something that helped a lot of people have more satisfying lives. I want to be "the Thomas Edison of having fun times with people!" To that end I've managed to invent a few social concepts in this book. Hopefully I've gone beyond a bare bulb of an idea, and I've lit up a football stadium-sized arena with floodlights that'll help you see your way to better socializing and connections.

I'm a person who cooks a lot because I thoroughly enjoy eating and I like having a well-fed family. And my mother-in-law (whom I adore) always used to say "If you get one good recipe out of a cookbook, it's worth the price." And she's so right! My mother-in-law is an awesome cook, 100 percent Italian, whose mother came from Italy. She was kind enough to pass down some of her recipes, so I as a non-Italian person of Irish-German-Polish descent, have been blessed to know how to make "the meatballs and sauce." My own mother has some great recipes too.

Well that's what I want to tell you today — how to "make the meatballs and sauce" of socializing. And if I only give you ONE great tip that you can remember, but it changes your life for the better, it's worth the time you took to read my book. I hope to leave you with more great ideas than that though. Let's make this thing a smorgasbord of socializing successes!

The title "Change Your Vibe" is my way of expressing what really needs to be transformed if you want to have more fun and better connections with people socially. What is THE most important thing that people will notice about you being in the same room with them that they may or may not even consciously realize?

It's your Vibe, plain and simple. I'll be talking about that more later in the book.

On my subtitle: "How to Lifehack Your Way To Social Success." The term 'Lifehack' simply means finding ways to get you the results you want. Even if they're weird, unconventional, or you have to trick your brain into thinking something or doing something differently. My brain and I are in this constant war over how we do things.

Now, what do I mean by "Social Success?" I'm going to let you define that for yourself. For one person it may mean feeling comfortable at a party or in a large social setting. For another it may mean being able to interact effectively at work or school. Or connecting better within your family or extended family. Or making a friend. That's a huge improvement over no friends, or a zillion acquaintances who don't really care about you.

So, social success is how you define it for yourself, and what you want it to be. My job is to suggest ways you can get to that place. And it can be an evolving goal. Start small, and work your way up to charismatic world leader who charms everyone in his or her path!

But even if your goal is simply to "look at life differently in a way that makes me happier," that's a great goal to have, and it happens to be one of my specialties.

As to whether my ideas work for you, that will be for you to decide. But it doesn't get any easier than I make it! My goal is to give you super simple ideas that will actually work. And then motivate you to do the things by being your cheerleader on this topic. No studies. No complications. No droning on and on about stuff that won't fit in your brain anyway. Just easy ideas and a fun vibe. Yeah. We're gonna have fun as if you were sitting right next to me.

Hopefully you can Catch My Vibe as I'm writing this. I'm excited. I'm mildly amused. I'm lightly caffeinated. And I'm thrilled that you've decided to join me on this journey to easier socializing and better connections.

Come on in, and let's get started!

LET'S MAKE A CHANGE

Why change? Change is hard. It's so much easier to just keep doing things the way we've always done them. It's called a Comfort Zone for a reason. We're comfortable there. Don't touch the thermostat! Maybe tomorrow. Possibly next week. Or maybe I'll just put it off forever. That's what happens when we "mean to do" something and never get around to it. Life continues on, and The Problem stays the same.

Well I don't care if you're eight or ninety-eight. If you want something to be different, you have to DO something differently. If you're eight, you have your whole life ahead of you to learn to live in a fun and effective way. If you're ninety-eight, should you bother trying? I vote YES! I'm planning to be very chatty and social, even if I'm stuck in a nursing home somewhere. Somebody has to cheer up those dutiful caregivers!

I regard people as special creatures. It's easy to forget that because the GLOBE has seven billion-plus humans. What's so special about that? Well, the odds of you being born are so small as to be almost negligible. Based on human biology, the likelihood of you personally showing up is ridiculously small. Yet, here you are! Yes we take it for granted because by the time you're born you're already crossing that finish line. But it's still highly unlikely that you even exist. So, that suggests to me that you're special, and have a unique reason for being here.

Second, in order for you to have made it far enough that you're reading this book, every single one of your ancestors needed to survive to the point of reproducing. Considering we didn't even have chlorinated water until about a century ago, the odds of all of your ancestors surviving into adulthood are shockingly, impossibly low. And yet, here you are!

You're unique, I'm unique, and we've got special things to do with this life. So, don't waste it! Even if you've sleepwalked through part of your life already, so what? All any of us has is today. So work on doing the best you can with the rest of your life starting now. Tomorrow is theoretical at best, and it's another gift if you manage to wake up in the morning. Don't sit around regretting, agonizing, fuming, or hating. It's bad for your body chemistry, not to mention your skin. And it'll make your brain shrivel in unacceptable ways.

For those who are constitutionally shy, how is it even possible to overcome your tendencies in ways that make you comfortable? Shyness and/or social anxiety can put this barrier between you and other people. The frustrating part is it's completely invisible but YOU can feel it's there. An impenetrable wall that no one knows is there but you. In fact, if there were a REAL wall in front of you, I'll bet you'd have an easier time breaking through the wood, plaster or concrete with a pickaxe than you would being able to penetrate that invisible wall of social anxiety. It's a real problem, but YOU CAN FIX IT.

Other people might not consider themselves shy, or socially anxious at all, but still might not have the ability to make the types of social connections they'd like to have. It seems it should be an easy and natural process, but for some reason it just isn't. So your results aren't terrible, but they aren't great either. They're just "meh." And you end up thinking 'well that's just me, that's how my life is.' It's something that you've accepted about yourself, but YOU DON'T HAVE TO.

Then there are people who have no trouble at all with socializing. It does seem that some people emerge from the womb with their social natures switched to "ON." I have definitely seen gregarious toddlers! Furthermore, there are people who find socializing easy. Which is great, but they can STILL DO BETTER. And there's a lot we can learn from these types of people, too.

I remember my niece Isabelle when she was eight years old. We were vacationing near a lake and there were a bunch of other families there. The next thing we knew Isabelle had waded into the lake with her swimsuit on, and she was busily chatting with these Stranger Families and all their kids. And they welcomed it!

She has always been like that, a gregarious person who has no problem approaching people and fitting right in. She is 'a natural' when it comes to socializing. But there's a lesson to be learned from Isabelle. And it is this: she assumes people will like her! She never goes into an interaction thinking they won't. And she's usually correct, in part because that's her foundational attitude.

In fact, what she actually did was a great metaphor for some awesome socializing technique. She WADED right in and made a SPLASH. She didn't worry about whether she'd be welcome, or if they would like her, or if she was fascinating enough for them. She didn't even worry if she'd be disturbing their Family Thing going on. Instead she splashed her way into the festivities with a big smile on her face and a boatload of friendly attitude.

They. Loved. Her.

How could you not love an attitude like THAT?

She didn't have the disadvantage of knowing there was anything to worry about. She wasn't packing any impressive knowledge, exotic experiences or special acumen. She was only equipped with an interest in others and a happy vibe. (Safety Note: Family members were nearby. We do not let eight-year-olds wander off with strangers.)

When you live a life of positivity, life tends to reward you by fulfilling your expectations. Then when you run into the occasional person who doesn't care for you, it's an anomaly. Like, "Wow, that's weird, but whatever, maybe they're having a bad day."

> *"When you live a life of positivity, life tends to reward you by fulfilling your expectations."*

That's the attitude I take today, myself, although it took me a lot longer to get to that point. Isabelle's Vibe is one of fun, friendly, and with the assumption that people will like her. Sounds super simple! And for her it really is. But what about for the rest of us? Those of us who come out of the womb thinking that life is like a big, scary beachball?

That was me. When I was a toddler I was deathly afraid of beachballs. I only know about it because my mother told me the story of when Aunt Jan came over to pick us up for a beach day, and offered me a shiny, colorful beachball, because what toddler doesn't like a beachball? Well, apparently my reaction was as if I just got offered a Live Action Monster From Under The Bed. I fled in terror, and wouldn't stop screaming until they hid the offending beachball in another room. Maybe if it had been a Beachglobe the story would've been different, but that's water under the swim accessory.

Consider that humanity didn't get to the point of overpopulating the planet by embracing every new thing or person as a "friendly phenomenon." Humans are naturally cautious creatures, and there are a lot of really good reasons for that!

In more primitive times, you certainly didn't want to treat every strange person, tribe, animal, or whatever, as something that couldn't hurt you. Quite the opposite! You had to approach new people and things with extreme caution before putting down your guard. Otherwise you'd end up dead.

However this tendency to be cautious is something that impedes us today when we try to make social connections with people. We're standoffish. We're reserved. We hide who we truly are. We're skeptical. We may be suspicious. And even if we make an effort to appear friendly (Smile! Shake hands! Make small talk!), if our brain is feeling uncertain or fearful, then that will unconsciously be apparent even if we're trying to communicate otherwise.

Thus you end up with the insincere smile, the awkward body language, the unenthusiastic tone of voice. You may not even realize you're doing it, and the other person may not be able to figure out what is "off" either, but they will sense it. They may think you're cold, or standoffish, or uncomfortable, or just plain don't like them. And probably none of that is true! It's just our Evolutionary Brain trying to keep us from being killed. Can you blame us?

That leads into a central concept in terms of being able to connect with people successfully. And there are two sides to this Social Coin that I want to flip for you. One is the assumption that THEY will like you. Yes, I know it isn't as easy as just snapping your fingers and saying, "Okay, people will like me when I meet them!" Especially if you're used to the opposite.

So what's important to know is that this ultimately is where you want to be when you get out there with your Changed Vibe. I have many ways to help you get there. But that's where we're heading. To a point where you will approach every social interaction with the idea that people will like you.

Of course they will! You're a fun, interesting and likeable person, and when they meet you they will soon realize that. I can sense it! You just have to make sure they're meeting your best self. We will get there. I'll show you how.

Trust me when I say that truly believing people will like you will help you create a Vibe where people actually WILL like you. It worked for Isabelle at age eight. It will work for you no matter what your age is. But there's lots more to discuss before we try that out.

Okay, the second side of the coin is getting rid of this whole "awkward stage" of meeting people. You know that whole period where you're not sure if the person likes you, nor are you sure you will like them either. You're stuck in an endless loop of small talk, and you both can't wait to escape to a safer environment. Or the bathroom. Or snacks. Or, heck with it, I'll just pretend I got an important text and stare at my phone! Why are you AT this party, anyway? Oh. Someone made you go. Well, sorry about that. Let's make the best of it!

And for some people Awkward is not a stage. It's just a constant state of not quite being able to connect in a way they would like. How do we overcome any of that? How do we make things comfortable?

Again I'll to refer to my niece Isabelle. How did she make friends in such a quick and effortless fashion? Why was she able to attain an instant comfort level with total strangers? I watched how she did it and made a mental note. And I use the technique to this day. Mostly with good success. Here is the secret: treat the other person like they're already your friend.

Yes! You've known them a long time and are happy to see them! Ridiculous, right? Why would anyone do that? Well, it's to get rid of all that stuff that makes meeting people mildly uncomfortable for most. The hesitations, the standoffishness, the hiding of who you are, the keeping to safe topics.

When you treat people like they're a friend already, it helps both you and them take down their guard. You still have to have certain caution in place. Like, don't go telling them all your inner secrets, turmoils or dreams. That isn't what I mean by treating them as an old friend.

I mean showing them warmth before you feel that way about them. Being open even thought it's technically a risk. Smiling in a genuine and friendly manner before you can have any inkling that it will be reciprocated.

But here's how not to do it. Don't put on a fake smile and "pretend" that they're a friend. Instead tell your brain this IS a friend (even though you just learned their name, and may have to ask it again when you've forgotten it halfway through the conversation), and you ARE happy to spend time with them, and you can't wait to find out what makes them tick.

That's an easy thing for me, because I AM fascinated with what makes people tick. I'm thrilled to hear "their story" and any background they're comfortable sharing with me. I love cool details. And I'm capable of remembering details for DECADES, so be careful what you tell me!

If you want to get to know people this is a great way to make a connection. Hearing their details. Sharing some of yours. Asking good relevant questions. Without getting too personal. You don't want to make people uncomfortable when you're just getting to know them.

When in doubt ask about their pet. That gives people an opportunity to talk with enthusiasm about a topic that won't feel too personal, yet really gives some insight into them. Because a pet is a family member, but it's almost impossible to reveal something too personal about pets. I don't think pets have secrets or confidences that can't be shared.

But you can still learn a lot about a person by how they talk about their pets. And I love hearing about pets anyway. I'm a sucker for a good pet story! We have four cats. One of whom (Maple) is so friendly that I think she thinks she's a dog. She never met a repair person she didn't like. While the other three cats are hiding under the beds until the repair people go away, Maple is up in their face trying to help out with the repair! Maple is the ultimate in a feline social, friendly vibe. And, no surprise, she assumes everyone will like her, and treats EVERYONE like an old friend! See how that works?

Many people are inherently cautious like cats. It's just wired into our vigilant "I want to live at least another day" natures. But to have more success socially we need to act more like dogs. Why are people so attached to dogs? They're friendly! They're happy to see you. They're loyal. They're enthusiastic. They're mankind's best friend.

It's no coincidence that they've attained this status. These qualities come naturally to most dogs. These are the qualities we need to cultivate within ourselves to have the social success that dogs do. Yes. I said it. Dogs are better at socializing than we are. At least when it comes to attitude. So start tapping your Inner Canine!

I'LL HAVE A SLICE OF PIE

What frame of mind do you need to be in for making friends? Well I'm a food-oriented person, so I made up a handy acronym to help us remember this concept. It is PIE: Positivity, Interest in others and Enthusiasm. Let's break that down further.

Positivity. Now, I'm not suggesting life is 100 percent roses. Anyone who's been on the planet for more than two seconds knows that it isn't. Life is constantly throwing big scary beachballs at us! And usually annoying stuff happens at least daily, if not on an hourly basis. So where is this positivity coming from? Well, friendships are supposed to be a relief from the crapola of life. Something to help us weather the storms, and laugh at our troubles. If your friendships don't bring positivity into your life, what in the world is the POINT?

That isn't to say there isn't room for talking about unhappy things. One of the other purposes of friendship is to give us space to feel sad, to give us support for our hardships, to give us a shoulder to cry on when we need it. Friendships do all that and more, too. BUT. A friendship shouldn't be focused primarily on the negative. That brings both people down. So although we may need the opportunity to sing the blues, we also need to focus on what's good in life and whistle a happy tune while we're doing it.

We may also go through a "season" where dealing with some awful is unavoidable. Friends will help you deal with that too. Because good friends are in it for the long haul, and they recognize that if you're going through a bad stretch, well, everyone has their turn, and eventually we come up for air and the sunshine breaks brightly again.

But if you're starting a friendship, it's certainly recommended to begin it with positivity. And vital to bring that to your long-standing friendships too. Because negativity can creep in almost without us noticing it, whereas positivity is something you have to work at. And it's worth the effort.

There was this woman I knew many years ago. She was well known as a complainer. Note: I am not against complaining in general. I actually do this to blow off steam. The difference is I try to make my complaints creative and entertaining. They make me laugh at life. Like the time I did a printer firmware update "just because."

We all know the rule of computer-related things. If it ain't broke, don't fix it! I was distracted and agreed to a firmware update because I wasn't in my right mind. Probably was on a sugar high or something when I clicked on it.

Well the next thing you know, my normally reliable printer wasn't recognizing any of my off-brand printer inks! And I was scheduled to print out several homemade birthday cards the next day. What a rookie mistake! So I said nasty things about the printer manufacturer. Each insult more creative than the next. I described ways in which I would destroy the printer on my lawn in a spectacular conflagration if I couldn't figure out a way to "undo the firmware update."

My teenaged son came into the room to marvel at my frustration. "You realize this is your own fault," he said.

"I KNOW," I hissed through gritted teeth as I poked ineffectually at various obnoxiously blinking printer display buttons. "Don't you think I know that?"

He rolled his eyes. "Well you can't do anything about it. Why don't you just buy the more expensive ink?"

Buy the more expensive ink? HA! Who does he think I am? A hedge fund?

I glared at him. "I need you to help me insult the printer manufacturer," I said pointedly. "That's the kind of support I need right now."

"What good is that going to do?"

"It keeps my blood pressure low, and when I'm done maybe I can figure out a way to get this stupid machine to accept the off-brand inks."

He shook his head. He knows I have my rituals.

I consider that sort of complaining to be therapeutic. And I DID get the printer to accept my off-brand inks. Eventually. After a lot of internet searching, rooting around in the plasticky innards of the machine, and use of a kitchen tool that probably invalidated the printer's warranty. But I was only successful because I kept searching for solutions instead of immediately burning the machine in the front yard and melting it into a plastic lawn ornament like I wanted to.

Anyway, back to this woman I knew from years ago. The difference between me and her is that I look for the good in life. So an incident like the Unfortunate Firmware Update is an aberration, and I treat it as such. Even when I'm frustrated I see the humor in life's annoyances. It helps to have an outlook of general positivity while expecting setbacks. Then when they happen it's like, oh yeah, I ordered blue, and got PLAID. Life is always trying to wipe that smile right off your face. Don't let it!

" Life is always trying to wipe that smile

right off your face. Don't let it! "

Apparently this woman came from a Family of Complainers. (It was actually explained to me this way. "Yeah, she complains a lot, but her whole family is like that.") They were of the Constantly Complaining Subspecies of Human Beings. So, maybe it was genetic. Possibly it was a really bad ingrained family habit. Or even a point of pride. "Nobody complains better than we do! We're the BEST at being unhappy!" They probably have a book in them entitled: "The Power of Negative Thinking: You stink, and eventually we'll all be dead anyway." Great title!

She was a friend of someone I knew, and we all ended up golfing together. A couple of us were beginners. Nobody in our female foursome would rise to the level of being "good" at golf. We were there for the sunshine and the conversation. There were cows grazing in a pasture next to the course. Sometimes my ball would fly into the cow pasture. Once one of my drives HIT A COW. It sort of looked up as if a super large fly had landed on it.

I was (and am) a terrible golfer. But that didn't bother me that day. I was having fun! At least until Complainer Gal got her Complaint Engine revved up. Turns out, we weren't having fun at all. Everything was terrible! It took too long to get our rented equipment. The clubs we were given were inferior. (Who knew!) The cashier wasn't helpful. It was too sunny and she had forgotten her sunglasses. (It was sunny! Up north! And I wasn't freezing my butt off!)

But that wasn't the worst part. As we hacked our way around the course, losing balls, raining divots and scaring the cows, a group of guys was behind us, was gaining on us, was finally waiting for us to finish the next hole, and eventually one of them politely asked if it would be okay if they "played through." (Hallelujah! We were just out there to socialize, gaze at cows and maybe get a little sun. Of course you can play through!)

But oh no. Complainer Gal had a lot of sharp words for them. They tried to placate her. She argued back. They pressed their case. She escalated the invective at them. The other three of us finally intervened and said please, by all means, play through. Some of us are just beginners after all.

Complainer Gal was smoldering. She complained about us "giving in." She complained about them "rudely asking." She complained about how we were going to have to "wait," while they "took advantage" and got ahead. We were all going to get extra sunburned. Etc.

What form of torture is this, that someone has such an exquisitely honed sense of injustice that they are just looking to be offended by life, and get satisfaction out of complaining to the point where everyone around her might think that cows are better company than she is?

Negativity as a way of life affects not only the person wallowing in it, but also the people around them. And the habit may be so ingrained they may not even realize it.

POSITIVITY

Positivity is a key to getting through life. It's also a key to healthy relationships. So it's one of the first things I look for in a solid friendship. Does the person have a sense of positivity? Even if they are experiencing a situation that is negative, can they find a way to bring positivity in terms of dealing with it, coping with it, transforming it, or even just accepting it without being 100 percent stuck in gloom?

Because the default position of life is troubles, challenges, annoyances and unpleasant surprises. Not to mention rips, tears, short circuits, shrinkage, stains, spills, trips, falls, sprains, strains, leaks, fender benders, things breaking down just past the warranty date and the occasional completely bombed test. Plus stuff much more serious than all of that. It takes a positive person to make life worth living in spite of the troubles life regularly throws at us.

INTEREST IN OTHERS

It's tough to make friends if you don't take interest in other people. I think that's one of the best parts of friendship, getting to know someone who's different from you and finding out how they came to be who they are. I think it's neat when friends have strengths, talents and skills that I don't. It's cool to watch them excel in things I could never consider even being halfway good at. They can advise me on things I'm really bad at, too! And inspire me to be a better person.

Every individual is unique, and they all have a fascinating background story that you might get to hear if you're patient enough and ask the right questions. You don't ask for deep background when you're first meeting someone, but eventually you'll get to trade bits of personal information that will help you know and understand each other. This extra knowledge will help you care about the person too, which is essentially what friendship is all about.

ENTHUSIASM

Enthusiasm. When I look at the PIE-Chart, this is the slice that is often the smallest, or it may be missing entirely. Then you are left with just PI, which is a math concept instead of a sweet treat and way to have fun playing with others!

Enthusiasm is more of a rare quality in people. Why is that? One is the thing I mentioned earlier. We humans are cautious by nature. We're enthusiastic as kids, and then we train ourselves to hide or suppress it. Enthusiasm means "putting yourself out there" where you can be rejected. Nobody wants that!

Enthusiasm also requires a certain confidence. Ah, back to early childhood days when we didn't have a care in the world and were confident about everything. Including that we could run down a hill and not end up in a tangled heap of limbs and bruises at the bottom. I can almost feel the scraped knees now!

Enthusiasm is energy. It's motion, it's action, it's life itself!

But anyone can feel a lack of enthusiasm for any number of reasons. Let's be honest, a lot of life's challenges work against a feeling of enthusiasm. It's something you have to fight daily to conjure up.

Enthusiasm can be a thing that needs to be actively watered and cultivated. It needs the right nurturing in order to come out. Now it's as natural as breathing to me, but there definitely have been times in my life where I've had to work a lot harder to maintain my sense of enthusiasm. The early childhood years raising my kids definitely left me feeling energy-depleted on many days! In an overall sense it was a less energetic period of life for me as each day was more oriented toward "surviving it" with everyone being fed, safe, happy and clothed. (I had at least one toddler who was famous for triumphantly shedding his clothes and pull-ups all over the house. It was a constant battle against nudity!) And don't get me wrong, I loved my kids' younger years and everything associated with raising them. It's just one example of life's challenges that can constrain your sense of energy. But it's still worth trying to overcome that.

Enthusiasm creates joy, and the joy creates enthusiasm. Like an endless motion machine, maybe. But a sense of enthusiasm is definitely something you'll want to have in order to be able to socialize well. And I'd also argue it isn't something you should just wait to hopefully feel. There are ways to make that feeling happen.

Where do you get the confidence to express enthusiasm? I guess I'd flip it the other way around. Begin expressing enthusiasm, and your confidence will grow.

So taken together, Positivity, Interest in others and Enthusiasm, you will have a fertile soil for friendship. That isn't all it takes, of course, but it's a very viable starting point.

This chapter is meant as an introduction to the concept of "Changing Your Vibe," what it means, what it might look like and why you'd want to do that. In the succeeding chapters we'll take a look at how you can get there, broken down in a very nitty gritty way. But before we move on to the next chapter I will do some Q&A. Because I've accumulated a lot of questions that people have asked over the years. I figure if one person is asking, plenty of other people have the same question. So here we go!

*

Question: I'm a very quiet person. I like talking to people, I'm just not great at it. I love social situations, but never know how to act once I'm there. I feel like people don't like me and I can't have a great connection with them, even though I want that. I think even my own friends consider me boring. I have no idea how to try to be interesting. Can I fix this?

Answer: There's no requirement to be interesting. Being dull, boring, regular, normal, nothing special – whatever you want to call it – is pretty much a default option for a lot of people. Life is tough and challenging, sometimes monotonous and just plain hard. So the idea of being "interesting" on top of everything else can sometimes feel like too much. And there's nothing wrong with that.

It definitely sounds like you want something different – friends who value you, and a social life you enjoy. So it's worth making the effort to try something new. (The whole Einstein adage: Don't expect different results if you keep doing the same thing.) Make sure this is something YOU want to change, not because "the world" expects you to have friends and a social life. Because that isn't enough motivation.

So here's a question back at you. (Yes I realize you'll have to answer it in your head, but still, go ahead and answer it!) What sort of person do YOU find interesting? What are the topics that you're eager to hear about? What is it about that person's delivery that makes the discussion fun and interesting instead of dull, boring or a dead end?

Being boring is fairly easy. No work required! Remain silent, stare at your phone, or hit a few obvious overused topics. Another sure path to boredom: too much information on a topic that other people aren't informed about. Sometimes people get too deep into a topic and people end up glazing over or tuning out.

So consider your audience. If you're going to talk about your job, for example, pick the aspects to it that people would find most interesting to hear. If you're going to mention your college classes, don't just say what you're taking, mention what you really enjoy, or what you hope to do with it. Or mention something unusual you learned in a class, or share a funny story about something that happened to you on campus. Every campus has its idiosyncrasies and crazy well known characters.

If you're talking to someone at school, mention anything going on out of the ordinary. Be on the lookout for that squirrel that almost caused the Unfortunate Incident, or the person wearing the Weird Thing worth talking about, or the bit of news that might help out a fellow student. Do you have any inside info that would be okay to share that would be interesting to others?

One of my brothers is a Chicago firefighter. He tells great dead body stories. And rescue stories. And safety stories. And weird drama you never knew firefighters dealt with. Pretty much ALL of his stories are interesting. Even his stories about cooking in the firehouse kitchen come with terrific culinary tips!

So, know your audience. Try to stick to the interesting aspects. Also anything funny that happens. Whenever something ridiculous happens in your life, that's a great opportunity to share a bit of humor. Slice of life frustration is generally easy on other people's ears. They don't have to deal with the irritation, but they get to enjoy hearing how you dealt with it.

Put yourself in your listener's shoes before you go on and on about meaningless details. Don't get lost in exact numbers, statistics, how many days or hours something took. Nobody cares about that! Visuals work well for any story. Sights, sounds, emotions. Whatever brings the scene to life.

Being interesting does sometimes require a little more work/initiative. It would be helpful to read up on current events, popular culture, possibly sports. But you don't need to be an encyclopedia on any topic. I would just skim popular current topics for general awareness.

A good conversation also requires energy. On a scale of Icy to Incandescent, what level of energy do you normally bring? Interesting people usually speak with enthusiasm, or at least a certain amount of animation. They vary their tone.

The closer you sound to robotic, the harder it will be for people to listen to you. The voice is a musical instrument. Take advantage of its range. Find someone who you think is interesting, and listen to the way they speak. The highs, the lows, the emphasis. The level of enthusiasm. Notice what they are bringing, and compare that to how you usually speak. There may be a significant difference in animation level.

Someone speaking with enthusiasm will smile. They engage people with their body language and their attitude. If you're not used to doing this, it might sound like a lot of work. But as you try it out and get better at it, you'll find it will become easier and easier, until it eventually becomes second nature.

"On a scale of Icy to Incandescent, what level of energy do you normally bring?"

I'm going to make more than one trip into the Star Wars universe, but think about the non-human droid C-3P0. He's literally a robot. (With a charming British accent, no less). His speech pattern and personality are anything but robotic! In fact, he conveys plenty of emotion with his tone. I'd argue that's one of the reasons he's a beloved character in that series.

So if your voice tends toward the monotonous, take some inspiration from one of Star Wars' famous droids!

Question: I'm nervous in conversations because I'm not unique. If you asked what makes me stand out, I have no answer. It's like I have zero personality. How do you get an interesting personality if you don't already have one?

Answer: There are two aspects to this. One is the effort to discover new interests, try new activities and develop new passions. That's worth doing for YOURSELF, not because others will find it interesting. So try out new things, read widely, get out of your comfort zone. Join other people in their adventures to see what sizzles your bacon. You can literally take classes online on almost any topic. I'd start exploring that. So yes, become more interesting, but the main goal should be to be more interesting to yourself more so than to anyone else.

The second aspect is what gives you "zero personality." Without knowing you I'm just going to venture a guess that your energy level is stuck on zero. Because the Real You is in there just waiting to be discovered and lit up. Everyone has a story. Everyone has stuff they care about that matters to them. Everyone has opinions.

Think of your inner self as a venue of some sort, you pick which one. A nightclub. A sports stadium. A museum. A library. A coffee shop. A comedy club. A restaurant. Now think of those places as being empty and dark. Pretty dull, right? Zero personality. Now picture the same places lit up, with workers bustling around, a crowd starting to filter in with happy conversation. Totally different place, right?

Well snap on the lights! Don't keep your inner, interesting self hidden in the dark. Light = Life = Passion = Enthusiasm. C'mon get happy! Welcome to my place.

Anyone would be delighted to join you, but you need an excitement about THEM, and an eagerness to share your inner self with others. Most people who think they have bland personalities are just suffering a serious lack of social energy. I address this concept more fully later in this book.

One of the reasons for that is not that they're incapable of having that energy, but from a young age we're used to suppressing the exuberant parts of ourselves in the interest of fitting in, not rocking the boat and going along to get along. It becomes this incredibly ingrained habit. You almost can't picture yourself operating with less caution and more gusto.

So start a little bit at a time. I'm not suggesting you go from zero to 100 overnight. (And if you're at 100 you probably need to hit the dimmer switch.) Bump up your energy level 10-20 percent and see what effect that has on your outlook and attitude. If you're afraid to do that with people, initially, then start with your dog or cat. They are GREAT audiences when you want to try out a new way of being!

Question: I feel like I don't click with people. No one wants be my friend because I have no great hobbies or cool experiences. I'm just boring. Whenever I'm with new people I want to connect, but I can't because I feel incredibly pathetic. How do I make friends when I don't have much to share?

Answer: I'm starting to sense a trend here. There are no dull people! Just less interesting ways of expressing what's fascinating about you. And you can always fix that!

When I look for friends I'm not looking for people with "interesting hobbies" or "fascinating careers." Those are peripheral topics at best, and I don't care if the person is a Safari Expert, a Professional Sky-Diver or a Coral Reef Reclaimer. What makes someone 'interesting' is their ability to ask good questions, follow up on the answers, and to comment in an engaging manner. And their ability to share the things about themselves that people can relate to, or laugh about, or connect with.

If you don't have anything inherently fascinating to contribute, then offer the little things in life that happen every day. I can count on our cats to do at least one thing daily worth reporting to others. Something funny, alarming or ridiculous. Daily traffic and weather usually has something worth commenting on. Life is funny, fascinating, frustrating and full of surprises. NOTICE what's going on around you!

> ## *"Life is funny, fascinating, frustrating and full of surprises. NOTICE what's going on around you!"*

But people are usually more than willing to share what's going on with them as long as you're truly interested in the answers. So approach new conversations with the idea that you're going to find out interesting things about people, rather than feeling compelled to share things you think you don't have. If you look for the humor around you, even small things in life become worth sharing.

Question: I'd like to bring a better energy level to my social life, but I don't know how. There's nothing that I'm enthusiastic about.

Answer: There are a lot of ways to raise your energy level. I try to put myself in a good mood before I see people. That seems like a better habit than counting on other people to adjust my mood for me when I get there.

Here are some ways I put myself in a good mood:

1) Put on tunes I like and play 'em loud. I will also sing lead vocals using a wooden spoon or a hairbrush as a microphone. Dancing is optional, but

it does get your blood moving! 2) Try to remember everything good that happened to me that day or that week. 3) Wear a new clothing item or an old favorite. 4) Watch a funny online video. (This can also double as a conversation starter if the video is cute enough) 5) Notice all the parts of my body that don't hurt in any way. As silly as this sounds, it can be very helpful to think of a time of pain or sickness and compare that to how great I'm feeling in the moment. It's an Automatic Gratitude Thing. 6) Think of a fun friend or relative and how they bring a smile to my face. 7) Remember nice things people have said to me. 8) Picture bringing a smile to people's faces when I bring my enthusiasm to them. 9) Think about a goal I achieved and imagine myself going after an even better one. 10) SMILE to myself. 11) Play with a pet. 12) Remember I'm better off than many people in the world who don't have running water, trash pickup, internet service...so many things we take for granted. (GRATITUDE making another appearance. No coincidence!) This list isn't even all-inclusive.

I don't wait to feel naturally enthusiastic. I create it, then I bring it. You know how people can get trapped in a 'downward spiral' of depression, negativism and failure? Well you can also create your own 'upward trajectory.' You start bringing "a little more energy" than you're used to traveling with. You discover this magically helps you to have a better time than you thought you would. You keep at it. Then it feeds on itself and compounds. Suddenly you're bringing a Fun Vibe everywhere you go. It may not happen overnight, but it WILL happen.

It'll happen because you changed what you're doing, and created a positive habit. Many people operate at a 'steady state' that's not particularly excited about life. If you try to bring an energy level a bit above that you'd be surprised to see how much that shows!

Question: I'm quiet and don't contribute much. My sense of humor is hit and miss, so I gave up on being funny. When I'm with a group people will make plans without me. It's like I'm not interesting enough for them. I have a hard time making friends. What can I do?

Answer: I'll be talking about group dynamics later in the book. It's difficult to be friends with "a group" without having individual friends inside that group. Instead of being a valued group member, you become a part of the scenery that gets forgotten. I guess there's a theme with this set of questions, and I keep bringing it back to the two "E"s, Energy and Enthusiasm.

Life is not a movie where you buy a ticket, get your popcorn, and settle quietly into your seat to 'watch the show.' It's a participation sport. It's like a stage play where YOU are one of the actors! Yes your name is in the playbill, you've got a character and a role to play. Even if you don't have the biggest role, you still have a speaking part. And about that pesky script. Guess what, you can rewrite it to make your part bigger. Yep. The play that is your social life hasn't been copyrighted yet, so no one can stop you from giving yourself a few more juicy lines. Wow, the wonders of life!

> *"Life is not a movie where you buy a ticket, get your popcorn and settle quietly into your seat to 'watch the show.'"*

So, what does Enthusiasm look like? Again, when I talk about this I have to emphasize that 'a little goes a long way.' No one is expecting you to be an entertainer, or do stand-up comedy, or give a speech, or have so much energy that people are contemplating a Caffeine Intervention.

Enthusiasm looks like this: 1) Good eye contact. Not 100 percent, but more often than not. It shows people you're interested and paying attention. Also the eyes are the window to the soul, if you're interested in connecting with people's souls, which I ultimately am. 2) A nice AUTHENTIC smile. This means using your eyes, not just your mouth. You can use the internet to search the difference between a real and a fake smile if you can't picture it. Look at the difference in your own mirror to see what I mean. 3) Dynamic tone of voice. You don't need to be saying anything particularly fascinating, but you have to have an interesting and interested attitude in your tone of voice. Whether you are asking questions or making comments. When you do this you raise the energy level of the group.

The idea is to communicate positive emotion. And emotions are contagious. It isn't what you know or do that makes you interesting. It's your attitude toward other people that matters. And when it comes to humor not everyone is great at telling jokes. Although some people do have awesome humorous stories, that tends to be more rare. Most of the humor I hear in everyday conversation just comes from what people observe, and their willingness to be entertained by that.

Like the time I almost got hit by a runaway kayak in traffic. After my life flashed before my eyes and I survived the incident, I was able to view it as funny. (It was at least mildly funny WHILE it was happening, too, although I also saw our insurance rates flash before my eyes.) Particularly because my car was still intact. Turns out, kayaks bounce weirdly like footballs! Who knew? Always secure your kayak before taking to the road with it.

Then there was this time I was following a truck carrying five loosely secured mattresses that were flapping madly in the lane in front of me like yammering lips! I pictured them wailing, "Help, we're being kidnapped by someone in a pickup truck who obviously has no respect for bedding!"

So humor doesn't need to be a big story; a small observation is just as good. I consider myself to have an excellent sense of humor not because I'm terribly funny or have any jokes at my disposal. In fact, I'm not even close to being the funniest person in my extended family. Instead I consider my sense of humor to be excellent because life makes me laugh, and other people tell me things that are funny too, and I laugh easily at these things. So I'm more amused than amusing, and that works just as well when it comes to humor.

Whew! I answered a lot of questions about enthusiasm, energy and being interesting. The topic is important. And even though I've numbered things up there, I don't expect you to memorize it or try to focus on a bunch of concepts simultaneously while you're making eye contact with someone. The ideas are there for you to think about and try to work into your life in small ways until they become habits.

I also understand that we're still in the big picture here. This isn't a transformation that happens overnight just by changing your mindset (although your mindset IS something that needs to change). You'll need to practice specific things to get comfortable talking to people and being in groups, and I will show you some easy-to-implement ways to practice the skills you need.

Onward in our Upward Trajectory!

CHAPTER 1: TAKEAWAYS

1. *Serve a slice of PIE:*
   Positivity (bring joy to your social interactions, while minimizing negativity)
   Interest in others (Take a genuine interest in others and what they have to say)
   Enthusiasm (Bump up your social energy level 10-20 percent)
2. *Assume people will like you.*
3. *When first meeting people, make an effort to treat them like an 'old friend'*
4. *You don't need an exotic resume to be interesting; you DO need to take a genuine interest in others and find topics that you can connect on.*
5. *Don't go to a social gathering with whatever your default mood is. Create a positive mood and bring that.*
6. *There is a lot of humor in everyday life.*

THE MEATBALLS & SAUCE OF SOCIALIZING

The first chapter was fairly philosophical. I showed you the goal, the transformation that needs to happen. It's about energy, enthusiasm, VIBE. But what about the practical hurdles between Point A and Point V? What if your persona is A for Awkward, and you have no idea how to take the first step toward the goal of V for Vibe?

This is where my focus on knocking big, difficult challenges down into small, manageable pieces comes into play. Here's where we start Life Hacking our way to success.

Before I tell you the next step toward building some confidence with people, let me first tell you about a difficulty I had when I started college. At that point I was quite sure I wanted to be a journalism major. I couldn't even imagine doing a job that didn't have a large writing component to it. Journalism was a natural fit! Or so I thought. Remember this was before I started my transformation from very shy to whatever kind of energetic idiosyncrasies I bring now. I had no problem talking to my family or small circle of friends, or the girls on my dorm hall, but when it came to total strangers I was a mess!

So guess what majoring in journalism involves? Yep. Talking to strangers. All the time. How did I not anticipate THAT little detail? Ugh. So I had a big decision to make at the very beginning of my freshman year at Lehigh University. Was I going to stick with journalism? Or was I going to change my major to something else that didn't involve constantly talking to strangers?

I was determined to remain a journalism major. The key would be to find a way to get through the part where I had to be outgoing and comfortable talking to strangers. The phone was another problem, especially in the pre-cell phone era when texting had not yet been invented.

I had to call these total strangers on the phone to arrange interviews. In addition to a Stranger Antipathy, I also had a full-blown Phone Phobia. I really didn't know how I was going to get through this. At all. Because why would any of these strangers want to talk to me? I would be taking up their time! Asking for a favor they wouldn't want to give. Insisting that they meet with me, another total stranger. Why would they want to do that? They'd probably reject me straight away.

It was impossible to solve. So I made my problem much smaller. I decided I didn't have to 'succeed' in anything at all. The only thing I needed to do was make a single phone call and try to set up an appointment. I HAD to make voice contact. But I didn't even have to successfully make the appointment. I didn't have to impress them with my phone skills. They didn't have to like me. All I had to do is: Make. The. Call. That alone would be the measure of success. That I made the call, no matter what the outcome.

How did I ensure that I made the call? Easy! I promised myself a reward. That reward was dinner. I love food. I am highly motivated by meals and foods of all kinds. So depriving myself of my next meal was the perfect way to get myself to make the dreaded call.

Suddenly, the whole thing became less about the call, and it became more about the approaching dinner hour. Would I be joining my hallmates for the meal? You can imagine how motivating I found that. The heck with my interview subjects and their perceptions of me. I was getting hungry. The call must be made!

So the key was to literally take my mind off the myriad ways the call could go wrong. Yes, those were still out there waiting to happen. But as the dinner hour approached I cared a whole lot less about my interview subject's feelings (and whatever imaginary danger that represented), and a whole lot more about getting to dinner on time. That's what motivated me. And you will have to pick something for yourself that you find highly motivating.

I made the call. And it wasn't nearly as dreadful as I had anticipated in my feverish overactive imagination. It wasn't perfect. But I made a few notes to myself as to what to say and how to start and end the call, and the person on the other end of the phone actually sounded like they'd be happy to talk to me. Who knew that people liked to be interviewed! Not me.

This ordeal had to be repeated at least once a week, sometimes more often if I also had an article to do for the school newspaper, the Brown & White. But instead of promoting weekly bouts of pre-dinner indigestion, what I soon discovered is that the process became easier. Turns out, repetition and familiarity breed both success and a certain comfort level.

By the end of that first semester I was so used to setting up interviews that I didn't need to goad myself into it. I just made the calls. By the second semester I was looking forward to making the calls. I was starting to get good at conducting the interviews too. Because after the first few I learned that they had a particular pattern and rhythm to them. And most people really seemed to enjoy being interviewed.

This story is a perfect illustration of Getting Out of Your Comfort Zone. It would've been easier to simply change majors and find a different way to indulge my love for writing. But I wouldn't have grown as a person if I had done that.

What I didn't know then, but which became increasingly obvious as time went on, is that I became a LOT more comfortable talking to complete strangers. While I thought I was "pretending" to be comfortable talking to strangers, Life had another idea. It actually did make me comfortable talking to strangers. I had started the transformation from an essentially shy person, to someone who can talk to anyone. I didn't think it was possible, but clearly it was.

Do something rarely and it's a persistent problem. Do something daily and it becomes routine.

> ## "Do something rarely and it's a persistent problem. Do something daily and it becomes routine."

Okay, so most of you aren't journalism majors in your freshman year of college. What can you do to gain a comfort level with things like initiating conversations, finding random things to say to people, and projecting the type of tone and body language that people will find welcoming?

*

Let's go to a question.

Question: I want to change how I interact, but when I try, it makes me extremely uncomfortable. It's like people notice, so I retreat back to my usual self. I feel like I'm stuck in a vicious circle.

Answer: It's always awful when socializing feels more like work than like fun! The problem is that you've decided to make a change, and you're working on that while you're AT the social activity that matters to you. Sometimes that's fine if you already have a certain confidence level in how you're presenting yourself. But if you feel you're starting at the beginning, then AT a social event is a terrible place to practice.

It's like saying to yourself, "Hey, I'm going to learn to play baseball. I think I'll start at the World Series!" Even pro baseball players don't learn their craft that way. They have years of practice from the playground to little league to high school sports. It's a gradual process.

No one would be successful walking onto a professional field for the first time and expecting to excel without any practice. And while socializing is a lot easier than learning to hit a 96-mile-per-hour fastball whizzing at your head, you can still benefit from practicing in a situation other than the very one you want to succeed in. My idea on that is something I call "PHASE." Although it's a fun acronym, there's no need to memorize it.

PHASE: PRACTICE HAPPILY APPROACHING STRANGERS ENTHUSIASTICALLY

I'm a simple person looking for simple solutions. I use off-brand printer inks, so clearly I'm going to come up with a fun, effective and FREE way for you to do this. What you need is daily practice working on certain basic social skills that need to become second nature for you. One great way to do this is in your brief everyday interactions that happen normally, and that a lot of people put zero effort into. Because the interactions are extremely low stakes, there's no consequence to doing well or not.

I'm talking about interactions with grocery cashiers, store clerks, coffee baristas, restaurant servers, mail carriers, bank tellers, librarians, bus drivers, gym attendants, dining hall workers, etc. People you have a brief no-stakes conversation with, and then it's over. So the first rule is: NO self-service. The idea is to actually interact. So skip the self-checkout lane. The nice part is you can practice daily, or at least several times a week.

All you have to do is be intentional about what you're trying to accomplish.

And the beauty of it is that you're not risking anything. If your interaction is a complete, embarrassing failure, well, so what? At least you got your groceries! Or your coffee. Or your dry cleaning. Or your library books. Or your deposit slip.

At the outset there are three things and three things only you need to be ready to bring to the interaction: 1) A smile, 2) a friendly (warm!) tone of voice, and 3) at least a modest level of energy. With those three things you can charm the world.

You'll use your brief, relatively anonymous errands to work on your: smile (authentic), greeting (energetic), comments, compliments, humor, etc. See if you can get the person to smile and enjoy the interaction. Note which comments get better reactions than others. Try to find a legitimate compliment you can give the person.

Have a brief remark about *something* to pass as small talk. (e.g. about how busy the store is, what's the weather like outside, does the place seem to be crowded) See which sort of comments go over better than others. You can even work on some mild humor. This is how you can develop a skill for just bantering with people for the fun of it.

A note on the smile, do that WHILE making eye contact with the person. That is the most effective time to light up your smile.

Don't practice everything at the same time, pick one or two things to improve on. As you get better you will notice you can make these things a fun encounter and you can affect the other person's mood! That's the key to doing the same in a real social situation. It will also improve your confidence as you get better at it. And if you have a 'failure' or run into someone who's unresponsive, no big deal! Try again with someone else.

I've been doing this sort of thing for years. It isn't because I need the social skills practice. It keeps me sharp and on my game. It makes these errands more fun for me, and usually for the other person also. Sometimes I'll receive a bonus, such as the occasional extra grocery coupon, a quick recipe or a hot tip. People are happy to help you out if you're having a fun and friendly time with them!

The key is to leave the other person with a smile and a feeling of having enjoyed the brief time you interacted. That's the only goal. And it's a sincere goal on my part. I'm trying to make their day brighter, and by extension, my own. It's the perfect place to obtain some social skills practice. When you think about how often people put ZERO energy into this, it's really a shame people don't get more benefit from it.

The grocery store (or the bank, restaurant, fitness center, cafeteria) is your playground. That's where you'll work on your basic social skills and get some instant feedback with no real social consequences. The feedback is in the form of their reaction to you. Did you get them to smile? Did they make a comment back, or answer a question? Did they seem to be in a good mood?

It's helpful to watch other people, perhaps someone who is ahead of you, to see how they do it. Some people are old pros at this (my father was one!). They can chat up a storm in the grocery aisle. See who is doing it well, and what they're saying. You can get some great ideas for future Bank Banter! Or Cafeteria Convos. Or Dining Hall Dialogue. Or Grocery Gab.

This is all working toward your end goal, which is developing and strengthening the skills you need to be successful in large and small social settings where the stakes are higher. Having confidence is a critical component of that success. There's no excuse not to be practicing this every time you go out for an errand. You can also do it in the drive-through lane at fast food restaurants or the bank.

Suppose the customer service person you're dealing with was in a bad mood. Your brief moment of happy interaction may make their day better, or take their mind off their worries. Having cheerful interactions with people with no goal other than to make them happy is a "pay it forward" exercise. I like to think it can ripple across the grocery store, the city, maybe even the country!

The bonus is your social skills are getting better while you're at it. And, little secret here: trying to make someone else's day better will do the same for yours. Part of my overall philosophy is that of making life better one moment at a time. So it's a win/win situation. And it's free social skills practice with no extra charge!

> *"Trying to make someone else's day better*
>
> *will do the same for yours."*

Persistence and gradual improvement are the keys to success.

Okay, so maybe you're sitting there thinking, "So what do I say in those situations? Help me out with some ideas!"

I will pick literally any little thing to start a conversation. I put emphasis on certain words to give off a friendlier vibe.

"Hi, how ARE you?"

"Hey, how's it GOING?"

"Looks like you saved this lane just for ME." (when I stroll into an empty checkout line)

"GREAT to see you!" (if I recognize them from previous transactions)

"Hi [NAME]," (if I know who they are, or can see their nametag and there aren't any pronunciation issues with the name.)

"Well I shopped too much again. When are you people going to stop me?"

"Has it been busy today?"

"Hey I like your (article of clothing or accessory, if in fact I do like something)"

"The weather's getting a little CRAZY out there." (If it is)

"Any great sales I should know about for next time?"

"Got any plans for later today?" (If I've already established that they're comfortable bantering with me, or they recognize me from prior interactions. Sometimes cashiers or baggers will ask me what I'm cooking based on what I'm buying, so I will use that as a cue that it's okay to be a little more inquisitive than normal)

Obviously the grocery store is my favorite place due to the food obsession, but I'm just as likely to interact with a bank teller, or a restaurant server, or the dry cleaning clerk, or the vegetable stand proprietor. If anything remotely interesting is visible, or is an obvious current event, I may comment on it. I might ask them if they get any breaks on the job. Or how their day is going. Or if their shift just started or is almost over.

But all of those statements are variations on the theme, which is really just the first statement. "How ARE you?"

What is contained in that statement? By itself, nothing. But notice I wrote it with an emphasis. (font body language!) How ARE you? Or it also could be said, "How are YOU?" Either one of those implies you're actually willing to hear an answer. It's just a little bit "extra" from saying it with no special emphasis.

But in order to get the engine of a good social encounter running, you need more than the statement. You need the correct VIBE. You need the feeling in your heart that you're having a joyful moment, and you want the other person to be able to sense that. You're happy to see them, and have a brief chat with them!

Because this is such an important point I'm going highlight it. There is a tremendous amount of energy and friendliness contained in the tone of your voice. Do you know what a friendly tone sounds like?

It sounds happy to be here, pleased to meet you, thrilled to be alive and on the planet. Basically you're trying to reach out and embrace the other person with your voice. It's like the vocal equivalent of a hug. That's why people respond so positively to it, whether over the phone or in person.

I had a sense in my mind of exactly what this tone of voice sounds like. I finally figured out who has it perfected, and who has ALWAYS had it perfected. It's my cousin Lynn McDonnell. (The same is true of her mother, my Aunt Margie.) They're naturals, the both of them, but that tone welcomes everyone in their vicinity.

"You're trying to reach out and embrace the other person with your voice. It's like the vocal equivalent of a hug."

If you feel like you're not sure what a friendly tone of voice sounds like, then you need to pick out a super friendly person in your own life and listen to them for a while. Hear the highs and lows, the pitch and the tone, the energy and brightness. Listen not to what they're saying, but HOW they're saying it. You need to be able to duplicate that when you're trying out this friendly and energetic greeting around town. Your tone should signal that you're ready to engage.

And because you're feeling this way, your statement will be accompanied by a GENUINE SMILE.

SMILE! YOU'VE BEEN BLESSED WITH THIS GREAT TOOL...

I mentioned it earlier, but it cannot be over-emphasized. I could put it at the top of the page as a header with a smiley face as an every page reminder, and it probably wouldn't be overkill. A genuine smile is a great form of communication that smooths over so many rough edges of life and creates good feelings out of thin air. So put the fake, forced smile away, stuff it into the back of the cupboard underneath some truly awful fad kitchen gadgets that you don't have much use for, and practice generating a friendly, sincere smile so you can produce one at will.

It's hard to create that kind of smile without feeling some of the joy I'm talking about, so when you're talking to your Clerk of Choice at your Store of the Day, what you're actually bringing with you is some Real Joy. Sure, I guess I could do Fake Joy, but you know what, I'm not that great of an actress. For me it's just easier to generate the real thing and then spread it around.

What's the point of faking being a happy person when you could just take that extra step and BE a happy person? That's a whole other book that I definitely have in me, but my point is feel the joy, bring the joy, and communicate it with your happy genuine smile. You can internet search this to see what a genuine smile looks like if you're not quite sure. The difference is the involvement of your eyes, they sort of crinkle up because you're actually happy, not just pretending you are, or wishing you were, or resenting that you're not.

It's much easier to socialize, have fun and connect with people if you make an effort to be a happy person. If you follow my methods on this you may find yourself becoming happy against your will. Like you were perfectly okay, maybe even famous for being crabby most of the time. And now that you're having to follow these socializing ideas you're becoming happy in spite of yourself. Take THAT, Golf Gal from a long time ago!

Anyway, to return to that simple opening statement. "How ARE you?" Or, "How are YOU?" said with a bit of emphasis to indicate you'd be happy to hear anything the person had to say. Now you are accompanying it with a genuine smile. And you're making eye contact, or at least attempting to, while you're doing it.

But there's more! See, a simple transaction contains a lot of the things that ANY social situation would. It's just that people will downgrade the whole thing to a "boring transaction," and, guess what. It WILL be a boring transaction if you take that attitude. But you can do so much more with it if you try!

So what have we got: opening statement with slight emphasis. Check. Genuine smile. Check. Eye contact made. Check. What else? You need to bring your energy level up to something a bit more than your default or maintenance level.

You see, life is like a long distance race. We know we have a lot more of it to go (hopefully), so we try to get through the mundane stuff with as little effort as possible. So, default mode is Low Energy. Or, as little as you can put in and still get stuff done. I don't blame anyone. Energy uses up calories. (Oh. Did I really just throw down that gauntlet? Did I just suggest an idea for the Happy To Be On Planet Earth Diet?)

Obviously I'm not asking you to come with a crazy level of energy. It's a store transaction, not a talk show host tryout. Let's be realistic. But still! You need to bring more energy than you normally bring. I'm going to suggest 10-20 percent more, depending. You can experiment with it to see what gets you good results. Extra energy communicates positive emotion: happiness, friendliness, a good mood. It lightens the atmosphere and spreads joy. It elevates people's moods.

Emotions are contagious! (That's why I'm allowing myself the liberal use of exclamation points and all caps in this book.) So you can either spread a positive one or a negative one. It all depends on whether you prefer endorphins or cortisol running around in your bloodstream. I'll let you look those up for yourself just for the fun of it. Homework!

Wow. All you did is walk up to the (grocery checkout, fast food line, teller window, ordering place), and suddenly you find yourself working on four or five essential social nuances! Who knew you could find all that in such an everyday place? I'll stop you right here and say if you aren't used to treating daily transactions as a social tour de force, then pick one or two aspects of what we discussed above and work on just those.

Don't feel like you have to pull this off perfectly at first. So maybe at the beginning you work on just saying something extra, and also making brief eye contact. That's it! Or, try saying "Hi," and popping out that genuine smile. Whatever you feel you want to work on.

Gradually you will want to be able to put it all together and really enjoy having a good time with total strangers. Because once you start getting it right, you WILL get positive feedback from people, and you'll recognize your ability to start connecting with people. Which is the whole point. That's what you want to get good at, so you can gain confidence and carry your newfound skills to your social life. Confidence gained interacting with strangers turns into a tremendous positive feedback loop.

Even if you're a great socializer already, sometimes we get lazy, so there's benefit in reviewing what you're doing, and maybe trying to do it better. Or more consistently. Or being more intentional about making the world around you happier. These ideas are not just for beginners, they're for EVERYBODY. All the humans.

Anyone can turn a perfunctory encounter into a fun, albeit brief social encounter so that we interact as human beings, not as automatons, cogs in the machine, perfunctory people. At its core two things are necessary. One is the expression on your face. That would be a welcoming one with a genuine smile.

The rest of your body language tends to flow with your face, as long as the feeling (Vibe!) behind that is genuine. You don't want to 'pretend' to be open to the other person, you want to BE open to the other person. In your brain. Which starts from your heart. You have to train your heart to be open to people instead of protecting itself. So when I say at its CORE, I truly mean the CORE.

The other thing that is critically important is the tone of your voice. That literally means the difference between "I'd love to talk to you" and "this is a boring automatic encounter, whatever, just get me through."

Note: if you're wanting a boring automatic encounter because that's what kind of mood you're in, or that's what you need that day, or you're in a rush – no problem! Many people do it that way anyway.

There's nothing wrong with just getting your stuff done and getting out of there. Life is all about flexibility and what is needed in the moment. Your tone of voice either invites people to engage or just keeps them at arm's length. Inviting them to engage means your tone is animated, it sounds a little brighter. It is friendly, personal, engaged. People are much more likely to banter with you if you sound happy.

The difference is a tone that literally reaches out and invites a response from the other person, instead of a tone that is much more perfunctory, or static. A low energy tone is a tone that wants to hide, almost. A tone that just does the bare minimum to get the job done.

It's like the difference in saying "hi" when you're depressed or bored, vs Excited To Be Here Because Ain't Life Grand. There's a big difference in terms of reaction depending on which tone you use. It isn't complicated but it IS important!

To reiterate, there are THREE things that are critically necessary for creating a connection with a total stranger: a genuine smile, an energetic demeanor and a welcoming tone of voice. Once you learn to do that with strangers on a regular basis, it will become a lot easier to do the same with acquaintances or people you'd like to get to know better.

> *"There are THREE things that are critically important to creating a connection with a total stranger: a genuine smile, an energetic demeanor and a welcoming tone of voice."*

Above I've outlined details of what you need to do in order to start practicing those basic social skills (whether you need that practice or not!), and to start bringing that Vibe I'd like you to have. But it's really important to explain what I'm actually having you create. It's something I call a Circle Of Warmth.

When you approach someone with a genuine smile, a welcoming attitude and an engaging tone of voice that reaches out to them, you're creating this incredibly positive Social Space that invites people in to interact with you. The warmer this circle is, the more it melts any Social Barrier that is up. There's always a certain amount of invisible barrier that exists between two people who are strangers, or who don't know each other very well.

Once you get good at creating this Circle of Warmth, you'll have great success melting those barriers and starting to connect with people. And I want you working on this with brief encounters with service people because it's the perfect place to practice this with no repercussions. And you'll get instant feedback on how well you're doing with it. You'll be practicing it over and over until you get really GREAT at it.

Your ability to create this and bring it with you everywhere will give you tremendous confidence because you can do the exact same thing with your social life. (You'll need some extra skills for that though, and I address those conversational aspects in later chapters.)

It's true that not everyone will respond to your Circle of Warmth. Some people may remain ice cold for reasons we may never know. But as always I say this: Don't Judge. And be confident that more than 90 percent of people WILL respond positively when you create a Circle of Warmth. That's what having a Great Vibe is all about. Creating this and bringing it everywhere you go.

What the Circle of Warmth does is it generates a Sphere of Engagement. (Don't ask me why my mind just went Full Geometry on this. It's just a helpful visual.) Do those things mean the same thing? Maybe. But Circle of Warmth relates more to YOU and what you're trying to bring with your social skills. Sphere of Engagement is what results from it. The warmer your Circle of Warmth is, the larger your Sphere of Engagement grows. (which you will see toward the end of this book when I tell one of my grocery checkout stories)

If you're someone who doesn't engage much, or you feel shy, introverted or anxious in a way that keeps you from reaching out to others, then your Sphere of Engagement is quite small. In fact it might extend only as far out as your clothing! (In other words, you're not putting any welcoming signals out there. You're existing as your own solitary monolith with little to no social warmth emanating from you.) The Circle of Warmth concept is an attempt to EXPAND your reach until it hits other people and starts warming them up and inviting them in. Once they feel that, they may just step into your Sphere of Engagement. (I can picture this all in my head but clearly I will one day be asked to create a workbook involving pretty geometric shapes. Finally I found a good use for geometry!)

So your Circle of Warmth may be small at first. But as you start interacting with one person at a time, you'll learn to make it bigger. It'll happen naturally once you start doing the things that allow people to connect with each other.

So we start the process one brief interaction at a time.

ANY TOPIC WORKS...EVEN THE WEATHER

I made a remark earlier that sort of implied that 'the weather' is a traditional boring topic. It does get a bad rap that way, and I probably didn't do it any favors by intimating that it belongs in that category. And yet! There's a reason why 'the weather' is a time-honored favorite. For one, everyone has weather. Nobody lives in a vacuum. Even astronauts (who are sometimes floating in a vacuum) can report on 'space weather.'

Weather is always out there. It's always changing. And we're all affected by it. Even the mega-wealthy and celebrities get rained on. And if you're indoors you still have access to the excitement if you are blessed with a window. So 'the weather' is a fantastic all-purpose tool for conversation. It's the Swiss Army Knife of conversational topics!

Also the weather is close to my heart, being from Buffalo. Now that I live in Florida, knowing the weather from hour to hour is not strictly necessary. It's 'sunny and nice' the majority of the time, unless the occasional hurricane is bearing down on us.

When I lived in Buffalo it was absolutely necessary to check on the weather at least three times per day. When you got up, at some point midday, and later at night. If you did not do this you would run a huge risk of being completely blind-sided by an unexpected weather event. Because Buffalo sits on the tail end of Lake Erie, where the unpredictable effect of the lake can hurl random weirdness out of the sky at the city and its suburbs.

So in Buffalo 'the weather' is more than a topic. It's a vital lifeline to knowing how many changes of clothes you're going to need that day.

But even here in Florida I love the topic of weather and I can get quite enthusiastic about it. Heck, I'll even stare at the sky and start jabbering about cloud formations and what they remind me of. Yes, the sky is the biggest and best ever blank canvas upon which to spill random thoughts!

Whatever you choose to talk about doesn't have to be the most fascinating thing. It just has to be something you can get enthused about, something that reminds you of something else, something you can use to connect with the person in front of you. That's it. For you it might be something entirely different. Like pets! Or what you're making for dinner. Or traffic. Or the local sports team. Or some detail of what's in the room you're in or what the person in front of you is wearing.

Any. Little. Thing. Works.

A fascinating conversation is all in the attitude you bring to the topic. We all know people who can make an interesting topic boring, or can make a boring topic interesting. It's all in your sense of interest, engagement, readiness to draw the other person in and hear their thoughts, and just an aura of fun energy.

And yes, I get it that if you're not used to doing that it may seem impossible to get there. But it really is NOT impossible. All it takes is starting small and practicing daily on all those cashiers, restaurant servers, bank tellers and gym attendants who are this captive audience, and a lot of whom would welcome a brief, entertaining conversation with you. I've worked in customer service, and it was always a treat to have a fun customer who was ready to engage!

One caveat though. You do have to 'take the temperature' of the checkout lane. Or the restaurant. Or the Wherever-You-Are. If the person you're dealing with seems uninterested, or not in a good mood, or rushed, or overly focused on something else, then it's up to you to notice that. So if you don't get much of a response to your friendly greeting or random comment, then interpret that as the person is not ready to engage much in that moment.

And don't judge the reason why! There could be so many reasons. Everything from having a bad day, experiencing physical discomfort, being distracted for any reason. You just can't know. The important thing is to not attribute that to yourself. Because my experience is that upwards of 90 percent of people will engage with me (to varying degrees) in a fun manner. So for the others I just hope that the rest of their day goes well for them.

*

Question: I'd like to be better at socializing, but I've been shy all my life. That's just me. As an introvert I'm not sure I can change. What exactly is the definition of "good social skills," and how can I obtain them?

Answer: I'm just pondering the idea of shyness, or of social anxiety, or introversion, and people's tendency to say, "That's just who I am." And I believed that myself years ago during my school years. It felt like something that was impossible to change.

But, shyness is not Who You Are. Social Anxiety doesn't come with the package. And introversion may be a tendency, but it isn't who you are either. I tend to regard all these things as barriers to communicating your true self to people. Who you are is what's deep down inside you. These other things are just obstacles in the way.

I would've described myself as an introvert many years ago because many large social situations made me uncomfortable, tired me out, and I couldn't wait to escape them. And I enjoyed solitude with books. (I still enjoy solitude with books to this day!) But it turns out I wasn't an introvert at all. What tired me out about social situations was the fact that I wasn't very good at them, so I dreaded them.

"Shyness is not who you are."

As I made my gradual transformation and began to get a whole lot better at connecting with people, these same situations I used to avoid became fun for me. I could now recharge with books, and I could also recharge with people! I really needed both things in my life. I'm just going to insist that "shy" is not Who You Are. It's just something that needs to be overcome so you can help people SEE who you are.

Lacking social skills is not "Who You Are" either. We all came out of the womb with Zero Manners. But do people run around claiming Bad Manners is "just who I am?" No, we don't get away with that. Because parents and other authority figures drill into us that you need manners to get along in life.

Yes, you can try to get by without ever saying please, thank you or excuse me, but you will get a lot of stink eyes thrown at you if you attempt it. And no one will give you the benefit of the doubt on anything, ever. We just take for granted that a certain amount of manners is required if you don't want your life to be a trainwreck.

I do think it's odd that we don't place the same level of importance on social skills. The only advice I ever remember getting on the topic was, "Stop being so shy and go talk to someone." Problem is, "Just do it" doesn't really qualify as an action plan unless you're up in a plane with a parachute strapped on your back and the door open. And for me "talking to people" felt a little bit like skydiving WITHOUT a parachute.

Just as an aside, it feels like our schools spend so much time teaching us things that are rarely used. I know they're required to teach it all so I certainly understand why they do. But why are social skills almost completely ignored when it's the very thing that could make a huge difference for kids?

For example they start telling you about "parts of the plant" as early as 3rd grade. So you're memorizing words like "phloem" and "xylem." For what? (Note: these can be useful when playing Scrabble™.) You don't even need to know the technical terms for "parts of a plant" in order to be a great gardener or a successful farmer!

Yet we learn this stuff over and over, to the detriment of subjects that would be useful. Why couldn't "Social Skills" be a special subject like art or music or phys ed? What's more important, social skills or knowing who Picasso is? Social skills or knowing music notes? Social skills or parts of the plant? I will boldly state that other than reading, writing and arithmetic, the entirety of the rest of grammar school could be devoted to social skills, and kids could wait until highschool to learn about social studies, science and all the rest.

I have no idea why our educational system still seems to be stuck in a model developed more than 100 years ago, but I guarantee you that as long as you learn the three R's, the very next best thing to be good at would be social skills. The heck with the pistil, the stamen and the carpel tunnel. (small science joke right there. I may not have been great at socializing back in grammar school days, but I knew my parts of the flower!)

Well that's my rant about that. But like any good conversation, this discussion will often meander in various directions, so it's your job to just go with the flow!

Okay, suppose you're not getting out on a regular basis. The daily practice is not happening. What then? If you live with other people—family, roommates, boarding house buddy, you can still practice your nascent social skills.

You may get a reaction of "What's gotten into you lately," or "Why are you in such a good mood?" or "Lay off the coffee dude! (or dudette)." But as long as you're not over the top with your interactions you're good to keep greeting your very own family members with added positivity and joy.

Yes. It's true. There's no penalty for treating the people you take for granted nicely. Although in a closed setting where behavior patterns are firmly established, I'd suggest raising your energy level only a modest 5-10 percent. You don't want to startle them, or make them think you won the Lotto™ and decided to keep it to yourself. You can always take it up another notch later when they're used to the New More Cheerful and Social You.

Now, what if you live alone and there's nobody to realistically practice on? Ha! We're not going to let a little thing like solitude stop us, are we? No of course not. There are some other practice accessories that many people have at their disposal. Pets and mirrors!

A lot of people talk to their pets already. Why shouldn't they? They're family members, and they're sentient beings. They can hear you, and, if they're a dog, they'll respond! Cats are a whole other story. Cats are like trying to deal with your worst ever blind date. You can't even tell if they're enjoying themselves! And when you say something directly to them they MIGHT look in your direction and think, "Meh!"

But you can still practice on them. The idea is to pretend in your mind that they can process your wittiness and social repartee. They're definitely appreciating the one-sided conversation you've got going on! Really it's only your own brain you're trying to fool, and the pets are a useful tool for helping. That's why it works even to talk to hamsters, parakeets and tropical fish. Pets are great for practicing speeches on, too.

It's one thing to imagine being more fun and energetic in your head. (Visualization of what you're working on is good practice!) But it's another to actually hear your voice saying the things in your head. You could record yourself with your opening lines, and see how that sounds. Or put it on video and see if you're succeeding in having an expression that is friendly and approachable.

RESTING 'BORED' FACE

That brings us back to the bathroom or bedroom mirror. A very valuable tool indeed! I'd like to digress into the topic of what your resting face looks like. There's this phenomenon out there called "RBF." It actually stands for something as an acronym, but I don't want to go off in a politically incorrect direction, nor do I want a "PG" label slapped on my book. So I will just describe it as having a Resting Face that is not very pleasant. It's having a normal resting fact that looks like it's in a very bad mood.

I will describe a pretty severe case of this. There was a retail situation I was involved in that caused me to be in a particular store a couple times a year. (Notice how vague I am being here!) The amount of time interacting with the customer service people was probably a solid 5-10 minutes each time. More words than normal would be exchanged. But it was a pretty routine transaction. Anybody in the store could do it.

The customer service in this store was very good and I was happy to deal with any of the cheerful guys and gals there. Except this one person. The first time I saw her I assumed she was having a terrible day. (Maybe even a "Terrible Horrible No Good Very Bad Day.") The next time I saw her she had that same (angry? frustrated? perturbed? irritated? Hold on a sec while I grab my thesaurus. Vexed! Irked! Aggrieved!) look on her face. I was starting think that this was just how she normally looked. It wasn't a Bad Day, it was more like a Bad Decade.

I made every effort to avoid dealing with this person. Until one day I couldn't because the others were busy, and she was the only one available, so I reluctantly dealt with her. Well! Her tone of voice was at least neutral, if not exactly spilling over into friendly territory. She was professional and efficient. There really didn't seem to be any internal negativity going on with her that I could tell. But. That face! What did it mean, I pondered. How could she not know that her normal resting face had this extremely off-putting vibe?

Life usually contains a bell curve of variation, and I honestly don't know what the "normal" resting face is at the peak of the bell curve. Probably just "busy," I'm not really sure. And there are plenty of people who have "somewhat" off-putting expressions, but it doesn't rise to the level of me asking them if there's anything I can do to help.

This woman really fell a couple of standard deviations away from that, more toward the Angry End of the bell curve. Without actually feeling that way, best as I could tell. I've never seen her without the angry resting face, even though it did brighten up slightly when she was speaking to me.

It makes me wonder if anyone in her life has mentioned it to her. "Hey, Aphrodite, I think your resting facial expression could use some work. Normally it looks like you're suffering from food poisoning, or just had a fender bender."

I'll be the first to admit that most people probably don't give their natural expression a whole lot of thought. Once the concept became known to me, many years ago, I relaxed my face into what I thought was the most natural, least effort expression I could. I pretended I was studying in a college library and didn't care to be bothered by anyone. Then I looked into the mirror.

Lo! What do you think I saw? Well fortunately it wasn't a bad case of Angry Face. Yay. But it *was* a form of RBF nonetheless. It was Resting BORED Face. Yeah, I looked sort of bored with life! Then I got a bit paranoid about what that meant for my whole previous life up until that moment. Was I always looking bored? Or worse, BORING? Gah!

I decided I needed to change that straight away. In order to be open and approachable to the world, you need to express those very qualities. And the human face is remarkably expressive. It doesn't take that much work to go from a bored face to a playful face. In fact it probably takes less than a calorie of effort to do it. (Sorry, future best-selling diet book! I guess we won't be able to smile our way into smaller-size pants.)

> ## "It doesn't take much work to go from a
> ## bored face to a playful face."

So I put happy thoughts into my head. Not excessively happy. Not "I just won the Lotto™," or "You've been nominated for the Pulitzer Prize" or "We're pregnant with our first child" happy. But something along the lines of "I'm going to see a friend today," or "someone else fed the cats already," or "it's time for that first cup of coffee!" Small pleasures.

I imagined that type of small happiness, plus an attitude of being ready to engage someone in a friendly manner if they happened to wander into my sphere of influence. What did THAT face look like? I checked in the mirror. It was an almost barely noticeable smile, just the slightest upturn of my mouth, plus a slight smile with my eyes. I don't even know for sure that my eyes did anything different, to be honest. I just mentally "sent" happiness to them, on purpose, and they felt slightly different.

Well these barely perceptible changes made a HUGE difference in how I looked in a resting state. In my ridiculously opinionated opinion. Teeniest amount of effort. Huge difference. I now looked friendly and approachable. Ready to be amused. Ready to have a conversation. Ready to go off on an adventure. (Note: You probably do NOT want to use this expression if you're studying, assembling something with multi-page directions, or trying to pull a sliver out of your finger with tweezers.)

So as I was making this change I would check myself regularly when I passed a mirror. To make sure I had this subtle expression that I wanted. The key was to make this my intentional resting face instead of that bored expression that crept there when I was alone, and that I didn't want to bring to the world. So yes I absolutely put that playful expression on my face when I was alone, because that was the best place to practice it, and the only way to make it a true habit.

Guess what unexpected thing THAT did. (I'll wait. You've got three guesses. Make 'em good.) Okay, what it did was transform my resting mood to match what was going on with my face. That isn't to say I needed a major mood overhaul. I'm pretty happy go lucky in most ways. Still, it's pretty easy to fall into a blah, bored or "whatever" mood. But when I changed the look on my face in this most subtle of ways, I could feel my own internal mood shift into a more proactive positivity. It was like suddenly being in a Fun Bubble.

I found myself talking to myself more (aloud) and saying encouraging things to myself. I made myself more fun to myself. I know how totally weird that sounds. A slight smile on my face can do all that?

Well, yeah. And it does even more when you're out in public, because something about that smile (which I amp up slightly more in public) sends out this signal to people that you're ready to engage, you're ready to talk, you're ready to: comment, help out, laugh, hang out with you. It's like you've taken down the Force Field that tells people you are going about your business and you're not to be bothered and don't come near me.

That's my theory. I'm telling you what worked for me, and maybe the idea is homo sapiens-wide, so maybe it'll work for you too. You can certainly experiment with it and see what kind of results you get.

CHAPTER 2: TAKEAWAYS

1. *Use brief, low-stress daily interactions to work on social skills.*
2. *Places: Grocery, bank, dry cleaner, gym, coffee shop, store, restaurant, post office, dining hall etc. Skills: Eye contact, smile, greeting, energy level, comments, compliments, humor.*
3. *To get out of your comfort zone turn it into a game. Deprive yourself of something you really want until you DO THAT THING which you find difficult to do. Then reward yourself.*
4. *A genuine smile creates good feelings out of thin air.*
5. *Emotions are highly contagious, so try to spread a happy one.*
6. *Three things you need to connect with a stranger: a genuine smile, an energetic demeanor and a welcoming tone of voice.*
7. *Pay attention to the message that your resting face is sending to the world.*

CHAPTER 3

A GIFT FROM ME
TO YOU

I'm going to give you a gift in this chapter. It's a big gift. It's the best one I can think to give you from a distance (while probably not knowing you). And it's the same one I would give you if you were in front of me or already a good friend of mine.

I'm going to accept you for who you are.

That's it. Nothing more than that. Just acceptance. Acceptance for being the person who was put on this earth for a very good reason, and with skills and abilities and attributes that can, will and do make the world a better place. I accept all that because I know it's true, and I accept you because you deserve that from me.

So I will go off on a couple of tangents about that. Oh, who are we kidding, you know me well enough by now to realize I'm going off on a whole CARNIVAL SWING RIDE of tangents on this topic.

This gift of acceptance is something you deserve from others. However that doesn't mean you will always receive this gift. And oftentimes we don't. Some people spend their whole lives seeking acceptance from various people in their lives. Especially from parents who refuse to give it. (Color me confused by that one. Parents? What do you think your one job is on the planet?) Okay there are several other jobs, such as keeping the baby safe and teaching manners, but you get the drift.

The thing is, even though you can't really control whether or not your Essential Relatives accept you, at some point you will have to move past that and into a wider world that WILL accept you. At least, your goal should be to seek those people who will accept you, to "find your tribe" so to speak. And hopefully you can latch onto a Significant Other who will provide you the love and acceptance you need, and you can do the same for that person. Happily Ever After, Amen!

I feel like I'm really tripping into a psychological area here, but there's a lot of psychological aspects that go into socializing, so I claim this area as something I have a right to delve into!

So back to this acceptance thing. It's more essential than it might appear at first glance. Think about it. We're social beings. What is the one thing we all really want from each other? After we start scaling Maslow's hierarchy of needs and get past Level One (physiological needs such as food, water, shelter and an acceptable wardrobe), and Level Two (safety and security, an income and a pestilence-free environment). Level 3 is "love and belonging." In other words, ACCEPTANCE.

Problem is, if people have been lacking that in their lives, there's a risk that they'll go out into the wider world with the objective to seek out this acceptance that they have been missing. And you know how life is—uncooperative! So the irony is, the people who most need acceptance in their lives because they've been lacking it, are oftentimes the ones who have trouble getting it because they come across as "needy."

Oh, let me stop right there and address "needy." It's just so easy to think, "Oh, poor thing, she (he)'s so needy!" You've heard people say that, right, they're taking pity on someone. Well guess what. That someone is EVERYBODY. We're all needy. We were literally born that way, a bundle of needs. The needs change over time, of course, but they don't go anywhere.

So let's not pretend that somehow other people are needy and we're not. No, we're all needy. The only difference is, some people have a tendency to show it, and some are able to hide it better. But believe me, if the world, or your spouse, or your best friend, or your employer, withdrew something you needed, then it would be very obvious. We're needy!

It's also true that the needier you appear, for some reason, the less the world wants to give you what you need. Stupid irony! Truth, though. Just as confidence begets more confidence, neediness unfortunately tends to do the same. Appear needy, and watch yourself get needier. So frustrating!

But I have a solution for that. It's one of my favorites. It's called Flip The Script. I didn't make that term up, someone else did, but it's just so catchy, easy to remember and TRUE. So congrats, Flip The Script Inventor, I'm using your thing!

Here's how you flip it. If you're a person who needs acceptance pretty badly, and by some twist of fate, misfortune, bad luck, timing, or circumstance, you aren't getting the acceptance you crave, then do the opposite of what you need. Stop seeking acceptance.

Instead, you GIVE it. Find someone you can help, or make less lonely, or share with, do a favor for, or befriend. I don't care where you look. Nominate your least popular family member to be the beneficiary of your largesse. Maybe Cranky Uncle Fester. Or choose a housebound neighbor. Or pick someone in your class at school that few people talk to.

Oh. YOU'RE that person? Well you're not the only one. There's a bell curve. Find another person who is hanging out at the lonely end of the socialization curve with you. Or talk to the bus driver. Or better yet, do some volunteer work. At an old folks' home. Or at a children's cancer clinic. Or at an animal rescue place. Or at a food kitchen.

Once you put yourself in the position of GIVING acceptance, especially to people who don't get that much of it, suddenly you getting acceptance becomes a lot less important. Sure, you still have needs, everyone does, but now you can look at them with a sense of perspective. It isn't just the world's job to accept you. It's YOUR job to find someone else in the world to accept. Ha. How about that?

This will not be the only time I'll tell you to Flip The Script. I'm big on that concept. Sometimes we get so mired in our own telescopic perspective that we can't discern our way out of a paper bag. So that's why I'm constantly telling people to Flip The Script, or Bust Open The Bag, or Pretend You're A Fly On The Wall of Your Own Life. (Hmm. That's a mouthful. Probably won't catch on like Flip The Script, but, oh well!)

> *"Sometimes we get so mired in our own telescopic perspective that we can't discern our way out of a paper bag."*

Think about it. If you're out there seeking acceptance and fearful that you won't get it, and "try too hard," or are pushy, or start asking too much, or are "clingy," it's likely to backfire into people not accepting you at all. And then, annoyingly, they may even call you "needy." Blech. Who needs that. And you will feel dependent on the world, which is holding back what you want (acceptance) and this grows into resentment and/or apathy.

"Forget it! No one's going to accept me. I'm just a big loser."

People say that to themselves. But the truth is they hold the power within themselves to change that, and just don't realize it. I repeat. Become an Acceptance GIVER. When you get good at that, along with the help of some freshly cultivated social skills that I'm going to suggest, you will transform yourself. And then you will start accruing acceptance unto yourself naturally, without demanding it, begging for it, or trying to secretly find some way to get it. (Did that not just sound Biblical, with my use of "unto?" Go, Thou, and Start Accepting People!")

The purpose of me mentioning all of this is to discuss why we want to get better at socializing to begin with. What's the point? The point is to make connections, have fun, and feel accepted. And a lot of what I'm going to talk about is at its heart a mindset shift. You have to start looking at yourself, and life, a little differently to start making the type of transformation that'll give you a life that is a lot better than where you are now. Or, if you're currently operating at Extremely Awesomely Happy, then I only promise to make your life "a little better." But still new and improved. Such a deal!

Okay, so you're starting the job of accepting others instead of worrying so much about them accepting you. And hopefully you're interacting well in grocery stores, coffee shops, fitness centers and banks. Banks! I love talking to tellers. They have a serious job, and some of it involves counting accurately, so people don't joke around with them as much. But I do. It always gets a smile out of them, although occasionally they have to re-count.

How do you go about making friends? You're past the age where you just play with kids on your street, or your parents are arranging playdates for you. Once you no longer have childhood activities like scouts or sports teams or dance lessons or art club, how do you go about making friends?

The answer is slightly different when you're in high school or college. Then you're literally surrounded by potential friends. But it can still feel incredibly daunting to make friends even in those settings. So I'll address both of those.

Adult friendships! Is that even a thing? Who has the time? Plus, everyone already has friends from: their childhood, their school days, their place of employment, their former life, their previous planet they immigrated to Earth from. Heh. The excuses are endless! Even in college it can sometime feel like the friendship circles are made of iron; they're already established and static. Everyone's friendship dance card is full, right? There's no room for one more.

Oh, don't even go there! You know I'm just going to refute that. I've decided I'm literally the guru on this topic. I know what I'm talking about! I'm gonna go All Big Sis on you and lay down the law here. THERE'S ALWAYS ROOM FOR ONE MORE. Have you ever heard of a friend group with a size limit? There isn't one! Not unless they go everywhere by private jet with assigned seats. So get that thought out of your head right now. If you are a fun person, there is ALWAYS room for one more.

CAT: CARING, ACCESSIBILITY & TIME SPENT TOGETHER

Back to the question at hand. How does one make adult friends? As always, I'm going to get very basic on this and explain it to you like we're all in kindergarten. Getting started on a friendship pretty much requires three basic things: Caring, Accessibility and Time Spent Together, or CAT. (hat tip to our cat Maple, who is the friendliest cat ever.) I like easy-to-remember acronyms like that, which is why I put it in that order. But I'm going to explain it in a more chronological way, which makes more sense in terms of how it plays out.

Accessibility. Your friend candidates are people who you see on a regular basis. And you see them regularly enough that you can talk to them and interact a bit. So this could be people you see at work, in a class you're taking, at the gym, a neighbor, at a scheduled activity, while exercising etc. Certainly people in your dorm or apartment complex!

Obviously if you want to increase your chances of meeting someone who could be a friend, you need to expand the number of people you regularly see. By regularly I mean probably at least once a month. Ideally you'd see them more frequently than that, though. The more often you interact with someone the easier it is to get to know them.

So if you don't have a lot of great candidates at work, then you might want to try joining an activity, or a team sport, or do some volunteer work. For stay-at-home dads and moms, kids' play groups often provide great access to other parents. Volunteering at school also puts you in contact with other parents at essentially the same stage of life that you are in.

For college students you need to generate some face-time that doesn't involve a PHONE being between you and the other person. (Ironic Nag Alert!) There are many volunteer opportunities available on college campuses, and it's a great way to spend time with students who are interested in helping others, and who could be potential friends.

No matter what activity you choose, if you see people regularly, then they are accessible, and you can frequently strike up conversations with them, whether it's briefly or longer than that. The purpose is to get a feel for them, and they for you. You are putting your VIBE out there. And you're getting some sort of vibe from them. If you're suffering from a friendship shortage, (or even if you're not) don't get too judgy about people. There's no reason to reject someone unless they're really, really not your type.

In other words, give people a chance. You'd want them to do the same for you. You'd be surprised at how many people who don't initially seem to be 'your type' turn out to be fun and interesting! I'm fascinated by people who are nothing like me. Those who have skills, abilities and interests I've never dreamed of having. So, be open-minded on the subject of who is a friend candidate.

When you're in school, practically everyone is the same age. But when you become a working adult, then age is far less important. You can even be friends with someone a lot older or younger than yourself. True fact. I know, it seems astonishing until you've tried it.

Time spent together. Next on the list of requirements to make a friend is Time spent together. This is NOT the same as Accessibility. Time with them where you normally see them doesn't count as "time spent together." You might think it should, but it doesn't.

This is the part where people falter. And I don't blame them, actually, because it falls in that dreaded category of "putting yourself out there." But that's tough tiddlywinks. Friends don't grow on trees. You can't drive around in a field, pluck them off and stick them in your car. You actually have to take the next step. Which is (dramatic bass drum roll): INVITE THEM TO DO SOMETHING WITH YOU.

I probably shouldn't have put that in all caps. That's scary looking, isn't it? Dang. Well I did it because it's important. Friendships are made one-on-one. So unless you can get to a place where you can issue an invitation of some sort, then friendship isn't happening. Not unless you've been shipwrecked together and it's your turn to crack the coconuts open.

As an example, in college it's fairly rare to be in class with people and somehow generate a friendship simply from that. Why? Because you need to take the next step! Which is to do something OUTSIDE the place you know them from. Yes you'll have to utter the magic words, "Hey, do you wanna…(grab a bite to eat, go to the gym, get a coffee, swing by my place, hit the dining hall, etc.")

That is the official language of inviting someone to do something. "Hey do you wanna…"

Or, you can use the more formal version: "Would you like to/be interested in…" or even "Would you like to join me in…" Yes, you have to "pop the question" in some form or other. It can even be, "Hey, why don't we…" or "You know what, we really should…" or, "Why don't we…" You fill in the blank with some activity.

The issue with this for most of us is that it's an opportunity to be rejected. Blech. No one likes that. And if you focus all your mental energy on this acceptance vs rejection paradigm, you just might intimidate yourself into thinking friends aren't worth the trouble, so why even attempt it. Well I say NAY to that. Let's just reject that and move past it. Instead we will do another of my favorite things. (This is a Patti Lifehack Extraordinaire.)

We are going to downsize the problem. Yep. Magically zap it with our Mental Downsizing machine and make it a much smaller deal than it first appears. (I have an almost unlimited quantity of mental gadgets at my disposal to make life easier.)

How do we downsize this problem of issuing an invitation and maybe getting rejected? Well first off, don't make the invitation too big. Like don't start with something that's the adult equivalent of going to the prom. You don't want to spend 6-8 hours with someone right off the bat. Or do something that involves fancy clothing.

Make it something that's no big deal. How about a coffee? Or grabbing lunch? (an easy one if you want to get together with a co-worker, either in the lunchroom or eating out) What if your car is getting worked on? Maybe they can take you to drop the car off or pick it up. Or going for a walk. Keep it simple and keep it small.

Special Bonus Tip: If you want to make it even more casual, just say you're going someplace for lunch and ask if they'd like to join you. That way it's more of a suggestion than an explicit invitation. "Hey I'm going to Cicero's Diner for lunch. Want to come?" Or to a movie. Or out to shop somewhere. Or for a walk.

The key to this method is that there is no real pressure, nothing riding on that type of invitation. If they can't make it, well, you were going anyway, so no big deal. It isn't like the activity in question depends on them saying yes. So it's an easy thing to offer, and if you don't get a 'yes' this week, you may get one next week. So take the pressure off an invitation by asking someone if they want to tag along.

> ## *"Take the pressure off an invitation by asking someone if they want to tag along."*

You need to already establish a bit of a rapport with them before asking them to join you on something. So they're used to talking with you and could imagine having a fun conversation with you over coffee, or lunch, or during a walk. If you can't see this happening in your head, then you probably aren't ready to invite them someplace yet. It isn't like a cold call or a spin of a roulette wheel.

You should already enjoy your conversations when you do see them. Lay the groundwork for that first, and THEN invite them. So if you're in a class together of course you need to have a few pre- or post-class conversations before asking them to do something with you.

Now suppose they can't do your suggested thing for some reason. Is that the Dreaded Rejection? Maybe it is, maybe it isn't. One way to tell is the nuance of their reaction. Is it a simple no, they're busy? Or do they say not this time, maybe some other time?

The second holds out more promise than the first. If people regret not being able to do something you've suggested, they will often say so. But not always. I'd continue to invite them several more times before giving up. Sometimes people are distracted, or surprised, or tongue-tied. So you want to give them several opportunities to consider joining you for a one-on-one.

Another aspect of Downsizing the Rejection Problem is having several irons in the fire. Your whole social life does not ride on one particular person saying yes to you! If you put all your hope into one person and they don't agree to your thing, that may seem like a devastating response.

Well, it actually isn't. For one thing, you don't know what's going on with them. They may well be truly busy, or have too much going on in their life to have room for another friend. They may be in a bad place for a reason you don't know. It's never useful to attribute a rejection to yourself. It might have nothing to do with you. And it really doesn't matter anyway. There's another 7 billion people out there to meet. Don't invest all your hopes in one potential person.

Expand your activities and always have several people out there who might fit your friend profile. And get used to issuing invitations. The more often you do something, the easier it becomes. Familiarity siphons all the drama right out of it. No big deal.

"Wanna go for coffee? No? Maybe some other time!" See, YOU can be the one to say "maybe some other time."

Say it in a friendly manner, and maybe there WILL be another time. If you really want to make some friends you should be issuing a casual invitation to someone at least once a week. Maybe even more often. Keep doing it until you get a yes. Then, go have a good time with the person. Bring energy, excitement, a good vibe. Bring THE FUN. I enjoy myself wherever I go. Even if I'm just hanging with Me, Myself & I. You can do that too. Just change your mindset, and change your vibe.

In the development of friendship it's perfectly okay for you as the pro-active person to issue several invitations at first. Because you know you might want this person as a friend. They may or may not have thoughts on that. But if you two hit it off and have a good time, then at some point they will reach out to you in some way. Whether it's their own invitation, or maybe they'll text you, or call you on the phone. Or swing by your desk, stop by your place or show up at your car. SOMETHING.

At some point they will indicate to you that they enjoy your company and would be happy to hang out with you. They will not SAY that. "I will be happy to hang out with you." Only Coneheads would say that. (small SNL joke) But they'll do things that mean the same thing.

It isn't like in childhood where this new girl on my street ANNOUNCED to me that she was my best friend. I was taken aback by her proclamation, even at age 10. Then she grabbed my diary and wrote all about our friendship on many pages of the diary. Her handwriting was ENORMOUS. It was a five-year diary (How was that even a THING?) that had preprinted dates on the pages, and she randomly wrote several years into the future with her giant billboard-sized writing. I barely knew her, and there she was talking about our great friendship with a few (humongous!) words on each page. Then she'd skip ahead a few months or years and repeat herself. I have a vivid memory of this.

I also wondered at that time if we were best friends even though she never actually checked with me to see if I was okay with it. And I was too timid to contradict her. So I sort of lived with it for a few weeks until she got bored with me and then went off and attacked someone else's diary. True story!

I still have the diary somewhere in the back of my closet because I'm a packrat but DEFINITELY NOT A HOARDER. (That show has so frightened me that I cannot even consider hoarding.) So anyway, adults don't do it that way. They just invite you to do things, which you can do or not, and they check in with you because they care. Which leads us to the last necessary quality of a friendship.

Caring. (Or for guys I'll call it 'concern' because sometimes guys get squirrelly about admitting they care about their friends. Sexism alert. Whatever! I have four brothers. I know how guys operate.) That simply means they know about what's going on with you, and they care about it because they care about you.

That also implies you have to have conversations that go beyond small talk with them! Otherwise, what is there to care about? So you will have to talk about things like family, your job, your activities, your classes, your hobbies, your hopes and dreams, things you're good (and bad) at, things you care about. And they will do the same. When they tell you about their stuff, at least try to remember the important points, and ask about it later.

In any friendship, things are revealed gradually. You do not unload your whole horrible history of your childhood, or your whole fabulous history of your fantastic achievements, or your whole Whatever History of Whatever, because all of that sounds like too much too soon. If your new friend tells you something that's kind of personal, then that's permission (and maybe even encouragement) for you to do the same thing.

Just don't go overboard, because it's easy to get overwhelmed by things like that, especially when you're first getting to know someone. And it doesn't mean you need to do it in the same moment that they're telling you their Important Thing. Save your Important Thing for next time. So you should take your cues from each other. Friendship is about reciprocity. Friendships don't need to be equal, but they do need to be balanced.

"Friendships don't need to be equal, but they do need to be balanced."

Caring. Accessibility. Time spent Together. You need these three things to establish a friendship.

*

Let's look at some questions on friendship.

Question: I'm always the person in my friend group who does the inviting. I arrange something, and everybody will show up for it. If I stop texting them or arranging things, they never reach out to me. Then I find out on social media that they all went someplace without me. What am I doing wrong?

Answer: Friendships should be reciprocal, so you shouldn't be the only one putting in the work. However, reciprocal doesn't mean identical, at least not in a point-scoring, tit-for-tat sense. People bring different strengths to a relationship. Some are better at arranging cool outings or initiating get-togethers. Others might be better at a quick "how are you doing" text, or anticipating a need. It doesn't have to be exactly equal, but you do have to feel an essential sense of fairness. Both people need to care about the friendship and each other. Otherwise, it's just not worth it.

The second idea is that you're the person who arranges something, and invites everyone, and somehow you're left out when that group goes out somewhere else. That doesn't feel right to me at all. Even if it's something you couldn't have done, they should at least let you know about it and allow you to make the decision yourself.

What I'd conclude from that is that you perceive yourself as part of a group, but are not individual friends with the people IN that group. It's a common problem, and how people most often end up in the situation of "I'm always forgotten," or "my friends don't include me." Who in that group—as an INDIVDUAL—are you friends with?

Do not chalk this up to "life isn't always fair." The problem is that friendship is always, at its heart, a personal one-on-one thing, first. That's what you need to focus on in order to be included and not forgotten. It isn't a Fairness Thing, it's a Friendship Thing. Being friends "with a group" can give the illusion of friendship, but if you're routinely left out of group activities then you either need to start developing one-on-one friends within that group, or start over with new friends.

Question: When I'm around people I know, I can be myself. But when it's someone I've just met, or I don't know well, then I get uncomfortable and don't act like I normally do. That makes the interaction awkward. I don't know how to fix this.

Answer: That's a normal feeling. Even people who appear completely relaxed often have at least a little sense of nervousness about meeting someone new. So most people can relate to your situation.

My solution is to pretend that they're a friend already. So, rather than allow my actual emotion to drive my actions, I replace it with the emotion I want to feel. This results in them getting a bigger, more genuine smile and a more interested and friendly tone of voice.

So I inject an enthusiasm into the interaction that I may not fully feel at the beginning. I know what you're thinking. That's fake! Oh, how I hate that label. I don't like fake anything. I hate fake sugar, fake fat, fake smiles, fake anything. We all want the Real Thing. So how do I reconcile the two?

I do it by responding positively to the potential connection I want to make. I don't know for sure that this is a nice, friendly and fun person in front of me. But I'm HOPEFUL that they are. So I'm responding enthusiastically to the hope I have for a nice interaction, a great connection, maybe even a future friendship.

It's no different than the enthusiasm I express to the cashier in the grocery checkout lane. I don't know him or her, necessarily. On what basis do I greet them as a friend? Same thing. I'm expressing my enthusiasm that the person in front of me is a potentially fun connection. Someone I'm happy to see because they're a human who deserves my best effort to have a positive and productive interaction.

It's the difference between seeing people as Potential vs seeing them as Problems. When you view them as Potential, you give them your best, you have fun with them, you brighten their day. If you view them as a Problems, well, that's a downer. Or if you view them in a Perfunctory way, as just a moving part of the scenery, well, ugh, you can see why that transaction is a boring one. And yet, that's where a lot of people are. On autopilot! I'm not criticizing that, necessarily, just pointing it out.

You can get a lot more out of your interactions if you give people your best most of the time. It's just another way of doing things. You can connect with many more fun people using my method.

Sometimes people are going through problems, have a lot of burdens, and autopilot is the best they can manage at the moment. No judgments! Everybody's different, and so are their circumstances. It takes all kinds to Make The Globe Spin. Just remember that when it comes to a socially rewarding life, what you put into it is often what you get out of it. The choice is yours to make.

Happy In, Happy Out. Or as I call it, "Hi-Ho!" Hi-Ho, Hi-Ho, off to connect we go!

"Hi-Ho, Hi-Ho, off to connect we go!"

Question: People find me hard to talk to, even if I've known them a long time. It's like my friendships never get past the small talk/awkward phase. When these same friends meet someone else, (even if they hardly know them) somehow they start sharing things I've never heard from them. They love talking to these strangers. I'm like the leftovers nobody wants. They never open up to me, and even if I ask them directly, I barely get a sentence out of them. Then the conversation is over. I'd like to be someone people are comfortable talking to. Can you help?

Answer: Small talk is a quick opener for friends. It can be the entire conversation for strangers or acquaintances. If you're stuck on small talk with people you've known for years, then you're still technically in that mildly awkward phase that people who don't know each other well, and don't trust each other, remain in. In fact, you cite that yourself, calling it *awkward*. Usually time itself will resolve that, even for people who are more reserved. But it hasn't for you, so you've got an extra layer of protection going on there. That's something you're going to need to bust through. Because it's a barrier to a good social connection.

What makes people feel comfortable talking to another person? They are looking for a sense of ease, a comfort level, a feeling of acceptance, that the other person will understand, relate to them, and "get" what they are saying. So I'll speculate that there's something in your manner that communicates the opposite. A lack of comfort, lack of acceptance, lack of "getting" them. Now, it may not be that way in your head. But that's how it's coming across externally.

What might the problem be? Again, falling into Speculation Land here. What is the look on your face? Have you ever just put on your normal face, then looked in the mirror (without adjusting it in any way) and taken a good hard look? Is it possible you're sitting there with RBF? (Resting Bored Face. Or it could be more off-putting than that.) If that's how your face normally looks, you need to work on changing it to something more playful, approachable, welcoming.

What's your attitude toward these people? Are you excited to see them? Do you communicate that? Because what's going on in your head is unconsciously revealed in our body language. So if you're feeling uncomfortable, that will seep out and people will pick up on it, even if they can't quite put their finger on why. Body language technically includes your tone of voice. Is your voice warm? Is it animated?

These are some areas to start looking at. Your Social Sleuth At Work!

Question: I don't know how to keep a conversation going. They always fizzle out awkwardly. I'm worried I talk too quietly, but if I try to talk with more enthusiasm it just sounds fake and forced. I think I give off this "aura" that makes people immediately dislike me. I have some social anxiety and they probably pick up on that, but I want to hide it better so it doesn't ruin my chances.

Answer: I think you've stumbled upon some serious truths here. The idea of "aura" really catches my eye. In a sense, that's what my entire book is about. That's what I'm referring to when I say to change your "vibe." It's this unspoken thing that's floating out there that people can somehow sense. I'm not sure if it's an actual thing, or it's all in my head. But YOU can sense it, and I can sense it, so I'm convinced it's there. Extending several feet outside us like some weird force field. This vibe/aura thing we're projecting to other people based on our internal state.

This is why I think it's important to transform your internal state into one of approachability, one of positivity, one of confidence. It isn't as easy as saying "voilà!" That's what I'm gonna do. Change my mind about myself."

It requires you to work on your thought patterns AND your social skills so you can build both the positive vibe and the confidence to pull that off without even thinking about it. It might sound impossible from where you are right now, but it really IS possible.

There's a huge difference between a fun, enthusiastic vibe and an awkward, bored, defensive or apathetic vibe. I'm not suggesting you're any of those negative things, but you could be if you feel you're projecting a vibe that people dislike. You really never want to be in the position where you have to hide your true self, or fake someone you're completely not. You want to slowly transform yourself into an improved, better, then BEST version of yourself.

That might look a lot different than where you are now, but the key is to earn your way there through practice, dedication, and just a sense of intentionality about what you're trying to do. Remember you're not just moving around as an individual in space. You're actually moving with that whole vibe. Whether it's positive, negative or apathetic. So you really need to cultivate the vibe you want to put out there to have the effect you would like to have. I have seen the difference. I have lived the difference.

Imagine arriving someplace and trying to not make any waves, or wishing you won't be asked a question you can't answer, or hoping to not do something ridiculous that you'll have to dwell on for hours, if not days. The opposite of that is looking forward to being with people because you're going to bring your positive, happy energy with you and help uplift whatever's going on. Don't let the crowd dictate how you're going to feel. YOU affect the crowd with your positive vibe.

This is admittedly hard to do when you're still in the beginning stages of trying to change your way of thinking, acting and connecting. For example, you can't just say, "Okay, I'll try this, attempt to fake a positive attitude," and then you can't really carry it off because you don't really believe it. So you falter, and fail. And then you declare "SEE, I knew it couldn't be done."

> *"Don't let the crowd dictate how you're going to feel. YOU affect the crowd with your positive vibe."*

No, no, no. You have to practice, practice, practice until you are utterly confident you can do it for real. Then you'll go out there and do it, and it WILL be real. At the beginning stages you are only doing small things. Like, you are going to give the cashier a great smile and greeting. And then he or she will give you a return smile, and maybe say something friendly. At first, maybe that's the only thing you can be confident of. So you build that confidence one interaction at a time. It becomes easier and easier. You are amazed at your newfound superpower.

You try it out on some acquaintance from a meeting. To your utter amazement THAT person responds positively, just like the grocery cashier did. Amazing! That's how it works. One stage at a time. Don't rush it! Wait until you reach Expert Level with what you're practicing. Whether you're King of Conversation. Emperor of Eye Contact. Baron of Body Language. Sultan of Small Talk. Princess of Positivity. (I am also known at the Alliteration Amiga.)

We're so worried about what others will think of us. By gosh, like something's actually riding on that. Flip. That. Script. How about considering what YOU think of THEM? Ha. Let them sweat that for a while. Oh, they're not? Well, then why should you? Just bring your best self, your best vibe, and let it fly!

If someone doesn't like you it isn't the end of the world. A 50-mile chunk of asteroid splashing into the ocean is the end of the world. Do you see any asteroids at that meeting? In school? At work? At the party? No? Then it isn't the end of the world. As long as you have good table manners and you're not insulting anyone, no one has any reason to judge you.

This is the mindset you'll have once you're more confident in your social skills. Which are just skills, dagnabbit! They're not Miracle Qualities that only a select few royal people can have. It's stuff you can practice like kickball, or knitting or kayaking. Feel you just can't put it all together yet? Then just practice one thing. Practice your eye contact. Practice it on your mom, your sibling. Creep out the mail carrier if you have to. Practice on your pets. You could practice on a potato, for Spuds McKenzie's sake! (small root vegetable joke) See I'm even telegraphing my ridiculous jokes so I don't have to worry about whether you'll laugh.

Question: I looked at a list of deep questions for getting to know people better. Things like "What's an example of an embarrassing moment for you," I couldn't think of an answer. I'm not much for thinking on my feet. How do I solve this problem?

Answer: Deep questions aren't like a pop quiz. You don't have to "pass," and you aren't being graded. How's this for an embarrassing moment: "Someone asks me a 'deep' question and I couldn't think of an answer." Heh.

You know, just because someone asks you a question doesn't mean you have to answer it. Like if they ask you something you're really good at, and you don't have a quick answer. You can always say, "I'm not sure," or "I'll give that some thought," or "I'll consider that," or "Interesting question!" or "I'll pass to the next team." (small board game joke) How about having fun with it, coming up with a non-serious answer? "I'm really great at getting the lids off jars!"

Maybe you could pick a different deep question that you DO have an answer to, and offer that one up (both question and answer) instead of what they asked. There's no social law that says you have to answer what they asked. This isn't a job interview. Instead tell them your favorite thing about yourself. Like, "I often say unexpectedly off-the-wall things!" Or "I travel with dog treats!" or "Children like me!" Whatever your thing is.

Question: I have to confront someone who hasn't been a good friend. I ask to hang out with him. Then says he'll let me know and he never does. I'm the one that has to start conversations and he doesn't seem as interested. He claims he's busy, but then I see him on social media making time for everyone else. What should I say?

Answer: If you've been good friends, there's nothing wrong with letting him know you miss him and would like to get together more. I don't think I'd view it as a confrontation though, so much as a statement of what you need from him. Because ultimately people are going to feel what they feel, and they're going to do what they're going to do. So make your statement. Your friend may or may not give you the kind of answer you're looking for.

In a perfect world he'd slap his forehead and say, "I had no idea you felt that way, I've been so distracted, sure, let's hang out more often!" And then you would. But another very possible scenario is that he says yeah I'll be better about that, and then he keeps neglecting you. Or he may even outright deny that there's a problem and tell you that you shouldn't feel that way. (That happens surprisingly often. People implying that you're imagining things, and that you shouldn't be feeling what you LITERALLY ARE FEELING.) Frustrating!

But you know what? Who knows why he's less available. The fact is, if he is, he is. Being upset with him about it isn't going to change that. So state your case, give him a chance to meet your need, but be fully prepared to move on, and start expanding your social life in other directions. That's probably a good idea anyway. It isn't ideal for either person to be overly reliant on one friend. That sometimes feels like too much pressure.

It's also tempting to want to "dump him" or just cut off the connection. I'd suggest not doing that. If things don't change, just de-emphasize the friendship, but don't shut him out. People go through: distractions, problems, busy spells, depression, seasons, reasons, hubris, you-name-its. Maybe he gets downgraded from "close friend" to "casual friend."

That's okay! He may cycle back to close friend one day, or wind up in some sort of Celestial Fondly Remembered Acquaintance Orbit. There's no need to burn bridges. Save your matches for burning up piles of unwanted memories, bad habits or embarrassing moments.

Question: I feel like I'm searching for friendships, but I don't get approached by anybody for that. I have some casual friends, but not close ones, and even those friends I only see every once in a while. How can I get more people to see me as a potential friend?

Answer: People are like video games in a store, or books on a shelf, or snacks in a grocery aisle or TV shows and movies on the screen. If you had to pick one, which one would you pick? And why? My point being, there are billions of people on this earth. You have to give people a REASON to choose to spend time with you. In our fast-paced society, it sometimes feels even harder to "break through" to the point where you show up on someone's radar.

This does raise the sort of existential question of "do you have to CHANGE" to attract friends into your life? Why can't we be accepted for "who we are?" I'm actually sympathetic to both sides of this argument. I can definitely see why people should be able to have solid friendships being exactly who they are at this moment.

Doesn't that sound ideal? Like we're five years old again, and we're going to tumble into the street with all the other kids and start playing neighborhood games like kickball and freezetag and Monopoly, and by the end of the day we'll have a couple of hot and dusty best friends to go home with and drink Kool-aid™ on the front porch. That sounds so nice I might actually buy a kickball and start hanging out on my front lawn more, trying to attract passing friends into my yard!

On the other hand, I'm writing a whole book about change, and doing things better, and refining your social skills in a manner that allows people to actually see the real you in the best way possible. Feeling relaxed, happy, confident and ready to give people the best you've got.

We've all got some rough edges and things we don't express that well and aspects that can be super annoying to other people. (Like me yammering on about safety topics. I can't tell you how thrilled I was the other day when I was talking to my brother Andy on the phone, and I made some offhand mention of situational awareness. And he said, "That's funny, I was just talking to my girls this morning about situational awareness." I just about fell out of my chair with joy! But really. I need to put a sock in it.)

So we can either say, "That's just me," or we can work to change some of that stuff. I'm not saying that you should or shouldn't. Only that you CAN and maybe might benefit by doing that.

Bottom line is, you don't have control over whether or not people will be interested in you as a friend, but you DO have total control over how you present yourself to the world. You can always improve that. Notice I'm not saying change the deeper 'real you' part—just the part that shows the world who the Real You is. Change some external aspects of your presentation so that people will be tempted to hang out with you and find out more about who you really are.

I'd start with the ability to convey positive emotion. If you can communicate a good mood, some interest in others, and a certain amount of enthusiasm for life and other people, that is a big step forward. Then the next time they're in the snack aisle they'll choose "YOU" instead of the cookie dough ice cream!

So let's go on to more chapters in search of toppings! And we'll check out some places where we can actually FIND friends.

CHAPTER 3: TAKEAWAYS

1. *Instead of being an acceptance seeker, become an acceptance giver.*
2. *What is needed for friendship is CAT: Caring/Concern, Accessibility & Time spent together*
3. *Downsize the Rejection Problem by having multiple possibilities.*
4. *Take yourself off "autopilot" and give people your best self.*
5. *You have to give people a reason to choose to spend time with you.*

CHAPTER 4

FORAGING FOR FRIENDS

Not having friends is literally a health hazard. It's the equivalent of not exercising, or smoking half a pack of cigarettes daily, or treating sugar as a food group. (Source: AP, i.e. Alliterative Patti, a.k.a. "Your Social Sleuth") Friends support us, they help us relieve stress, they give us tips to make our lives better.

I firmly believe you can make friends at any age. The difference is that when you get past your early childhood years, you have to be a lot more deliberate about it. Because we aren't thrown into as many obvious situations that are ideal for friendships to form, and we're (rightly) more picky about who we want to spend time with.

Remember! You become like the people you surround yourself with. To a great extent we are products of "our environment." Well what do you think a friend or a friend group IS? A huge part of your social environment! So make sure you surround yourself with friends that you enjoy and are honored to pal around with.

"You become like the people you surround yourself with."

If you're feeling alone or lonely or not connected, probably the best prescription for you is a friend. Someone to talk to, someone to do things with. Someone who will listen to you and hear you. Someone who will share stuff about themselves. Someone who will support you, encourage you, and (sometimes) advise you, someone who will be your cheerleader. If we can't cheer for our friends, by what right do we even call ourselves friends? It's a major part of the job description!

So where, oh where, do we find friends?

I don't think online friends are enough. They don't fill the need I'm talking about. In fact, I'd like to quote fellow writer Mark Manson on the topic, because he said it so perfectly that I wish I had thought of it.

Mark said, "Connections online and through devices seem to be a poor replacement for the emotional and psychological sustenance we get from being around others. Social media and video games are like the diet soda of our emotional well-being — it tastes like we're hanging out with people, but there are no emotional calories. And in this case, no emotional calories is a bad thing… it's starving us."

I agree with that, 100 percent. Online connections are just are not enough to truly fill that human connection we all need. And to really punctuate that for me, I really hate the taste of diet pop. So online connections just cannot fully replace interacting with a real live human.

*

Question: It seems I'm always the one who has to begin the convo when texting. Even when the other person responds I get one-word answers like "yeah" or "ok" etc. Sometimes if the convo goes on for a few days we run out of things to talk about. They won't respond even though I know they've seen my message. Am I wrong to feel this way? Or should I just wait and not care that it's taking forever?

Answer: Wow, those convos were so dry I feel like I need to moisturize your phone! Texting is a tool. It doesn't take the place of a relationship. Ask yourself why you're texting to begin with. If you're getting one-word answers from people, that isn't a conversation. I think you need to head out into the great wide world and meet people, establish connections and form friendships. Then those are maintained (in part) by texting. Texting is a tool, not a substitute for doing the actual work of getting out there and forging relationships.

*

That question above is what I'm talking about when I say that the phone should be used as a tool not a crutch. Don't let it take the place of a sincere effort to invite people into your life for a real relationship.

"The phone should be used as a tool, not as a crutch."

So where do we find friends? All around us.

COMMON FRIEND HABITATS

Here are some sample places where friends can be found:
    Work – Co-workers at your stage of life or who share interests.
    Neighborhood – Next door, in your building or complex, up the street.
    School – School/campus events and groups; living spaces. Activities. Teams.
    Meetup – Online way to connect with people locally.

Recreational sports team – A great way to connect, whether single sex or co-ed. "Going out after the game/match." Need I say more?

Book club – Food, fun, friendship, oh, and books.

Farmers' market – You can zero in on your interests and meet people who are ready to talk.

Church group – Spirituality, socializing, service.

Take a class – Continuing/Adult Ed is a great way to meet people with similar interests and pick up some knowledge or skill. You have built-in things to talk about too! "How about a bite to eat after class…?"

Volunteer work – You might want to vet this first if you're looking to meet people in a similar age range or stage of life. Many groups can use a helping hand. Animal shelters are a terrific place to volunteer if you're a pet lover.

Local food or art festivals – Whether as a spectator, participant or volunteer, these draw like-minded people who are usually in a relaxed and friendly mood.

Tours – Local tours of wineries, breweries, art venues, restaurants, cultural locations all attract people who might want to connect.

Dog park – Is there anything more fun than someone admiring your dog? Or you bonding with someone else over their pet? We love our pets! We love PEOPLE who love our pets! Let Spot encourage you to be your most outgoing self. "See Spot. See Spot run. See Spot sniff everything in sight and make a gajillion dog friends, all of whom have owners…"

Trivia night – Head out to your local bar armed with your Secret Knowledge Area. You might be able to join up with a team that can use an extra. Or check out other teams and see "what they know," and get a feel for the personalities. Then make your friendly approach.

Exercise club – Become a regular at a certain time or for a particular class.

Fan club – Join a fan club of a local sports team. It doesn't have to be top of the line professional. It can be Triple A baseball or another junior league, or even the teams of a local college or university. Fans are devoted, and they love talking about the team.

Wine club – You can find a venue offering regular tastings. Or you can create your own club, picking either a spot to meet regularly, or try different places.

Special interest club – Many areas have groups ranging from sewing to politics to you-name-it. Pick your interest. Or develop a new one!

Outdoors club – You need a certain amount of stamina, good joints plus sunglasses for this. But if you have energy this is a fun way to meet people and get good exercise too. And somehow talking while enjoying nature helps conversations flow easily.

Networking group – whatever your job, there's probably a professional club you can join to meet people doing a similar thing.

Rotary! – This sounded so serious and mature to me before I was persuaded to join. (I'm seriously missing a major 'maturity gene' from my DNA) Rotary specializes in service projects, networking and civic contributions. Yes, still sounds mature. But along with a few friends we made it fun! In addition to helping the community and getting the word out about your business, we have regular socials and we do a lot of fun connecting. We have literally brought a special vibe to our Rotary chapter. We are a fun group! We laugh a lot. And do a lot of civic good in the process.

Local Race – Whether runners, bikers, or others, people who like to race usually like to connect with others who do the same. Plus, no one has their guard up while they're sweating. They've literally just survived an event. And most races need volunteers for set-up and clean-up. More opportunities to connect if you don't want to train for it.

Dance class – More sweating, but these people are graceful at it!

Friends – If you already have one friend that you like, chances are good that the other people that they know are likely to be good people too. So you can meet a lot of additional friends this way, and also be introduced to new friend networks. I have seen people reluctant to connect that way because "that's not my friend group." Oh really? Is there an imaginary seating chart? At the same time, if you're going to connect with a friend of your friend, it's polite to let them know.

Martial arts classes/clubs – You can meet people while improving your personal security.

Bowling alley – If bowling is your thing, oftentimes leagues have teams looking for a player.

Places featuring live music – Including restaurants, bars and coffee houses.

Old friends & acquaintances – Yeah, those relationships that faded or died on the vine for some reason, we all get busy, I get it. Well you can reconnect with them! And they have probably moved on to make some other friends, acquaintances and contacts that you could also get to know. So the watchword is: REKINDLE.

Your kids – No, you don't have to pal around with young people. But you can hang out with their friends' parents. Invite them over to watch the college football team play. Or arrange a parents' lunch for whoever can come.

Community garden – It's a great way to meet people who are in tune with nature, and might lead to some great side dishes!

Local events – Scour your local newspaper and online sites to find interesting events to attend.

People not in your exact generation or stage of life can be great friends too! You may even learn things from them.

Meetings – People who attend community meetings are usually passionate about something. Whether it's about city beautification or street widening or affordable housing or attracting business to the area. Regulars get to know each other.

Shop at local businesses – Local stores often are more connected to the community and the people who work there can be knowledgeable about what's going on locally. Get to know the proprietor and get some hot tips.

Your Significant Other's Contacts – People they work with, hang out with, or just know in some way. You don't have to automatically categorize them as part of your significant other's life. They could become part of yours too.

Crafting group – Join one. Honestly, I'm pretty terrible at crafts. But I have been to events held by some crafty people I know. And these events have been fun. Even if something is not "your thing," you can still have fun at it and meet people.

Sales parties – This is the type of thing where you're supposed to buy things like jewelry, kitchen goods, storage containers, candles, gifty things, whatever. There's usually plenty of people to connect with. So if you're going to go and make a purchase, be sure you also come away with some contact information for some future new friends.

Politics – If changing the world is your thing, become a volunteer and meet others who are of similar political persuasion.

Community theater – Local community theater almost always needs volunteers to help out behind the scenes, at the box office, you name it. You can make a huge number of connections, and people in this area tend to be pretty social! It's a great excuse for regular contact and socializing. And all these people know other people. Once you're known by this crowd it seems like everybody knows you.

Start your own club – Yes it requires a bit more derring-do (vintage phrase!). But if the club you want doesn't exist yet, you can be the one to start it. In the internet era it's all the easier to publicize it.

Say Yes – When someone asks you to do something, say YES to it. For example, someone might need help moving. Well, you probably won't be the only one helping out. Say yes and go meet some people! Say yes to things you wouldn't normally do. You can both expand your horizons and meet people. Getting past that "automatic no" in your head is the biggest hurdle. You can always hibernate some other time.

Note: You can ignore this advice if your main problem is you don't know how to say 'no' to things. I'm not trying to make your life worse, I'm trying to rewire your brain so that you're more open to social opportunities.

It's helpful to look at people as potential friends, not whatever category you've slotted them into. For example, it's sometimes difficult to view your child's teacher as anything other than that. But, they could be a friend! Don't let your brain shove people into easily recognized boxes.

Anyone could be a friend. Even the person next door with grandkids. Or your hairdresser. Or your kid's baseball coach or dance instructor. Or the person teaching you in the pottery class. Or the minister at your church. Maybe that person is so busy ministering to others that they don't have anyone ministering to them with relaxing Friend Vibes. You could be their Friend Vibes person!

Friends can be found pretty much anywhere if you take the attitude that anyone could become a friend. But realistically in order for a friendship to develop you have to invite the person into your life. And before you do that you're going to have to have at least a good conversation. Preferably more than one, but if you're at a one-off event you may have to gather up the courage to issue the invitation, or at least offer contact information, right away.

That's why you already need decent social skills before you wade into the friendship arena. You don't want to go in there with this uncertain standoffish attitude. This idea that "Why would anyone want to be my friend. They probably already have a LIFE."

Yes, anyone who is past their teenage years already has a life. There's no choice but to have one after you're a teenager. Teenagers are allowed to not be sure about anything. Adults are expected to Have A Life. But that doesn't mean they don't need a friend, or aren't open to that. People almost always make time for someone they click with. So don't put a damper on the friendship before it even begins by assuming they don't have room for you in their life.

Although some people ARE too busy for new friends. It isn't that they don't like you. It's just that they've got a bunch of kids, they work, they volunteer at their kids' school and they have dogs. There's just no way. That person could still be an Occasional Friend. Someone that you get to see once in a while and have a great time with every time you manage to get together. They may not have time for a close friendship right now, but that doesn't mean you can't thoroughly enjoy them when life permits.

So don't give up on someone just because they're short on time. Be open to whatever people can give you. I know a few people who fall in the above category, and I am awesomely thrilled if I get to see them once in a while for coffee.

You do need to know if you click on a conversational level. That way when you get together at least you know you can carry on a fun conversation. That doesn't mean that everyone you do something with will become a friend. These days life is so busy that the planets practically have to align to give friendship time to flower. But if you keep inviting people to do things, at some point you will click enough to form a friendship.

If the person is new and you're inviting them to something, start with something small. Start with a coffee. Or shopping. An errand. A trip to the gym. Lunch. Going for a walk. Simple stuff.

As I mentioned in a prior chapter, you've got to put some time in to get to know someone well. You have to tell them about yourself in order for them to understand you. And the same with them. No, I don't mean an autobiographical sketch. Save the heavy stuff for when you know each other better. Keep things light at first. If a friendship develops they will be happy to hear the more serious stuff down the road. As always the key is reciprocity. And anything serious that they tell you stays confidential! If you're not sure, keep it to yourself. People expect friends to have their backs.

If life tends to get in the way of your friendships, try scheduling get-togethers. Like a weekly coffee date. Or a monthly lunch. Or a weekend text. Or a phone call. Or a gaming hang-out. Put it in your phone calendar. If you're trying to initiate something and it doesn't work out, just put it in your calendar to try again next week. Sometimes people go through really busy seasons and you have to keep trying.

Quality is more important than quantity. It's better to have one good friend than a dozen acquaintances or quasi-friends. Good friends want the best for you. They take the time to know your stuff, and care about it. They celebrate and hurt along with you. It's reciprocal. They should help you be your best self. Friends should be there to help celebrate your best moments, and they should also be there to help comfort you in your worst moments.

"It's better to have one good friend than a dozen acquaintances or quasi-friends."

What is that thing that makes people click, allows them to develop a friendship chemistry? It starts with good conversation. The ability to enjoy fun topics together, to share positivity. For me, it starts with a smile and a fun conversation. It's about taking an interest in each other. Putting out a fun vibe with social energy is important to get the spark going that will allow a friendship to flourish

It's also the feeling that neither of you is there to brag or show each other up. Even if you're the most successful person ever, that isn't why someone would want to be your friend. That might even be a bit of a detriment if you give off the impression you're an impossibly successful Super Busy person. We don't want to hang out with people who don't have any time for us. We just want a friend! Someone we can relate to. It's okay to be successful of course. But what's truly important in a friendship is your Friend Qualities, not any perceived external worldly success.

So the best way to get to know a new potential friend is simply to ask about them, all in a relaxed, friendly but interested manner. You're not interrogating them, but you are getting to know something about them. And it makes sense to throw in a bit about yourself as you go along. Without turning things into a monologue.

An initial question is important, but the follow-up question is more so. "So, what do you do for fun?" Suppose the answer is they like their exercise class, or their dog, or their craft that they're really good at. Or, a sports team. Then the next question might be, "What do you love about it?"

That should lead you to a really great fun answer. Which you can comment on, follow up on, or add to with experience of your own. And off you go, in a great conversation. The key in any really good conversation is to seriously listen to the person's answer. Not to drift off in your mind, or focus on the next thing you're going to say. Focus on them at first. That's how friendships are formed.

Sometimes in conversations people get stuck on facts. Facts, facts, facts. That can feel monotonous. That isn't how you create a meaningful conversation, although of course some facts are necessary. What's more important is how the other person feels about the facts!

So for example if you're asking about their job, okay get the gist of the thing, but then you might want to know what do they love about their job? What do they hate about it? What frustrates them? What aspects are they great at? What are their short- and long-term hopes? Do they feel fulfilled? Any hilarious work miscues? Triumphs? Heart-warming moments? There are so many directions you can go with this that don't involve a recitation of facts. When it comes to great conversations, FEELINGS trump FACTS every time! (And you don't have to ask all of those things at once. See which things the other person is more inclined to talk about.)

"When it comes to great conversations, FEELINGS trump FACTS every time!"

Likewise if they are asking you about your job, keep the same thing in mind! Don't just give them a recitation of facts, or answer the specific thing they asked. Tell them a great story related to your job. (funny? Heart-warming? Frustrating? Disastrous? Etc.) Or tell them what aspects of your job give you an emotional reaction, whether positive or negative. THAT is what they will relate to. Not the nitty gritty details.

You can pump that interesting energy into the conversation yourself with your great questions or your awesome answers. So give some thought to the things in your life that create an emotional reaction in you, no matter what it relates to. (job, pets, teachers, kids, family, team, class, home life, whatever!) If you're having an emotional reaction, there's probably a GREAT anecdote or story in there busting to come out.

*

Question: I'm decently famous. I'm currently in the music industry and my career is on the upswing. I'm trying to hit all the right notes, if you know what I mean. As part of that I'm in a public relationship with someone who's also pretty well known because it's good publicity for both of us, and sort of this career-boosting thing. But as you might've guessed the relationship isn't real.

The problem I'm having with it now is the longer this goes on the more uncomfortable I am with faking it when we're out in public. I never really know how to act. It feels like I'm making it up as I go along and I have no clue how it's coming across. She hasn't given me a lot of feedback either so I have no idea what she's thinking about it. Not sure how to handle this going forward.

Answer: Dang, a famous person! Are you more famous than Ross Perot? (He's my high water mark in celebrity interactions.) Anyway, doesn't matter. You haven't asked anything about the whole idea of perpetrating this fakery to begin with, so I guess I'll leave that alone and let it be the Ugly Vase in the room.

If you're a musician and not an actor I can certainly see why doing a regular acting job of this nature would be stressful. Not your skill set! Faking anything is a challenge. But I'll say this, there are many men and women who are NOT dating each other who are good friends. And they oftentimes develop an ease with each other, and a closeness that gives people the idea that they are a couple when in fact they're not.

That's because they demonstrate care and concern for each other, as well as a natural "vibe." How about going for the idea that you and she ARE actually friends. Essentially, get to know her as both a person and a friend. Maybe hang out together and exchange information as true friends would. Then your warmth will be real. Your concern for her will show. Then you can support each other in both the career and friendship aspect and let that vibe FLOW!

Not sure if I should be facilitating this fake thing, but from my perspective yeah, get out there and gain a friend because it would be good for your soul, never mind your career. As always, Bonus Big Sis Advice from me to you.

FRIEND GROUPS

Okay, what about friend "groups?" Well a lot of that can be organic luck. Pals from school who've stayed in touch and find time to get together. A work group that really clicks. People who've played on a sports team and love going out together. The neighborhood posse. A group that has formed naturally due to proximity, activity or interest. So if you've got that going, great! But what if you don't, and wish you did? You have to make the most of opportunities that present themselves.

I have definitely rolled into other people's already existing groups. Like this outsider who just appears out of nowhere. It's at least mildly daunting. But! My take on this is to not expect "the group" to do all the work in terms of acceptance or fitting in. The group already has a dynamic, its own vibe in place. So the question becomes, how does the new person fit in?

It's always helpful if the person who invites you along throws out a simple introduction. Like, "Hey guys, this is Cassandra. I know her from exercise class. She's great at scrapbooking!" or "Hermes and I work together. He's a runner." That gives people at least a little to latch onto.

Don't hang back and expect group members to do all the work. The best way to acquire some of the group's vibe is to say hello and then find out about them. That means talking to them one-on-one and getting to know them.

There's always the temptation to try to impress others with our wonderfulness. We keep thinking that's what gets us acceptance. See how wonderful I am? Accept me! I'm the awesome-est. Hmm. Now doesn't that sound just a *little* off? Doesn't it kind of ping your Needy Meter? (Again. Nothing wrong with being needy. We're all needy if we're breathing.) But our needy aspect is really something to leave on the back burner when we're trying to get to know a group of people and see if we like them and can connect with them.

It's Flip The Script Time. Instead go with the objective of discovering what they're about. Finding out what there is to enjoy about these people. Doesn't that sound more appealing? Instead of trying to work in a Humble Brag, or a Real Brag, or ANY Sort of Brag, find out what they've got going on that's great in their lives. Whether it be their job, their kid, their hobby, their house, their car, their classes or their pet. Find out what makes them smile.

That doesn't mean you shouldn't talk about yourself of course. Think of things ahead of time that are worth mentioning. Just avoid making it a bragfest or a boringfest on any level. So focus more on your interest in and acceptance of them, instead of the other way around. Flip. That. Script.

Obviously you're probably not going to have time to have an extensive conversation with everyone in a group when you first meet them. So pick someone, or a couple of someones. Then the next time get to know one or two more. Friendships are made one-on-one through personal conversations. They don't just magically happen while you're at the edge of a large circle simply listening. You have to engage on some level. And do it with 10-20 percent more enthusiasm than you were thinking.

So beyond existing groups, what can you do to create a friend group? Well, if you've got people you know from something (activity, volunteer work, school parents, co-workers, neighbors, exercise class) you can start your own thing. You can invite them to be on a recreational sports team, start a hobby club (books, knitting, scrapbooking, hunting, fishing, wood-working, gaming, outdoor activities), set a time for a regular walk and invite people along, schedule lunch (weekly? monthly? quarterly?).

You can have a regular event at your house. A Friday happy hour. A Saturday or Sunday football social. A Bible study. A discussion group. A crafty thing. Gaming. A casual potluck dinner. A gourmet club. You need to have something that will create the proximity and time spent together that people need to form friendships. Not everything will take right away, or at all, necessarily. You have to experiment. Even existing groups will transform, with members coming and going. Flexibility is key when it comes to groups.

This is more of a pitfall in a younger crowd, but what if you're part of a group but you feel like you're being left out of things? It's a pretty common scenario. It means you've failed to make friends with individuals within the group. That's the thing you need to fix. Or else move on from that group and join another. Or start your own.

Remember individual friendships come first. Group friendships develop organically from that. Otherwise you risk being a peripheral group member who is acquainted with everyone and friends with no one.

So grow those friendships one relationship at a time. And remember there's room in life for different kinds of friendships. Not everyone will be your best buddy, nor will they need to be. Close friendships tend to develop from fortunate circumstances and compatible temperaments. Life doesn't always provide the perfect opportunity for that.

You may need to expand your reach to include more potential people, or simply have more patience. There have definitely been periods of my life where my main conversational companion was a toddler. But circumstantial friends and occasional friends also have their place in life. They fill a need in a moment, and even if the connection isn't as deep as you might prefer, it can still benefit both parties.

COLLEGE DOESN'T HAVE TO BE LONELY

I want to make a special comment about people feeling lonely at college. I had the most fun and friendly dormitory hall a person could ever hope to have. (Dravo A-4 forever!) But that might not be your experience. And even if you happen to have a great hall, you still need to develop good social habits to make some friends in college.

It may seem that everyone already has friends from high school. Or that groups form quickly and somehow you get left out. You just don't find people to click with. And yet you're surrounded by hundreds of people at the same age/stage of life! Literally doing the same thing, getting your college degrees in the same place at the same time. What's wrong with this particular Social Petri Dish? Why isn't the friendship culture growing?

This situation suffers from the same intimidating factors that any social situation would. Fear of rejection. Reluctance to reach out. Some people being self-absorbed or indifferent to those around them. Clinging to a prior group due to discomfort with growth and change. And if you're feeling shy or anxious, these obstacles can seem insurmountable.

College is still a great place to meet people and develop friendships. The mistake people make is expecting it to 'just happen,' or experiencing an initial rejection and giving up. Note: If your social skills need work I'd still suggest doing the exercise I outlined in Chapter 2, where you have BRIEF energetic social interactions with service people. Such as dining hall employees, gym attendants, fast food servers, campus security, the dorm manager, library staff, T.A.s, custodial staff etc. Work at this consistently until you're confident you can bring a friendly and enthusiastic vibe that will make each interaction fun.

Once you feel you can have friendly banter with strangers, then you should turn your attention to specific campus venues for friend-making. I'm sure everyone has heard the advice, "JOIN A CLUB." It's literally the first thing anyone shouts at you when you say you're feeling lonely at college.

So it's a cliché, sure, but it's a true one! The thing is, you can't go to a club meeting and just wait for friends to materialize like Star Trek visitors beaming in. You still have to engage other students in conversation. And ultimately you will need to invite them to do something with you, and that something needs to be outside the confines of the club.

Ideally you want a club that meets frequently, at least weekly if possible. The key is to have some regular conversations, then INVITE them to something. Grab a bite to eat, go for a walk, invite them to study together, or to just swing by your living space for a snack or a chat. There are all kinds of campus events to go to, from sporting events to shows to arts programs to guest lectures to outdoorsy stuff. And give it several shots before giving up on it. Have several people in mind and keep working at it. Make sure your tone of voice is open and interested. Bring that fun and friendly vibe and make some friends!

Another way to make campus connections is to instill a Regular Intentionality to some of your actions. For example, on a dorm hall, make it a point to say hello to the people hanging out in the lounge. Make conversation in the kitchen. Knock on someone's door and offer to share the popcorn. Check in with people even if they are at first not all that responsive.

If you bring a positive and friendly vibe, most people will welcome that. The more of a regular you become, the greater chance you will kindle a connection. Don't stick to your own hall! Visit a floor above or below. Ask a favor. Offer to share something. Ask a question. The more regularly you put your fun and friendly vibe out there, the more likely you will make a connection.

We ignore the importance of connections at our peril.

We have the ability to create our own personal networks to take the place of being in a neighborhood you've grown up in, or being with an extended family that just isn't in your immediate vicinity. Fortunately we also live in a time where we can maintain our connections with physically distant family and friends via technology. But having in-person friends that you can count on and interact with regularly is equally important.

It's good for your longevity, it's good for your mental health and it's good for your social health. After your own personal spirituality, expanding your network of friends (whether it be one or many) is the single most important thing you can do to add value and meaning to your life.

What is the purpose of friendship? They're there to cheer for you when you have success. To sorrow with you when you get bad news or something's got you down. To help you when you're frazzled or overwhelmed, or in a bad spot or just plain in need. To talk you up when others are asking about you. To talk you down when you're on the ledge. To be a role model when you need one. To be a buddy when you need someone at your side. To help you when you're having trouble being your best self. To encourage you if you feel you've failed, and to remind you that it's going to be okay.

To give you a hug for no reason other than that you need one, or want one, or weren't expecting one. To give you the benefit of their experience so you don't make identical mistakes. To give you hope that tomorrow can be better. To remind you that "you've got this." To be early to your parties either to help out or to get the party started. To be the last to leave to help you clean up. To be gentle with your weaknesses. To be there for you through thick and thin, lose and win. To remind you of the big picture when your nose is smashed up against the glass of a horrible problem. Friends provide companionship, entertainment, a hand to hold onto, a shoulder to cry on.

Friends are there to insist on the truth when you forget why life is worth living. These are friends who are behaving as true friends and operating at that level.

"Friends are there to insist on the truth

when you forget why life is worth living."

FLAWED FRIENDS

I would not be Worth My Weight in Bold if I didn't also acknowledge that there are plenty of not-so-great friends out there. Ones who either didn't learn the Friendship Code, or don't know or care enough to follow it. People whom you've accumulated into your life who have somehow attained "friend" status without corresponding to what the title really means.

These are people who have come from childhood or school years, or they've latched on through some sibling or significant other, or they've just been in your life so long that there's no other way to describe what they're doing there, yet they are still a far cry from the ideal that I'm talking about.

I almost hate to delve into this area because it's a bit negative, yet I realize there are plenty of you who have such people in your lives, and they're technically "friends," so what about THAT? Am I going to ignore the obvious, that there are a lot of really crappy friends out there? Some of whom we seem to be stuck with for one reason or another?

Yeah, I'll address it. I'm just not going to overly dwell on it though, because Beating Back The Negativity Out of Your Life sounds like the subject of a whole other book. Which I also probably have in me. I'm like Wonder Woman in that regard. I dodge those Negativity Bullets and they bounce off the magic bracelets, and then I lasso the Happiness as I fly around in my invisible plane keeping an eye on things. I'm sure you'll be wanting to read THAT book.

So what about these quasi-friends, poor excuses for friends, people who populate our lives because they've just been there so long, but they really aren't all that friend-like when it comes right down to it?

First of all one of the main points of this current book is to teach you how to portray your best self so that you can BE a great friend to other people, and attract great friends into your own life. So that's a Full Steam Ahead project for you.

But what about this Social Yard of yours littered with people who have questionable friend tendencies. To what extent do we need to clear that yard?

Well people aren't objects, so I'm going to shut this metaphor down right now and start talking about these quasi-friends as the PEOPLE they are. People are not objects to be used, tossed aside or disrespected. At the same time, if someone is not acting like a true friend, or if they're bringing a lot of negativity to your relationship, or if they are simply a bad influence, that doesn't mean you need to keep them in your life in a prominent spot. Nor is it your job to "fix" them. You aren't their parent, their counselor, their parole officer or their life coach.

However what you do have domain over is which people you permit into your life, and at what level they're allowed to function. In other words, the relationship you have with that person IS your business, and you have every right to determine what you'll put up with and what you won't.

Most of the time it isn't useful to burn bridges, cut people off or drop them. Yes, sometimes that's absolutely necessary, but it's an extreme action and I view it as a last resort. Usually it's more helpful to place less priority on a relationship that isn't working right. So you downgrade it. Spend less time on it. Deprioritize it. Put it on hiatus. It's placed on "injured reserve" (to use a sports metaphor). And replace that person with healthier relationships.

Examples of such crappy stuff (NOT all -inclusive!): gossips a lot, says mean things to you, makes jokes that hurt your feelings, doesn't stop (whatever) when you inform them you don't like it, takes you for granted, spends most of their time staring at their phone while you're trying to talk to them, habitually lies to you, is only there for you when they're bored with everything else, disappears when you need them most, rarely shows up on time for anything, more likely to cancel than show up, promises X and delivers Y or nothing at all for the most part, disparages people whom you love or things you're crazy about, always talks about his or her stuff and doesn't care about any of your stuff, views you as competition instead of a pal, talks behind your back, blames you for things indiscriminately, doesn't keep your private stuff private, brings you down, etc.

So if Old Friend Dionysus does things that fall into the above categories and it's really wearing on you, then you absolutely need to find healthier relationships and put this one on the back burner. That doesn't mean you have to burn that bridge. There are any number of reasons why you might not want to do that.

They may be connected to others you know and want to hang out with. They may be tolerable as an occasional friend. They may have positive traits that you value, and you can deal with this person in small doses. And they may want to change their negative ways, and just haven't succeeded yet. Bad habits can be difficult to extinguish.

So I'm not someone who readily gives up on people. But for the sake of my mental health and peace of mind I won't spend a lot of time with someone who brings many of those negative things to the table. It's not my job to judge anyone, but it IS my job to protect myself from excess negativity as I perceive it.

And heck, we've all done variations of the above at one time or another, we're human and we've failed people at times. I'm just saying if the negative outweighs the positive in terms of how a person normally operates, it's best to keep him or her at a certain distance, or see them sparingly. And if you recognize any of those Bad Friend Habits as something you are too often guilty of yourself, then it's time for some self-reflection and a vow for a new beginning.

> *"If you recognize any of those Bad Friend Habits as something you are too often guilty of yourself, then it's time for some self-reflection and a vow for a new beginning."*

Promote the healthy, de-prioritize the unhealthy. When you have healthy friendships it's incredibly easy to see the difference! Seek out good friends, and BE that kind of good friend yourself.

INVITING PEOPLE IN

On to a more positive thought. When reaching out to make a friend, I'm essentially suggesting that you throw caution to the wind. I'm coaxing you to "put yourself out there." That's certainly a phrase you've heard before, and probably with some well-earned skepticism. Because the idea of 'putting yourself out there' fifty gazillion times in the hope of the Numbers Game yielding you a friend or two in the process, well, doesn't that sound downright EXHAUSTING? It does to me.

That method operates on the assumption that there will be some small percentage of the population that will be more or less a 'perfect' friend candidate for you. So you just have to spread yourself far and wide, searching high and low, beating the bushes until you've defoliated them in the effort to "find" friends. Again, exhausting! I need a nap right now just thinking about it.

That's why my approach is diametrically opposed to that. Instead of "putting yourself out there" an endless number of times in the hope of finding the one or two people you *might* click with because they're basically the same as you, I want you to polish your social skills until the Real You can emerge with just about anybody you come across.

I'm not a person who believes we need clones of ourselves, or just a "certain kind" of person to make up our team, our tribe, our posse. You can actually be friends with all different sorts of people, and have just as much fun that way.

So when I say to "put yourself out there" what I mean is simply to lower your natural "defenses" and give yourself a chance to shine and allow others an opportunity to know you. So to the extent that putting yourself out there means getting out of your comfort zone, then yes, you need to do that. But I think it needs to go a step further than that. You need to be comfortable "inviting people in."

That's the whole point of "being out there" to begin with. So you can create that space with other people where you can exchange happy energy, have fun conversations, can 'click' with people, and can say, "hey, let's do this again!" And you don't just want that once so you can make a friend, you want it every time so you can enjoy life, and make great connections. So Putting Yourself Out There is important, but Inviting People In is vital.

"Putting Yourself Out There is important, but Inviting People In is vital."

For many people the Comfort Zone lies in keeping to yourself, remaining unobtrusive, not saying too much, and certainly not drawing attention to yourself. Why? Because this posture is one in which you 1) Won't make a mistake, and 2) You won't be rejected.

Well. I have NEWS for you.

That's ALREADY a mistake. In fact, it's like pre-rejecting yourself. So it's a big fat fail on both levels. From a 'making friends' and 'connecting with people' standpoint, anyway. It probably does give you a better angle at the snack bowl, though, since you won't be as distracted with pesky conversations.

When you think of it that way, there's no good reason not to get out there and meet people, have great conversations, and try to generate some fun. Once you've worked on those social skills to the point where you can have awesome conversations in the grocery store, the gym, the bank, the coffeeshop, there's absolutely no reason you can't have the same type of conversations in your social life.

Look at strangers as friends you just haven't met yet. Realize the value you can bring to people's lives just by taking an interest in them, sharing what's fun and friendly about you, and connecting with them. Life is better with happy companions at your side.

Be somewhat selective about whom you let into your life. It isn't important that they're identical to you, but it IS important that they value friendship in the same way you do, and that they bring more positive qualities to the relationship than negative ones.

Not everyone will want your friendship, but sincerely making that attempt and sometimes failing is not a mistake.

The biggest mistake is to not try.

CHAPTER 4: TAKEAWAYS

1. *You become like the people you surround yourself with.*

2. *The phone should be used as a tool, not a crutch. Don't let it take the place of a sincere effort to invite people into your life for a real relationship.*

3. *You can find friends almost anywhere if you keep your mind open to that possibility.*

4. *Don't try to impress potential friends with your awesomeness. Instead impress them with your friendliness and interest in them.*

5. *De-prioritize the negative relationships in your life without burning bridges.*

6. *Putting yourself out there is important, but inviting people in is vital.*

THE POWER OF POSITIVITY

In some ways this chapter on Positivity should be the opening chapter, because it's the basis for much of what I recommend. Or it could be the final chapter, since it's the explanation for a lot of what I say. So I will defy both of those options and plop the chapter in the center, in the HEART of this book. Hmm. Maybe there is a method to my madness. Just as there is a method to people's sadness.

I have to be legitimately careful about how I discuss this, because there are plenty of serious conditions out there, one of them being chronic depression, that I'm in no way qualified to speak to. Anyone suffering from something that is affecting them in a highly negative way should seek out a competent therapist for individual treatment. That's what those professionals are there for!

Plus, many situational things can cause someone to go through a really down period. Sometimes crazy bad stuff happens, and no amount of reading or optimism or walks along a sunny beach are going to fix it. I wouldn't dare to claim otherwise. So for everyone suffering from things, large and small, or battling depression, or just stuck in a pit without knowing how to climb out, I encourage you to seek the help you need. I'm with you in spirit.

I also want to make clear that while a general attitude of positivity is helpful when it comes to both living and socializing, it isn't a cure-all. Some stuff is frankly so bad there's no putting a happy face on it. And don't let Positivity Gurus tell you otherwise. Every one of us has things that go wrong each and every day. I'm not asking you to slap a Fresh Coat of Positivity on everything like a cheap paint only to have it wash off like a watercolor.

I'm a self-taught expert on having a Positive Vibe. I have a humorous outlook to begin with, so the minute things start going wrong, I begin seeing the comedic aspects. I think life is pretty funny, except for the tragic parts.

There's nothing as hilarious as a near-disaster you've survived with all body parts intact! Recently I've experienced at least three potential conflagrations involving me and the car. It would be four if I counted the Unexpected Christmas Tree Obstacle Course, but my husband was driving for that one, so that goes on his scorecard. My friends are getting tired of hearing about my Near Death Experiences!

So let's pull out of the driveway of our day (metaphorically), and gun the engine as we face the open highway of our lives. We are Licensed To Thrive!

I believe in starting the day on a good note. For me it's prayer. For you it might be meditation, or a bit of exercise, or a great cup of coffee or tea. (I'll be joining you shortly for the coffee!) But I think it's helpful to start the day with a focusing element that will get you in the proper mood.

It's far too easy to just leap out of bed and start immediately attending to things, and not even notice the fact that you survived the night and you've been given another day. With each day being a new gift. And I have definitely been guilty of starting some of my crazier days in exactly the wrong way. Maybe a baby started crying, or we were getting up late and I had to rush the kids to school, or I just got plain lazy and didn't do a good opener to my day.

Life is habit-forming. So if you want a new habit, you have to promise yourself you're going to do it faithfully for 4-6 weeks in order for the habit to take root. Maybe write yourself a big note and attach it to the ceiling. It will say, "Be Glad I'm Alive Again Today," or something to that effect. Or maybe put it on your bathroom mirror so it doesn't fall off in the middle of the night and create a really freaky effect on your sleep.

Also, give yourself some leeway. Maybe you had to rush in the early morning, but now it's mid-morning and you're having a coffee break at work, or you have some time before or after a class, or there's just a break in your day somewhere. Start fresh! Do your morning meditation/prayer/gratitude thing right then.

You don't have to penalize yourself for not making it first thing, even though that's more ideal. Do it whenever you can squeeze it in! But still try to make it a first thing habit. It's helpful to have a Long Form and a Short Form version of this. Maybe even an Express Version! Sometimes life presents challenges that can only be responded to with Emergency Gratitude. Or Capsule Gratitude. I am nothing if not relentlessly flexible and creative with my stuff.

Gratitude. Whole books have been written on the subject, so its importance cannot be overstated. It's helpful to have a mental list of the things you're most grateful for. Write them down, because sometimes you think of things that didn't occur to you before. Also a great exercise to do with family or friends is to write down what they are most grateful about for EACH OTHER. What a wonderful gift to receive from another person! You can even do updates.

Pick a body part of the day and be glad it's working correctly. We usually only pay attention to what's going wrong. Admire your Properly Working Pancreas, your Fully Functioning Frontal Lobe, your Effortlessly Effective Esophagus.

And even if you have stuff that isn't going right with your body (which is pretty much all of us), you still have a gazillion body parts working correctly. If that weren't the case, you wouldn't even be alive to read this. I'm amazed how many body parts actually work the way they're supposed to the vast majority of the time. It's truly impressive!

In any case, why not focus on the things that are going right?

As a person who cooks enthusiastically, I'm amazed at the sheer variety that is available to us in grocery stores. Compared to 50, 100, 1000 years ago, we can eat like some kind of weird royalty! We don't even need to go to an exclusive restaurant. The exotic things we have available to us locally would be incomprehensible to people from most of our recorded history.

Even though I consider myself a decently good cook, I have definitely had moments where I've concocted a dish where the ingredients all fused together and tasted like building products! Or that one thing I made that had four different textures, and none of them tasted good! I still suffer the occasional Cooking Disaster to this day. The point being, don't let missteps get you down, socially speaking. Failure is just part of life. And when you've experienced that it makes the successes so much sweeter, whether they be in the social or culinary realm!

"Why not focus on the things that are going right?"

How about that tall glass of water? Did you know water didn't start becoming widely chlorinated until the 20th century? Before then you were playing Drinking Glass Roulette! So I'm grateful for the very basics of life, the people who populate it, and too many other positives to count. So how do we balance that against the negatives? Well the negatives are just things to deal with. Some of them can be turned into positives depending on how they're approached. Others can just be endured.

I've found, though, that sometimes when you have to deal with difficult people, it's helpful to look at the bigger picture. It's so easy to affect others' moods in a negative way. Pump a lot of negativity out there, and watch people flee to escape it. People are like rubberbands. If you snap at them, very likely they'll snap back. And the sum total of negativity will increase!

But I like to work on changing the overall dynamic. Why let the negative person dictate my mood? I don't have to! So, sometimes I will encounter negativity and: 1) Pretend I didn't notice it, or 2) Let it bounce harmlessly off my self-imposed Positivity Force Field, or 3) Make a deliberate attempt to respond neutrally or positively despite what I just heard. These are all viable choices!

I like having options, not feeling like I need to respond in kind. Also, if someone is really upset about something, it's helpful to sit with them and work through where that came from and if there's anything you can do to help. It's a judgment call though. If they're just ranting and raving, and firing negative stuff, then maybe it's too soon for a talk. Sometimes only isolation and ice cream can help.

I do try to limit the sheer amount of time I spend with negativity. If someone has a grievance with me I will certainly hear them out, and offer any apologies that may be warranted, and try to fix the thing if it's fixable. But what I'm NOT going to do is put up with endless complaints about the same thing, or suffer unjust invective.

You can be mad at me, but please watch your tone! Short aggravations should be dealt with in 10 minutes or less. Cloudburst, apology, done. Bigger complaints can go longer if your anger is really eloquent and you have a lot of important points to make about a complex situation. But my tolerance for dealing with unabated Bad Crap expires after that.

You will have to buy another ticket or token for the following day. You may even have to make a case for me having to listen to more, because unless the argument has changed, just tell me it's Irritation #5, I'll make a mental note and we can skip the repeat unpleasant conversation.

Seriously! Just deal with The Thing. Don't invite The Bad Thing to be a member of the household if it isn't paying rent or taking out the garbage. (I think I'm working my way up to a completely ill-advised therapy book now.)

"Just deal with The Thing. Don't invite the Bad Thing to be a member of the household if it isn't paying rent or taking out the garbage."

It can be easy to fall into this bad pattern of people sniping at each other, or blaming each other, or taking out their frustrations on those around them, or people simply not treating each other as human beings deserving of respect. You should treat your family members at least as well as you would a total stranger. Not worse because you're taking them for granted.

So I will put up with a certain amount of negativity (even from myself) because we all have bad days. But at some point I will retreat from excess negativity because it's just not healthy for me. That's a good time to take a walk, or go out for a coffee, or stop by the church, or shop for obscure vitamins.

With family members, the situation is what it is, so excess negativity might have to be dealt with just by trying to de-escalate. But when it comes to social life and your friendships, you can actually choose to be around people who bring a lot more positives to your life than negatives.

It's always a tough call when you've got a long-time or close friend who is "in some ways" toxic. Toxic. That isn't one of my favorite terms. I hear the term Toxic People being tossed around like a really unhealthy salad. I like to think there are Toxic Traits rather than Toxic People. But. I know there are some real examples out there of what can only be called Toxic People. So I'm not going to argue that they don't exist. Just that if you're aware of a hugely negative effect when you're in the presence of certain people, you really need to avoid, limit or prevent spending much time with them.

Hmm. Why does a chapter on Positivity have to spend so much time talking about these Negatives? Probably because life isn't perfect, and people are dealing with a lot of things. There are even people who are Temporarily Toxic because of stuff they're going through.

Even in those cases though, it's good to set limits for yourself as to how much negativity you will endure before telling them you've reached your quota that day. Because none of us is impervious to negativity. If you sit there and listen to it hour after hour, it's going to make you crazy. And the results won't be good for either you, or the person you're indulging in their Ventfest. So limit that stuff! I'm going to arbitrarily say half an hour. After 30 minutes of venting/negativity, I call we have to take a break for snacks, or better yet, positivity.

If the other person can't think of one nice/positive thing to say after venting for half an hour, then that's it. Time's up! Limit reached. Someone go walk the dog, feed the cat or change the birdcage. My own limit on a negative conversation is more like 15 minutes. If it's taking longer than that I will require a flowchart and maybe a Powerpoint to keep all the negativity straight. I'll start making hand-drawn illustrations on the back of paper plates! With fascinating cartoon noses!

Take a breather and come up for some positivity! How about take a timeout and PRAY together? Whatever form your spirituality takes. It's difficult to keep hurling negativity at people when God's in the middle.

I described slightly adjusting the look on my face when I'm by myself. I made it just the teeniest bit more positive. From a physical perspective it's fairly subtle. But the effect on my mood was pretty large! That sounds almost crazy. But I would definitely prescribe it, like a mood-enhancing drug.

"Smile a bit to yourself when you're alone. Like a fun surprise is coming. Or you know the secret to happiness." Take 4x daily as needed. Unlimited Refills.

"It's difficult to keep hurling negativity at people when God's in the middle."

So a small smile did that for me. Made me more joyful than my Normal Joyful. It increased my energy. My readiness to do things. My mood. My willingness to engage people.

Do I have anything else in my grab bag of Positivity Tricks? I'm picturing a bag like the one Mary Poppins uses, where she pulls out a full-sized floor lamp. I do actually, although it isn't related to socializing per se. It can be used in that manner though, so I'll include it.

Each year my husband and I clean our garage. It accumulates random stuff, because we're originally northerners from Buffalo who are used to having basements, and we have no basement in Florida. So we accumulate a LOT of stuff that doesn't belong.

So we declare a Garage Clean-Out day. We do it together, just he and I, even though we have two college-aged sons. We summon them to help us move heavy things. It's an opportunity to get the garage just how we want it, plus we don't want to hear any whining about "how long is this going to take," and "when is this going to be over." But here's the thing. You can view this as an unfortunate task. Or you can view it as a Fun Tradition!

So we have transformed it into a Fun Tradition. I decided we must have a Parent-centric soundtrack from decades earlier. (another reason to leave the college kids mostly out of this picture) We open up our garage and start pulling everything out onto the driveway and lawn.

I look forward to our annual garage clean-out tradition. Doing it together as a team is much more fun than either of us tackling it by ourselves, or doing it alone in gradual parts. The picture of us doing it has made our annual Christmas card!

Doing difficult tasks can often be more fun with family and friends. Anything done from a place of "we're going to have fun with this" is much more satisfying than focusing on it being drudgery, or boring, or endless. That's what makes the annual Thanksgiving feast such a joy to cook. Everyone's pitching in with something! It's social. It's fun. It's joyful. It isn't just me alone in the kitchen doing ju jitsu with the giblets.

This can really be extrapolated to any task in life. Find the social element. Find the fun. Turn it into a game. Turn on the tunes. Give yourself interim awards and prizes. Pretend you're being televised. "I'd like to explain to our audience just why we have so MANY bags of cat litter out here…" One of the days we were working on the garage I'm going to conservatively estimate it was sunny, 99 hot Florida degrees, plus bonus humidity. We turned the hose on each other.

So there are ways to take essentially negative situations and transform them into positive ones.

*

Question: My husband and I got married right after college and recently we moved near his hometown, about 30 minutes away. My in-laws want us closer. They can't seem to accept that we're happy where we are. They ask why we can't be like my husband's brother who's "only five minutes away." Now they're always making rude comments and blaming me. What's the best way to respond?

Answer: Ouch! I can see where they're coming from, but it's your life to live, not theirs. I don't think I'd want to live any closer to THAT attitude, certainly not "five minutes away!" However you don't need to respond to every comment. If anyone does, have your husband do it. Just let it fall on Otherwise Joy-Filled Ears. I suggest NOT trying to appease them because you can't.

But, you CAN respond with kindness. You can visit. Call weekly. Send cute texts. Even if they're cold or mean, you don't have to respond in kind. Pretend they're loving and supportive even when they aren't. That'll help your own peace of mind. So like them "in spite" of themselves, not because of it. Make it a fun job that you're determined to do well, and don't invest *anything* in the outcome. Just treat it like an interesting game you play. They do or say something awful? Make them some brownies, or buy them something they like "just because." Don't even expect a thank you. Seek your own satisfaction in doing a nice thing.

So, that's how we turn a negative into a positive. Don't respond in kind to negativity. Turn it into a game, complete with prizes. You're not trying to win anyone else's approval; you're trying to win your OWN approval. It's hard when someone's firing slings and arrows at you, but remember you can put up a Kindness Force Field that will cause them to bounce off.

Most people aren't totally ill-tempered. They may just be stuck in a bad habit. Or suffering from something physically. It's tempting to keep them at arm's length for your own self-protection. That's human nature. But what if you tried to overcome your human nature? Actually went of your way to SINCERELY compliment them? Or responded to their negativity with something "as if" what they just said was pleasant? (and not in a sarcastic manner) The power of love and positivity can do amazing things if you try to persistently apply it. Think of love as a Behavior Balm. It might not clear up that Rancorous Rash right away, but give it time! And it will certainly do good things for your peace of mind regardless.

Question: I'm a college student who commutes. I live with my family, and my grandfather is here on a long-term visit. My parents claim my grandfather thinks I'm cold and rude to him. I know I don't talk much, but I'm not ignoring anybody. I can never think of anything to say. I'm just uninteresting. Pretending to smile is getting old, and now they're saying I'm rude! And it's hard to fake being interested all the time. I do like my family but I can't stand the idea that they think I'm being rude just because I don't have much to say. How can I fix this?

Answer: I give you a lot of credit for wanting to make a change! That's how all change begins. Couple of things I picked up on in your question: "Pretending to smile." If you're smiling because you're "supposed to," or to create an effect of friendliness, it won't be genuine. So it will feel forced (to you) and it will seem forced (to them). Lose/lose situation.

It should come from a place of joy and happiness in your heart. You ARE glad to see them! And you are happy to be spreading your joy. So first you have to work on actually attaining that feeling within yourself. I get this mainly through gratitude. Every morning I think of all the things I take for granted that are huge gifts in my life. Health. Family. Running water. Air conditioning. The fact that we didn't accidentally burn our house down a couple weeks ago. Internet. Etc. How about grandpa? You won't have him forever. In 10-20 years he may be gone. He may be gone next year. Nobody knows! Value the fact that you have him now.

You call yourself "uninteresting." You know what, a world traveler, an astronaut, a wild animal trainer, or a feng shui consultant...they sound interesting but they could be total bores. They could go on and on about them and "their thing." Interesting people are ones who get the conversation started, ask good questions, ask relevant follow up questions, and are interested in the person and the conversation. That means good eye contact and a certain enthusiasm in your tone when you're asking questions and making comments.

It has ZERO to do with what you "know," or where you've been. When you share stuff about yourself, keep it short, and share the things that would interest or amuse others. Tell your grandfather how school is going, what your day is like, your hopes for the future. Then try asking her about HIS life, and what things were like many years ago. People love to talk about their memories of a bygone era. (Me, I like to talk about bygone meals! Bygone vacations! Bygone hilarious incidents! If it's "bygone" chances are I'm gonna recycle it! Nothing like having a 'green' conversation!)

Start small. Each day think of something to share with your grandfather about yourself. Also think of a question to ask him. Be interested, make solid eye contact, ask good follow-up questions, and use an enthusiastic tone of voice. Grandparents usually don't need much encouragement to get rolling on a story, so get him started and let it fly! These techniques also come in handy when you go off into the adult world.

Question: I hate bothering people because I don't want to cause anyone any trouble. So I don't ask for things I need. I don't reach out to people for friendships (they probably already have plenty of friends). I don't even like bothering people for things I should bother them about, like asking a professor a question. What can I do to improve this?

Answer: You don't solve this with a gradual approach. It works best if you Flip The Script, and desensitize yourself to That Thing You Fear. You're worried about imposing on other people's time. So you need to do the opposite of what you fear doing. Instead of "improving" by being "only a little bit bothersome," you need to fully embrace the idea of BECOMING bothersome. Yep. You heard that right.

Now why would anyone want to become bothersome? Well you can't properly socialize with people without intruding on their time, their consciousness, their presence, their attention. So by definition, socializing requires that you be 'bothersome.' The key is to make it a welcome bother, not an unpleasant one. So realize it's your duty to be bothersome.

"You need to fully embrace the idea of BECOMING bothersome."

Make yourself a plan. I'm going to bother at least one new person a day, one I haven't bothered before! Or I'm going to bother a different person at least once an hour with something like: a greeting, a question, a compliment. Something. You have to desensitize yourself to the idea of bothering people. Instead make it a valuable and valiant GOAL. If you need help with the social skills that will make it easier to have that be a welcome thing to people, then that's the next thing up on your list.

When I first started in public relations fresh out of college I was with a division of General Motors. One of my duties was to act as "company photographer." At first, the idea intimidated me. I had to take pictures of all kinds of things. People doing work on the job. Documentation of big meetings, special events, union agreements, etc. I was in these incredibly cavernous, loud, crowded, busy assembly and component parts plants. Wearing safety glasses. Schlepping around with a giant camera bag with a zillion heavy lenses. I was thinking, "Geesh, I'm going to be out there in the way bugging everybody with my camera." Well my boss put an end to that line of thinking quickly. "This is your job," he snarled at me. "No one will care that you're there. You're just doing what we need you to do."

And just like that, I had permission to bother every single person in the company. Even the company executives. It was liberating, actually. It was my job. Nobody could question me. In fact, I could order people around, explaining that I needed them to do this, that or the other. And I found that this mentality carried over into my regular life. It was my JOB to bother people, ask them things, interrupt whatever they were doing. As long as I wasn't rude, it was perfectly fine! So I'm going to assign you a task today. It's your job to bother people. Because you're on this planet at this particular time in history. And you're reading my book. So, obviously! Now get out there and BOTHER.

USING YOUR BRAIN FOR GOOD

The brain is an amazing instrument. It does incredible things that are too wondrous to contemplate. Things we tend to take for granted because we don't even "think" about them. Essentially if you didn't already own a brain you couldn't afford one. Take the hypothalamus for instance. The hypothalamus is basically like the brain's Cruise Director. It keeps your daily physiology in line, regulates appetite (the buffet!), guides the release of your hormones, controls body temperature, manages sexual behavior, and regulates emotional responses (good days and bad days on that one!). Yes we should have a lot of respect and gratitude for our hypothalamus.

The ability to express complex emotions in subtle (and sometimes not-so-subtle) ways is one of the things that separates humans from lower order animals. A lot of our communication with each other is emotion-based. It's part of what makes communicating sometimes complicated and frustrating, as well as rich and rewarding. If we were just robotically issuing statements at each other in a monotone with no facial expressions and zero body language, well there wouldn't be much to pick up on or misinterpret, would there? That's part of the whole mystery of human beings. What we're saying as contrasted with or emphasized by what we're *really* saying.

"If you didn't already own a brain you couldn't afford one. So be grateful for it!"

So we've got this complex bit of equipment called the human brain. Somehow we're allowed to operate it without a license and no specialized training. We don't even think to take special care of it until we're old enough to ride a bike and parents start reminding us to 'wear a helmet.'

The brain is a powerful enough instrument to make your life catastrophically miserable or unimaginably delightful. Most of us settle for brains that are 'pretty reliable but full of surprises.' But the thing is, if you don't get its remarkable power under control, you can inadvertently end up letting it take you down a dark path. (Worries! Obsessions! Resentments! Regrets! Envies! Jealousies! Stress! Tendency to relive every last negative thing!) or you can unlock its potential to take you in a more positive direction (Gratitude! Joy! Healing! Delight! Connecting with our Creator! Reliving positive memories! Visualization! Developing good habits! Extinguishing bad habits!)

The extent to which you can get your brain working with you instead of against you has a direct impact on your success and happiness in life. "Success" being defined as living the sort of life you want to live. It's easy to let bad brain habits overwhelm good brain habits if you don't realize that's what's going on. (Don't expect a book on neuroscience from me anytime soon. I know those need citations!).

Get your brain to work in your favor. It has been said that the brain doesn't know the difference between something you've experienced and something you imagined you experienced. This is why visualization is good practice. It's also why mentally practicing what you need to do in an emergency situation increases the odds of you doing the right thing if a real emergency breaks out.

I'm always trying to trick my brain into thinking life is more fun than it is. I turn boring and monotonous things into games. I turn things I don't want to do, or am afraid to do, into games. I turn unpleasant things into games. Basically, I'm into GAMES! Tricking your brain into thinking life is more fun than it is actually MAKES it more fun than it is!

> ## *"Tricking your brain into thinking life is more fun than it is actually MAKES life more fun than it is!"*

Here's another one of my secrets. I'm a pessimistic optimist. What that means is I expect wonderful things out of life. At the same time, I try to really lower my expectations of what the experience will consist of, or what will satisfy me. So I'm continually in this state of wonder that my expectations are exceeded.

I do expect good outcomes. And usually my brain does a wonderful job of helping the great outcome to materialize. It sounds contradictory, but it really helps me enjoy most experiences. I'm also a Make The Bester. Whatever the situation is, I'll try to wring something good out of it, even if it seems objectively terrible in the moment.

So I do whatever I can to trick my brain into working with me instead of against me. That's why I want us to "Life Hack Our Way To Social Success." It's the next best thing to a magic wand!

What happens in life is pretty much an objective thing. But what we tell ourselves about that event is up to us. Life doesn't write the story. WE write the story. The same event can be interpreted and processed by people in different ways.

Remember my golf outing with the acquaintance who was crabby about everything? She had a miserable time that day. I not only remember it as an amusing story, but I even further capitalized on it by using is as an illustration in this book as an example of How Not To Do Life. One person's Ostensible Humiliating Failure is another person's Life Lesson and Stepping Stone To Future Success. So the event itself is not changed, but our perception of it is.

Another of our bad brain habits is mentally revisiting past "social crimes." The time someone was telling a story and you interrupted. Or the time you asked a sincere question and you could tell by the look on their face it came across as rude. Or the time you called that new acquaintance by the wrong name. Or you said something intended to be funny that was truly awful—not just a tangle of the tongue, but a complete swan dive down the stairs and bellyflop off the bannister by your brain.

Our brains LOVE to hang out at the scenes of our every faux pas, re-running the show like a bad movie or a persistent pop tune lyric. We do this LONG after everyone else has completely forgotten about it. Yeah, we used to be Cave Dwellers, but in modern times we're now Comment Dwellers.

These things are truly awful in the moment, but you give them much more power than they deserve by re-living them. So apologize and then laugh at your human fallibility. Then, STAY OUT OF THE COMMENT CAVE. If you find yourself revisiting prior comments, then write yourself a fun, fresh script. Then bring THAT to your next social gathering.

What was the purpose of remembering bad events when we WERE Cave-

Dwellers? Simply to learn a lesson that would keep us alive the next time around. So allow yourself to replay a past Terrible Social Event once to examine it, and maybe a second time to re-do it in a NEW way for yourself. When you write yourself the fresh script, cast yourself as the hero/heroine who does and says the right thing. Feel free to play THAT scene in your head as many times as you want. I'll even provide the popcorn!

Take the attitude of cats. Cats are cool characters, always hanging out, completely in command of their emotions. Every once in a while I'll see one of our cats try to make an expert jump and miss, or try to steal another cat's treat and get whapped in the side of the head. Or it'll hurl up its dinner right in front of a crowd. The cat ought to be dying of embarrassment but it NEVER is! It just resumes its calm posture, looking at me like, "WHAT. You've got a problem with what I just did? I've got more where THAT came from."

If your brain is spending too much time Comment Dwelling, create the new script and channel your inner cat. Your brain doesn't know the difference between what actually happened and what you THOUGHT happened. So tell your brain to use the Winning Script instead of the Cringy Script.

You've probably heard the phrase "Nature abhors a vacuum." Well, so does your brain! So if you try to banish a negative thought by chasing it out of your brain, it'll keep trying to wriggle its way back in. That's why it's important to fill your brain with more positive images so there's no room for the negative thought.

Take your Social Mistake and REPLAY the thing as the way you wanted the interaction to go. Or better yet, create an entirely NEW interaction in your head, with you being the hero of the story. Visualize, internalize and memorize. (VIM!) Push out the bad thoughts and replace them with new, healthier thoughts that are part of the script for future fun interactions!

*

Question: I have no friends. My father died many years ago, I'm an only child, and my mother passed away this year. I'm working remotely, so I don't even have co-workers. In the past friends have either dumped all their problems and weren't interested in me, or I felt like I couldn't be myself around them, so I acted how I thought they wanted. That made me feel fake. Now I feel like if I had a friend, they would just put up with me, or hang out with others and not invite me to anything. I want to be confident, but due to my history I just don't feel that way. I'd like to discuss it with my mom, but obviously I can't. I'm worried about leaning too much on my husband, even though he's very supportive. Any ideas on where I can go from here?

Answer: Whew! That's a lot to deal with. I'm really sorry about your mom. That just adds to the whole aspect of not having people to rely on other than your husband. No one can replace your mom, and the grief from that goes on for a long time. Don't be afraid to have conversations with her even now. You won't get direct feedback, but she'll hear you.

I do feel your isolation. One way to slowly work your way out of this despair could be through some volunteer work. You might do it in honor of your mom. It will also allow you to help people who need it. You will grow your self-esteem through serving others. You can also get to know other volunteers. And it helps provide perspective on life, that yours may not be perfect, but many people are worse off. It's a good way to start some low-stress socializing, and you may even make friends from it.

As far as your prior experiences with friendship, those do sound unbalanced. Friendship is all about give-and-take, reciprocity, and being there for each other. So if you're dealing with someone who has very little interest in you, then you're better off moving on rather than continuing to pretend it's a friendship. Same thing with changing yourself to fit in with friends' expectations. A good friend will accept you for who you are, regardless of room for improvement. I'm sorry these early experiences with friends have been bad ones, but not everybody behaves that way.

Even though you consider yourself relatively friendless, that doesn't mean you're unworthy of friends, or you're in a position of having to take what you can get, no matter how awful and un-friendlike the person acts. I think you'll have more success if you get out there and just enjoy people and bring some positive interactions to them with no goal other than to brighten their day. Oftentimes if you do good things just for the heck of it and for no other reason, you'll find goodness attracts itself back to you. So bring joy, positivity and enthusiasm to those around you.

That means getting out of the house in some way and bringing your best self to your surroundings. I know it's hard to think about positivity and joy in a year in which you lost a parent. But, that's probably the one thing your mom would like to see you do right now. So, do it for her!

*

Why is positivity so important for friendships? For one, friendships are optional relationships. So there's no good reason to bring negativity into your life. What is a friend doing there, anyway, other than to add some bonus positivity to your life? If your life is not better off with the friend in it, you really need to go back and re-evaluate the purpose of hanging out with that person!

You know they've done studies on positivity. (Which I absolutely, positively am not going to cite.) They've learned things like sports teams that are positive about their upcoming season tend to do better than those who aren't. People who suffer difficult situations whether it be a health problem, divorce, business failure, unexpected catastrophe—all get better outcomes if they are able to find a positive framework and tell themselves a positive story, in spite of what they're dealing with.

Negative people blame themselves, give up on the situation and conclude that all is lost. Positive people blame the circumstances, learn the lessons, and think of the current problem as a temporary one-off. This is a monumental generalization of course, but I like it, so I'm going to flow with it! ("Don't cite me, dude." That's my version of "Don't tase me, bro.")

*

Question: What do you do when someone gets upset with you when you try to set boundaries? I have problems being assertive and have a difficult time standing up for myself because I avoid confrontations. What do I do when I try to tell someone they crossed a line with me, and then they get angry with me because I said something?

Answer: Setting boundaries and standing up for yourself is a good thing, not a bad thing, so you have nothing to apologize for in that regard. If someone gets angry at you for establishing a boundary, a good statement might be, "I'm sorry you feel that way, but this is how it needs to be FOR ME." Just because someone is angry doesn't mean you have to feel guilty about that. You're not responsible for alleviating someone else's anger. They've essentially created their own problem, so they need to own their anger. You're just responsible for you!

I realize it's hard to watch someone's anger, or feel like you're the target of that. I give people a certain amount of time to vent, and maybe another amount of time to cool off or calm down. If that doesn't happen I'll just move on. "Well I see you're having a tough time with this. We can talk some other day when we've both cooled down a bit."

Okay notice something else I did with that statement. I offered to help shoulder the person's burden on the anger. Even though I may not have been the angry one, I said we're BOTH going to cool down. Because when you tell someone that they need to cool down, or get into a better mood, that oftentimes fans the flames of anger even more because it implies the problem is "all them." Even if the problem IS "all them," (from your perspective) it's still generous to say we need to take a break from this and cool off. Consider it to be a good form of Anger Etiquette.

Yeah there are plenty of people who have a habit of throwing off a lot of negativity. And some of them don't even have very good aim! They just spray it around like shrapnel. Or a lead-based lawn sprinkler.

I imagine this polite conversation, "Do you mind if I share my poisonous thoughts with you?"

"Why no, go right ahead, I'm in the mood for a delicious downer!"

I'm not saying people can't have tough conversations, of course. But there are constructive ways to do it. So try to play fair, be honest, and take as much care with the other person's feelings as you would with your own! Constructive criticism gives people good feedback while building them up, not tearing them down. Constructive, right? It's sitting there right in the word!

Question: I feel like I don't have my own personality. I can't break out of my shell and act like myself. Everyone acts like I'm boring. That's partly because I'm afraid of people judging me, and I feel like I can't trust them. I don't even know where the real me is. Do you have any advice?

Answer: Yourself is in there, deep down, and it's meaningful and interesting. But it will take a sense of enthusiasm to communicate it properly. So you need to develop enthusiasm for life, enthusiasm for yourself, and enthusiasm for others. With those three things, you can connect, and you can socialize well while being true to yourself.

The 'External You' is fearful, is so afraid of being judged that your exterior comes across as a statue. Rigid, unmoving. Just "there" to be looked at, not interacted with. Maybe even 'pooped on' as birds tend to do with statues? I hate to throw something so scatological in there, but it just sort of emerged when I started going in the statue direction.

Anyway, let's move it over into the Star Wars Universe with Han Solo being frozen into carbonite on the orders of Darth Vader. Picture Darth Vader being your mortal enemy. (Not hard to do!) He's ordered your personality to be frozen into carbonite. Also picture what type of character Han Solo is. He's bold, active, engaging, a lot of FUN for someone who's rough around the edges! He has a starcruiser's worth of energy and passion!

So the person with THAT kind of energy is deep down inside you, but is encased in carbonite because Darth Vader doesn't want the world getting to know the Real You. Darth Vader represents nothing more than fear. No one's going to actually shoot you with a blaster if you start sharing more of yourself with others.

The way to begin unfreezing that carbonite is with some passion and social energy. And you get to practice it on all those Storm Troopers and Droids that you meet in your daily activities! When you get really good at these interactions, bring that passion to the rest of the universe.

Question: How do you become the sort of person people want to hang out with?

Answer: Earlier I used a beachball as a metaphor for random irrational fears. Well I believe in recycling! Now I'm going to re-purpose that same beachball for something positive. If you're going to go to a social gathering, what should you bring with you? I'm going to suggest you come with a beachball! No, not an actual plastic beachball. With the stuff that a beachball represents.

Number one, it's fun. So you go to any gathering with a sense of fun, joy and enthusiasm. Remember emotions are contagious! Second, a beachball is a toy. So you can bring a playful attitude, one that will turn things into a game. One that jokes around with people in a nice way. Third, beachballs are colorful. So that implies you will show up with an interesting topic or two. And a vibrant, interested tone of voice. Next, beachballs are multi-colored with different panels. That suggests an openness to other people and different points of view. Everything welcome to be considered! Beachballs are also resilient. If they get pushed, prodded or poked they will bounce back to the original shape.

Finally, remember that beachballs are ideally SHARED. No one should be hugging their beachball to themselves, refusing to play with others! If you really think about what a beachball represents, that means you are bringing a whole lot of goodness to any social event.

So if your beachball is flat, still stuck in the package (or worse, you haven't even bought it yet!), it's time to think about acquiring your very own Giant Metaphorical Fabulous Beachball. Use your social skills, energy and enthusiasm to INFLATE that thing and bring with you everywhere you go. It will be only in your head of course, unless you put it in your car for some weirdly idiosyncratic inspiration, (I suggest buckling it in for safety's sake!), but it's pretty hard to let go of the mental image of a giant beachball.

Do not go to any social gathering without your beachball.

CHAPTER 5: TAKEAWAYS

1. *Positivity is good for: your brain, your health, your outlook, your friendships, your survival.*

2. *Happiness Rx: Smile To Yourself. Take at least 4x daily. Unlimited Refills.*

3. *Indulge in gratitude daily. If you don't have time for a lengthy rendition, try Express Gratitude, Capsule Gratitude or Emergency Gratitude.*

4. *Tricking your brain into thinking life is more fun than it is actually MAKES life more fun than it is.*

5. *Think of love as a Behavior Balm. It might not clear up that Rancorous Rash right away, but give it time!*

6. *Don't get stuck in the Comment Cave of cringy social statements. Mentally rewrite the script into a winning scenario, then VIM: Visualize, Internalize, Memorize. Fill your brain with positive scenes so there's no room to replay the negative ones.*

7. *Bring your Metaphorical Beachball to all social opportunities.*

AWKWARD TO AWESOME

Being ignored on your birthday.

I'm putting this concept right in the middle of this book so we can all stare at it. It is an awkward concept. It may even be the most awkward of awkward social non-events. Because I figure this book exists to Iron the Awkward right out of your shirt, and having zero people wishing you a happy birthday is like pulling a linen blazer out of a scorching hot dryer. It is Wrinkle City.

There are also variations of this that feel almost as awful. Like the person who has a 'friend group' that is sort of hit and miss, so NO ONE in this amorphous group notices your birthday, so you have to put it on the calendar yourself, inform everyone of it, and then make actual plans to invite them to it. This is then followed by people not responding, bailing or flaking at the last minute. And then you end up with (if you're lucky) two impatient people who then either leave early or suggest doing something else. Or one person who decides to take pity on you and at least eat some food with you. Or, nobody but nobody shows up.

This. Is. The. Worst.

But it happens. I read and hear about it repeatedly. And you know what? Good for you! Anyone who has done some version of the above. Because at least you have the guts to give yourself a celebration that you deserve. And the fact that most of the world is indifferent to your special day, and unaware of your value, well, the world hasn't met the Real You that I know is deep inside you. Because if they HAD met that person, there would be plenty of people happy to celebrate with you.

So the point is: I want them to meet that person. The best version of the Real You.

"I want the world to meet the best version of the Real You."

And by the way, having nobody to celebrate your birthday with you is not a problem in itself. It's just one day, you're a year older. In the grand scheme it's not that big of a deal. If you're lucky the day will roll around again next year. However, it can be a symptom of a larger problem!

So don't focus on the birthday, uneaten cake and lack of presents, cards, or well wishes. (Would it kill someone to just send a text? Stupid insensitive friend group.) Instead let's think about the bigger point. For someone who is in a 'friend group' that ignores your birthday, it means one of two things. The first thing could be that this friend group doesn't do birthdays. Or doesn't do them consistently. Nothing wrong with that! Even in workplaces you'll see some work groups that do birthdays and some that don't. Or ones that have a "motivated subgroup" and an "indifferent subgroup."

But if your friend group generally does acknowledge birthdays and they all seem to melt into the ether when it comes to yours, then that indicates an interesting problem. (Let me also state the caveat that they need to be aware of the birthday. If you haven't told them when it is, don't expect them to read your mind or call your mother!)

The problem is that you are friends with a 'group,' but not a particular person IN the group. You're orbiting the social scene but don't have a secure place within it. If you had a true friend in the group, at a minimum THAT person would want to celebrate with you, and wouldn't force you to plan it all yourself. (although it could just be the two of you, and he or she might ask you where you want to go). The diagnosis is: Friend Group providing illusion of friendship, but the disappointing birthday scenario reveals this to be completely inadequate.

So, don't sit around and sulk about a horrible non-birthday celebration. It isn't the birthday that matters. It's what it reveals about the state of your social life. I'm not a person who believes you need a huge crowd to celebrate a birthday. For some, family members are enough. Or an outing with a close friend or two. It doesn't really matter how many as long as you have someone to celebrate with.

Really, a birthday event is just an excuse to have fun and celebrate the person that you're friends with. So if the people you hang out with don't want to have anything to do with you or your birthday, then it's time for some self-reflection. And I'm not going to judge how you ought to feel about it. Some people don't give two hoots about their birthday. Others don't like the attention. Some would just rather not. There's nothing wrong with any of that!

But if you're feeling sad that you don't have friends to celebrate with, then use the crappy birthday experience to motivate yourself to change things for next year. Not so much for the sake of the birthday. It's really for the sake of having the social connections you want to have in your life. The birthday is evidence of the problem, not the problem itself.

*

Question: I'm beginning to dread my birthday. Same thing every year. The family wishes me a happy birthday and I get a cake. But the so-called friends don't even care. No texts. No birthday plans. Nothing. Not even if I hint around about it the week before. I honestly can't wait for it to be over so I can resume my pathetic life.

Answer: First off, happy birthday! Please apply my well wishes to any under-celebrated year of your choice. Second, you don't have a pathetic life. You just have a lot of great life potential you haven't fully tapped yet. Third, the real problem isn't your birthday. The problem is you don't have enough people to care about you the other 364 days of the year. You mention having "friends," but none of them is reaching out, even with the help of HINTS. This is at best an Acquaintance Group, not a Friend Group.

So. How do we fix this?

You start by deciding you need to make friends within your own 'friend group.' Yeah. Sounds ironic and redundant, but it isn't. This group is Friendship In Name Only, or FINO, so you actually have to start from the beginning and make a friend as if you've just met them. Sure, they know your name and they see you hanging out there on the periphery like a bit of stage scenery, but who is your friend? Who is going to come to your house? Who's going to call you? Who's going to care about your stuff? Anybody? At the moment, no. Not until you reach out and start developing an actual friendship.

Maybe you don't feel ready for that yet. Maybe you need to work on your social skills first. As the Social Sleuth I'm going to suggest that's probably true, or you would've made friends in this group already. But, it's also possible you haven't asked any of them to hang out with you one-on-one. We're all busy, so maybe you just haven't had time to initiate something. So give that a try, and see if you get any takers.

If you feel you can work within your group on the key social skills I mentioned in prior chapters, great, go ahead. But I suggest working on these things daily. It's the only way to get good at this stuff. It might feel unnatural or uncomfortable at first. Most new skills do. But the more you practice, the better you'll get. With experience and success you'll gain confidence.

Funny thing about all of that. Once you actually learn how to connect with people you may actually find out that although you're willing to celebrate your birthday, suddenly it doesn't take on the importance it once did. Because once you have real friends, you already know you're valued by them. And sure, they'll help you celebrate a birthday, but if the timing doesn't work out, or circumstances interfere, you will realize that oh well, you missed out on that, but it doesn't really matter because you DO have people who care about you.

And that is enough.

Yep. It wasn't about the cake. It was about the friends.

Question: Just had another birthday. I'm 28. Nobody texted me. Two family members wished me a happy birthday though. I'm very independent, although obviously a bit of an introvert. Normally stuff like this doesn't bother me, but for some reason this year my lack of anyone to celebrate with just leaves me feeling depressed. I don't even really care except for the fact that it's embarrassing to admit to people I'm doing nothing for my birthday.

Answer: While the birthday thing hurts, what it really shows is a need to make the kind of connections that will lead to a group of people who care about you in general, not just on your birthday. A lot of independent people like you are pretty happy in their own company, and you get a lot of things done on your relatively solo journey. That can be a double-edged sword, though, because although it means you're very self-sufficient, it also tends to result in you not having a network of friends to rely on when you need that.

Even though it might not come naturally to you, or be something you want all the time, you need to learn how to BECOME the sort of person who does reach out. That doesn't take away from your independent nature. It just adds a multi-dimensional layer to what you've already got going on.

I'd use this year's birthday doldrums to motivate yourself to begin making those personal connections. It isn't like you'd need a huge squad, especially for someone who's as independent as you are. But it would still be great to have several people you can rely on. I'd start by looking at the people you currently have regular contact with to see if there are any potential friends that you could make an effort to do things with, keep in regular contact with, invite to things.

Wherever you're bumping into people regularly: work, the gym, a coffeeshop, an activity, at a minimum make sure you greet people with something friendly like "Hey, how's it going, what's your week been like, got anything going on?" etc. Remember what they say so you can follow up. Be the guy who has the friendly greeting, the sincere smile, the welcoming and enthusiastic tone. That's how you build rapport. That's how you make friends. That's how you create awesome birthday celebrations, or just friendly birthday texts.

One interaction at a time. And, happy birthday!

LIGHTS, CAMERA, ACTION!

So, how does one go from Awkward to Awesome?

It doesn't take that long if you put your mind to it. Yes, that fabulous and amazing brain that you received free of charge with your entrée onto the planet. So let's see if we can engage that marvelous brain for some positive effective action!

This is what is needed: 1) Awareness of what the essential social skills are, 2) Opportunity to practice the essential skills on a regular basis. Ideally daily, but at least several times per week. 3) Low-stress, low social risk settings in which to practice them. 4) Motivation to take it seriously and work hard and consistently at it. 5) Enlarging of the comfort zone. 6) Increase of confidence. 7) Extrapolating newly learned behaviors to target area, i.e., your social life. 8) Social skills go from drawback to superpower. 9) You are no longer concerned about what people with think of you because you have Flipped The Script. 10) You realize you have the ability to bring the fun to them. 11) You have no idea why you ever had a problem with your birthday.

How long can this take? It's a classic Your Mileage May Vary situation. It's tempting to say "a year" because that's how often the earth revolves around the sun. That seems pretty arbitrary though! A quick learner might be able to do it in 1-2 months. But I think more realistically it could be done in six months with consistent practice. Do you think I'm kidding? Well DO you?

I'm not. But I'm making the assumption you're going to actually follow my directions as outlined in other chapters and start deliberately engaging strangers on a regular basis with, at a minimum, a genuine smile and a greeting. I say that nonchalantly because I know you can do that much. It's simple. It's brief. It's a completely harmless activity. And unless you live in an extremely remote area, there are always strangers around you can practice on.

I wish I could tell you there was a much easier magic technique. Like, you could just say a certain sentence, and then everyone miraculously realizes what a great person you are and suddenly you are swimming in social acceptance. Or, if you just hold your head at a different angle, somehow you will look unbeatably confident. Or the problem was your clothes! Just change your wardrobe and it'll give you a whole fresh personality too! One that everyone wants to be friends with.

The thing is, if the magic sentence, the unbeatable body posture or the perfect wardrobe style existed, we'd already know about it. The secret would be out! And everybody would be uttering that sentence, cranking their neck, and wearing the same thing. It would be nauseatingly awful, now that I'm thinking about it. I can just picture us all bored, looking alike, and suffering some serious neck pain!

So be glad it isn't that easy.

Naturally, then, it's sort of hard. But it's only hard in a "persistent commitment to work at it" kind of way. Y'know. That virtue we used to call "fortitude." (No, not Fortnight. FORTITUDE) The actual things you have to work on aren't all that hard. They will only seem that way (a little bit) at first, because you aren't used to doing them. And you might be a little afraid of the reaction when you say hello to a coffee shop cashier with an energetic greeting and a big sincere smile. Maybe you'll stumble over it at first and it won't be perfect. (I'll bet it'll be pretty good, though.)

This is a long-range project that needs a long-term commitment in order to work properly. But I can pretty much guarantee you will make huge strides socially within a matter of months if you do this consistently. Because it's a slow build-up of essential social skills. As you get better at it in a practically no-risk situation, you will also (without even realizing it too much) build the confidence you need to make a real difference in your social life. Give it six months to work. I'll bet you'll see huge progress. I'll bet you'll see some progress well before six months.

Your best tool is something that can help you track your progress. A calendar, a notebook, an app or notepad in your phone. Keep track of how many strangers you approached that day, or that week. Note if you just did the basic thing (smile & greeting) or if you added anything to it. If you said something that got a particularly good reaction, write that down too! As you add more things to your repertoire, make notes on those. (A compliment! A question!) Seeing your progress written down is motivational.

Maybe you'll have to go on a late night snack run to get your Stranger Interaction in. Don't wait, go do it! Although I call these 'Stranger Interactions,' it's okay if it's someone like the usual coffee cashier or the same guy at the grocery store. The key is they're not some old buddy, they're distant enough that you're knocking through that Stranger Barrier each time you talk to them. Desensitizing your fears. Practicing your skills. Increasing your confidence. Manufacturing that magic wand.

I'm making the assumption that you'll be able to go from Zero to Charming and hold that pose for 60-120 seconds. Maybe you're sitting there thinking "I CAN'T. I haven't been charming for a single moment of my life since birth. I can't do it for 15 seconds. Much less a whole two minutes."

You know I'm going to have a handy life hack for that. I'm always fully equipped with solutions to make life easier! We will assume the idea of smiling and engaging a customer service person with an energetic greeting such as "Hi, how ARE you," feels like a bridge too far. Maybe it is. After all, it isn't part of your current persona. How are you going to make this appear natural?

I remember when I was a very young and fresh out of college professional, suddenly assigned (among other things) to be The Company Photographer for a large division of General Motors. One that had not just one huge physical industrial plant, but dozens of them. All filled with very intimidating-looking seasoned automotive professionals who were far more interested in getting their jobs done than worrying about the company photographer.

What it took was my snarly boss to give me permission to do my job. (Okay, it was a direct order. But it also felt breathtakingly like permission.) So if you're reading this, that changes our relationship for the duration of this book. I AM THE BOSS OF YOU. Ha. You probably didn't realize that when you started. Fact though. So if you're going to get the most out of this book, you're pretty much required to do what I tell you. To give it your best effort.

With that out of the way, you now know it's your job to greet various strangers and customer service personnel with a big genuine smile and an energetic statement. So that's helpful. But that isn't the only Life Hack I have on the subject. Of course not. I believe in redundant systems! Always prepared with backups. So now that you know this Greeting Thing is literally your job, as assigned by me, maybe you need an extra push transforming yourself into that character who does that.

Yes I used the word 'character' deliberately. I totally get the fact that fiddling with your normal everyday behavior is out of most people's comfort zone. "What, I can't just get my coffee like usual. I now have to start behaving totally differently?"

Just remember that change is growth. You don't grow without INDUCING a little discomfort into the equation. $Y = mx + b$ (I knew that equation would come in handy for something other than calculating line slopes someday! Thank you Sr. Paracleta!) WHY = Maxeffort + Boldness. Okay it's a stretch, but it's MY stretch. I don't calculate too many line slopes anymore.

Back to the character bit. I'm asking you to perform an action that doesn't feel like you. (It can't. Otherwise you'd already be doing it!) I know how important this is. This is the first and most basic thing I've asked you to practice. I realize my entire program collapses of its own weight if I can't get you to do that first thing. If you feel there's no way you can do this thing, so there's no way you can do any of it, so why bother. Downward spiral right there! Catastrophic thoughts! Let's purge that pronto.

And I promised I would give you the necessary life hacks, the simple explanations as if we were all in kindergarten (trust me we all need that in life!), and ways to smash the tasks down to sub-atomic particles, if necessary, to get the job done.

So this feels out of character for you. You're not sure you can pull it off, even for a minute. Even though I've given you permission and assigned you the task. Magnificent Brain, ready for action! This is what you tell your brain. Inform your brain that you've been hired for a movie. (I am the director. You're getting the BIG bucks, so you'd better be on time for your scene, ready to hit your mark and play your role!)

Your role in this movie is Mr. Ridiculously Friendly. Yes, your scene today is Ridiculously Friendly Dude greets cashier. It's only a 15-20 second bit, but you can do it! Or perhaps you're Ms. Happy Talk. Everywhere you go you bring that Friendly Vibe. Here's your scene. Let's study your lines!

Here they are, choose one of the three:

1. "Hi, how ARE you?"
2. "Hey, how's it GOING?"
3. "Hi."

Notice #3 is super simple in case you want to work on the smile first and work your way up to a full sentence later. Also for the sentences I've placed the emphasis where it needs to go. The emphasis makes the sentence more friendly. It implies that they can just respond with a hi or hello back, but they would also be welcome to answer the question with something simple like "Doing great," or "pretty good," or "Not bad." You may actually get one of those answers.

An important note about #3, if you are going with the abbreviated greeting, it needs to be uttered in a way that I would describe as "bright." It is not said with an air that could be considered low, down, falling away or with finality. It is an opener to an interaction. So it sounds a little higher, brighter, going up in tone, as an invitation.

Practice it this way. Say hi while looking down and lowering your voice. Then say it while looking up and raising your tone in a bright and more interested manner. That's the difference. I know it's only one word, but a journey of a million smiles starts with the first grin.

Another point about "Hi." (I am hilariously focused on one word, but it's important to get it right.) Don't clip the word. It's tempting to make this brief word even shorter because the quicker you finish the word the sooner you're done with the task. I know how your lazy mind works!

Well don't do that. Make the most out of this simple word. I know it is only one syllable, but the closer you can get it to sounding like two syllables, the friendlier it will sound. It will almost sound like, "Hi-ya." Because you're not anxious to abbreviate the interaction. You're implying that you'd love to extend it.

And if the person you're interacting with does come back to you with a similar greeting such as, "Great, how are YOU doing?" or something similar, then of course be prepared to at least simply answer that with your own "great," "pretty good," "not bad," "fine," or whatever. You can even add "I've got a lot going on today," if you get suddenly inspired to do so.

So, you've just been cast in a movie for a simple 15-second role. The part expands later as you learn to have a brief convo with people like this. Then it's more like a two-minute role. You're getting paid an unimaginably large sum for this role. So you really have no excuse not to pull this off. NONE.

It isn't even really you that's doing this interaction. It's your assigned character. That takes even more pressure off. Even if you don't execute perfectly the first few times, do you know how many times directors re-shoot movie scenes?

Lots! Yes, famous actors get their lines all screwed up, or the scene is not quite right. Over and over again! They get a zillion takes until they get it how the director wants it. And, so do YOU. It doesn't have to be perfect at first. You just have to do it. And do it repeatedly because that was my assignment to you. And trust me when I say if you do it every day for a month you will feel like an old pro by then. You could do it with your eyes closed.

The Smile. I feel you could almost write a book on the human smile. It is such an important part of our social selves. If you don't smile much you are missing an amazing aspect of your essential human ability to interact well. A genuine smile changes everything.

Let's start with the fact that animals, generally, don't smile. Dogs try, desperately, with their tails. But it just isn't the same. Cats never intended to smile. Let's be serious. Their attitudes are perpetually one of, "Uh-huh. Right."

"A genuine smile changes everything."

So the fact that we humans can do this is a huge benefit. You could almost be wondering what is the purpose? Well possibly to match our extremely cognitively developed brains, which are able to process so many subtle facial expressions in microseconds without us even being consciously aware of it. It tells us what we need to know about the person standing before us, are they friend or foe, busy or available, confident or less so, interested or bored. And so many other things.

Not only are we great at communicating our internal state via our expressions, we are also pretty good at reading those expressions on others. For example, you might not consciously realize why you have a certain impression of someone. But you might have the ability to describe them as "friendly," or "cold," or "thoughtful," or "pensive," or "fun," or "serious," or "irritated," or "joyful," or "impatient," or "concerned," or "agreeable," or "angry," or "confident," — so many things you can easily describe about people, oftentimes without them saying a word.

It's written on their face and it's punctuated by their body. And you pick up on it usually without any direct thought. It's just a feeling that you 'sense.' Ah, the wonders of human sensor bio-technology! That's how the human race has managed to stay viable for so long on this planet. We're able to pick up on what people are feeling without them having to say it.

The human smile is a marvelous tool that is able to impart a sense of friendliness, ease, joy, kindness, interest, approachability and so much more. It's a shame some people don't use this tool often enough. There's just such a huge difference between interacting with someone who smiles readily, and dealing with someone who smiles rarely. And maybe you've got a great reason, like you're a poker player, Nobel Prize laureate or an international spy. So you need this sense of mystery and gravitas. But, most of us don't have to have a stern face as part of our job description. So let's loosen up that smile and get ready to deploy it!

As I've mentioned elsewhere in this book, smiling not only communicates positivity to those around you, it can also improve your own mood. I've given an example of how even the smallest of smiles that can do this! So smiling is great for your mental health.

Socially, a genuine smile conveys acceptance, openness and a positive mood. People tend to trust you more if you smile. Not that this is necessarily warranted, but you can also be sure the opposite is true. They will trust you less if you don't smile. A smile enhances your approachability, and makes it seem more likely that you're open to conversation. What are the first things we do when we DON'T want to have a conversation? Break off eye contact and lose the smile.

But that reminds me of a story of when one of my kids was a toddler. He was regularly getting into all sorts of trouble involving suntan lotion, baby powder and artistic scribblings on the floor with Forbidden Sharpies.

When one of these sorts of incidents would break out, he caught on pretty quickly that I was no longer smiling at him. In fact, I looked downright stern, with creased eyebrows and everything. So whenever this happened he would come up to me, as I knelt on the floor frowning at him; and he'd put his chubby little hands on both sides of my face, and push upward, bellowing, "How about HAPPY!"

See, he knew how to fix the situation. Just get that smile back into place and everything would be right with the world. Smart toddler! That always made me laugh.

So yeah, if you're at a party, don't go around telling people to smile. But if you grab them by the face and push up, yelling, "How about Happy?" that should do the trick nicely!

*

Question: I'm trying to improve my social life, but everything I've done in the past month has gone wrong. Whenever I arrange something, it seems like the person I'm trying to get together with will text me that day and say they can't make it. Then I'll try to make it for the following week, only to find out they're completely busy, or sometimes what I reschedule gets canceled too. I'm starting to wonder if people are being honest with me or if these are just excuses not to get together.

I organized an evening out with about a dozen people. Everyone said they would be there. Then that night only I and one other friend showed. It was on okay time, but I could tell the other person was kind of shocked it was just us. Then there are the people who promise they'll make time to catch up with me, but when I try to arrange it they're never available. Most of the excuses I'm hearing are totally legit, so I know it isn't about me, it's about what's going on in their lives, but I can't help but take it personally. I never cancel on anyone. I'll arrange my whole day around someone being available. Yet nobody seems to meet me halfway. Sorry for such a long question but I'm really at a loss.

Answer: You're sensing that this is a pattern and so am I. It doesn't do much good to attribute this to people being busy and them having valid excuses. All of which may be true. The bottom line is that even if they're busy, people WILL make room for you in their lives if you're important to them. So I think we need to be very honest here and say these people place less importance on the relationship than you do.

But the good news is 1) This is fixable, 2) You're frustrated enough to want things to change, and 3) You seem to have decent planning/initiating skills. That's no small thing.

The main issue is BECOMING the sort of person people want to hang around with. You don't need to change who you are deep down (nor should you), but your self-presentation likely isn't allowing people to appreciate the best version of yourself. That's what has to change.

I mentioned in an earlier chapter PIE: Positivity, Interest in others and Enthusiasm. You need a certain level of social energy to achieve that enthusiasm, and also confidence in yourself. That means sharpening your social skills so you're confident in them, AND it means forgiving yourself for not being perfect. Because none of us is perfect, and dwelling on mistakes is a completely distracting downer.

You need to be able to engage with a welcoming, playful smile, and a true sense of acceptance of, and interest in others. Social energy is heard in the TONE of your voice. It's a voice that reaches out and gives the equivalent of a hug because you're excited to see people and are focused on what they're saying. It takes a bit of practice if you're not used to doing it, but this sort of person brings a contagious sense of enthusiasm to a group.

None of us is perfect, and dwelling on mistakes is a completely distracting downer.

People want that sort of person around, are happy to befriend them, and love to go to their events. So this is where I think you should be headed. Persistence is a great skill to have, but you first have to cultivate the ability to connect with people in a way that makes them want to hang out with you.

Question: Whenever I work on my conversational skills I feel like there are a crazy number of variables I have to manage in my head, and it's just too much for me to think about while I'm trying to talk to someone. It feels like the situation is too complex and people end up finding me boring, or they just forget me. I feel like the third wheel in every conversation. I really want to be a more fun person, but I can't figure out a way to do that.

Answer: The whole "many moving parts" thing is a real problem for a lot of people. That's what happens when you focus excessively on the outer aspects of your presentation. It becomes too much to keep track of! The key is to change your inner self first. You need to build confidence and develop a positive energy and enthusiasm inside you. Once you feel this inner power and enthusiasm, your external presentation will automatically shift to match your internal feelings. You'll then get positive feedback that will in turn give you even more confidence. Only then should you concentrate on nuances.

Positivity, fun and enthusiasm don't come from fiddling with externals. They come from a feeling of joy in your heart and mind that you want to share with others. Once you've got the basic social skills down and know you can brighten someone's day with a nice interaction, then share the FEELING, not the nuances. Details are secondary to communicating positivity and fun.

And don't think too far ahead in your conversations. Focus on what's being said in the moment and follow up on THAT, linking to it with another relevant question or comment of your own. Whatever they're talking about, you can comment on both "the thing," or even better, how they're feeling about "the thing." For example, "Wow, sounds like you're having a rough week!" or "That's fantastic news, I'd be celebrating with calories!" or "Really, you almost burned your house down? When did the sense of panic kick in?" (Yeah I'm still telling that story.)

Question: I've tried really hard to be friendly to people at college, but it feels like a façade. I'm having trouble making friends. People are either apathetic or creepy. I'm tired of pretending to be interested in people I don't like, and smiling for the stuff they say like it's a performance. Some are just into drugs and I don't want to get involved in that. I'm not sure what to do.

Answer: Sorry you've had so much to deal with! You don't need to perform for other people. You need to reach inside for your Inner Best Self and find a way to communicate that to others in a friendly and somewhat charismatic manner. That way healthier people will want your friendship and can truly appreciate the real you.

Inner work means reflecting on what really matters to you, and what your values are. Decide what you do and don't like about yourself and vow to improve the things you don't like, and build on the things you do. If your ideas and values aren't fully formed, take time to research and reflect.

Then, don't be anyone's chameleon. You don't have to agree with people to get them to like you. (You do have to be polite when you disagree though.) You don't need to smile inanely at everything. However you DO need to keep a mildly pleasant expression of your face. Save your genuine smiles for the people and comments that deserve them.

"Don't be anyone's chameleon. You don't have to agree with people to get them to like you."

How to attract people to the Inner You? My answer would be through some positivity and enthusiasm. This doesn't mean taking interest in things that bore you to tears, or people you don't like. If stuff is boring/meaningless, either change the topic or leave the conversation. If people are toxic, why keep smiling at them? Seek out healthy people with your positivity and enthusiasm for your Inner Values, and for people you're interested in befriending. Enthusiasm will change your body language and tone of voice for the better. Just make sure the people and topics are worth being enthusiastic about!

Question: I'm having a lot of trouble making friends at my high school. It seems like most of my conversations fizzle out awkwardly. I'm normally pretty quiet when I talk, but if I try to be louder or more enthusiastic it feels fake. People seem to immediately dislike me. That ruins my chances to make friends and just makes me feel more anxious. I try to hide my feelings but they still somehow pick up on it.

Answer: Hiding what's inside is difficult. It's actually more effective to CHANGE what's inside. Sounds more difficult but in the end it's the easier way to start giving off a good vibe that will help you make friends.

One way is to Flip The Script. Instead of worrying about what they think of you, start focusing more on what YOU think of them. In other words, develop a positive mindset and start focusing it on someone. It's VERY difficult to communicate a positivity or enthusiasm that you don't actually feel. So the trick is to develop that mindset of positivity and start sharing it with the world.

Obviously you don't try this with the popular people or the bullies. It's much easier to start with the "invisible people" or even the ones who get picked on. Who is nice to them? Usually no one! So why can't it be you? That's where you start working on your energetic vibe and your positivity toward others.

If you can offer PIE (Positivity, Interest in others and Enthusiasm), you can be a good friend to anyone. If you have trouble with conversations you'll have to practice that. But to keep it simple start with this: decide every day you're going to make at least 2-3 social efforts. Make it one in the morning, one at lunch and one in the afternoon. You're going to greet someone with enthusiasm and a big genuine smile, while using their name. Pick someone, anyone. Even a teacher. It doesn't matter who. But you must do it with enthusiasm.

"Hi Taylor! How's it going?" "Hey Mr. Smith, what do you have planned for us today?" "Yo Madison. Are you ready for class?" Etc. Inject 10-20 percent more energy into it than you normally would. The big smile is key. Do an internet search for 'genuine smile vs fake smile' if you're not sure what that looks like. Do this daily at least 2-3 times.

After you get this down cold, start adding comments or conversational starters. A comment, a funny remark. A COMPLIMENT. Those are always welcome. Keep working at this until you start getting some nice positive responses and smiles back. This is how you develop confidence. You can start turning these interactions into real conversations and start making some friends.

SOCIAL ENERGY

No chapter on Awkward to Awesome would be Worth Its Weight in Bold without a discussion of a concept I call Social Energy. What the heck is that, and how do you get it? Well, first of all, it's just a measure of something. Sort of like body warmth.

We're all at a certain number whether we're running a fever or have unfortunately declined to room temperature status. But unlike body temperature, which tells us whether we're normal, sick, dead or frozen into the peak of Mt. Everest, the Social Energy calculation measures something different. It tells us how much engagement we're putting out to the public. So everyone has social energy, it's just a matter of how much.

And just to clarify, social energy is not a measure of how loud, boisterous or ostentatious you are. It is not a "look at me" index. More decibels do not mean more Social Energy. It's a measure of your ability, willingness and inclination to engage with others. And how well you put out those signals.

Whether you're loud, quiet or somewhere in between (where most of us are), you're able to put out a significant amount of social energy if you have some basic social skills and the desire to do so. How do I know this? Well, I personally just made up this calculating tool, so I get to decide what it measures. It's a combination of warmth, and a willingness to push that warmth out there with enough energy to engage others.

Oftentimes when people tell me they're in a group but having trouble mixing with people, or they're at a party but they feel invisible, or with one or more people and don't 'click' with them, the thing I suspect is missing is this ethereal term I call Social Energy.

Perhaps it's better explained with a foray into the Periodic Table of elements. And the idea of "chemistry" between people, which I'm sure is a term you HAVE heard before. Whether it's between romantic partners, friends, teammates or colleagues, it's this quality that causes people to click and thoroughly enjoy each other's company.

It makes you feel like "yes, this person gets me," and I can really talk to them, and I'm enjoying our interaction enough that it seems like time flies. Like my first date with my husband. Our three-hour date (on a mid-week work night no less) felt like only minutes had passed. And then suddenly they were closing the restaurant, and we were like, what???

So if you look at the Periodic Table you will notice the elements running down the right-hand side. These are the Noble Gases. And for all their nobility, they are INERT. They don't mix with the other elements very readily. They are quite happy just being off by themselves not reacting with anyone or anything. They are the highly-paid supermodels of elements. They are all like "Just leave us alone!" So fine, Noble Gases. Be that way!

But the other elements are ready, willing and able to interact. Why? Because they have some spare electrons that are happy to meet you. They're excited! They have energy. And when they meet up with some like-minded element, they are happy to hang out, click and sometimes even form a "bond!"

Okay, as someone who is constantly griping about her Xylem and Phloem years, I'll end the analogy right there, because there's no need to start linking random molecules of esters together until we form a polyester suit. Those are still out of fashion.

You need some excitement, some Social Energy, in order to create that spark of life that gets people to enjoy the event, the conversation, the interaction, each other. If you sit around like an inert Noble Gas, well you may look perfectly fine but you won't engage anyone on a personal level. People won't grab you by the lapels and say, "Let's be friends!"

Well, a charismatic type might do that, but most people won't. So then you'll just sort of wander around refilling your drink, checking your phone, admiring the wall art and hoping the family dog maybe wants to hang out with you. (Answer to that: probably yes! Family dogs are awesome. Most are experts on Social Energy. You can learn a lot from the family dog. They could literally teach a class.)

So, Social Energy is the quality that allows you to bust out of your protective force field and engage others without worrying about them rejecting you. It's like the difference between moping around a cold campfire poking the gray ashes, and standing at a blazing hot bonfire.

Social Energy is basically enthusiasm for what's happening in your immediate vicinity. It means focusing on the people and things happening right in front of you. It's an enthusiastic focus. Not a half-hearted looking all around the room to see what's going on "over there."

Not reviewing your grocery list or to-do notes or class assignments or whatever else is roaming around in your head. It's being focused on the here and now, and the people you're with. And it's bringing your best self and happiest energy to the moment.

"Social Energy is enthusiasm for what's happening in your immediate vicinity."

It need not be loud. But it does need to be present. Available. Ready to engage. Happy to be there. Ready to reach out to whomever you're with. Even if you don't know them! If they're a human being and they speak your language, you can probably find a human element to connect on. I'm not going to list the human experiences that are common to us all, but there are a lot. So the ability to connect is there if you're even mildly creative.

That initial exercise I'm asking you to do, where you interact briefly with a service person and you try to engage and make it into a fun interaction. What do you think that little exercise is? It's an opportunity to create that moment I'm talking about. Where you bring a bit more social energy than you're used to doing, and you reach out, and you discover you can click with someone even in a brief interaction!

It might not happen the first time you try it, or with every person, but it WILL happen. You'll learn that by using an open approach, a welcoming smile, and an interested tone, you can have a fun, satisfying interaction with just about anybody. Once you realize you have that skill, you can then extrapolate that ability to your own social life, your own family, your own workplace, your own neighborhood, really, anyplace that you go. You could make friends on the International Space Station, for Neil Armstrong's sake!

You: "Hey, what's THAT button for?" Astronaut: "DON'T TOUCH THAT…."

You won't click with everyone. Nobody does. But you don't have to click with everyone. All you have to do is reach out, give it your best effort, and take whatever people give you, whether it's a little or a lot. And some you WILL really click with.

Be present. Be interested. Be approachable. Be friendly. Leave your phone in your pocket or purse. No one wants to interact with a phone. The phone is literally a barrier. If you need to look at your phone then apologize and say "hey I need to check something real quick." And maybe step aside while you do it. Then when you're done come back to the interaction. Let the person know they've got your full attention.

Bottom line is, the one thing you need to take with you to social interactions is some Social Energy. That's what allows you to click with people. That's what will give you a fun time and a memorable interaction. You can forget your purse, your wallet, your phone, your keys, probably even your shoes – those are all important things to have at a social interaction, but none of them is as important as bringing Social Energy.

CHAPTER 6: TAKEAWAYS

1. *Some friend groups are FINO: Friends In Name Only. You need to make one-on-one friends within your own friend group, or else find another group.*

2. *Improving your social skills requires persistence and fortitude.*

3. *Why? = MaxEffort + Boldness (slope of MY line)*

4. *Even a simple word like "Hi" can be said in an inviting and approachable way.*

5. *A genuine smile changes everything.*

6. *Social Energy is what helps people click with one another. It is enthusiasm for what's happening in your immediate vicinity.*

7. *The one thing you need to take with you to social interactions is Social Energy.*

CHAPTER 7

CAN WE TALK?

Small talk. Small talk gets dissed by people all the time! To hear people complain about it you'd think it was on the order of a telemarketing call. Or a traffic jam. Or a bad internet connection. Things nobody likes. The worst!

Well, not only do I see a very good purpose for small talk, I've actually grown to like it. I would no sooner leave the house without my small talk arsenal, than I would back out of the driveway at 60 mph without checking my mirrors.

There are exceptions to every rule. When the house is on fire, we can dispense with the small talk, and just yell "fire" in a crowded hallway and get out of there. (Like I did just this past month! True story. My advice: make sure you have a smoke detector in your garage. Especially if it's attached to your house.) But most social situations require at least some amount of small talk in order to function well. Why is that?

Once again we're going to hearken back to olden days and ancient times, when you couldn't always tell if the person you were dealing with was friend or foe. Or, even if they appeared friendly, you had to ensure they didn't have any latent Foe-like tendencies. So small talk is used to gather some basic information. Probably at this stage you're learning more about them from how they're saying things, rather than what they're saying.

Why does small talk even exist? Can't we just remain in stony silence, listening to the clock tick, the air conditioner whirr, the chairs scrape on the floor? (Mmm. Sounds like we're taking a test!) Small talk sets the foundation for establishing a relationship, which is the whole point of why we're conversing. It helps us trust each other.

For example, if you need something from someone, you can't just march in there and say, "I need this. Give me the THING."

Well you can, but it would feel rude, and you might not get "the thing."

So, pleasantries are exchanged. You form at least a surface level relationship. Notice the word "pleasantries." That implies you are being nice to each other. Not being abrupt, rude or simply making demands.

We don't even think about it, usually, but our entire demeanor in a small talk situation sets the tone for establishing a relationship and governs what the interaction will feel like both in that moment and going forward. I think if any of us stopped and pondered that, it might give us stage fright! But we're pretty used to this drill, so in general we don't overthink it.

However if you find that most of your small talk situations don't go that well, it's time to look at the scenario more closely. I would argue that whether you're dealing with a customer service person, or someone you've just encountered at a meeting or a party, you should treat the person in a friendly manner. Not because you want something from them, but because you're establishing a relationship of sorts.

There's value in creating a friendly connection regardless of what the future holds. Why? I think both people benefit from the warmth and good feelings people can share together, however briefly. It increases their willingness to help each other out either with information or direct action. Basically, it's why humans have done so well as a species. We're tribal! We flourish in groups. There are synergistic benefits that accrue from helping each other out.

So there's benefit to engaging in that manner most of the time. Generally speaking, you can go anywhere and come out with at least what I call a Surface Level Friend.

I don't even want to call them acquaintances, really, because even though a lot of people ARE acquaintances, that really feels like I'm keeping them at arm's length. Think about how we refer to them: "JUST an acquaintance." Just. Only. Merely. No, I don't want to be anyone's Just, Only or Merely. I'm there to connect. Even if we do it ONCE. Or, once in a while. So I like to think of acquaintances as "Friendlies." People I'm friendly with, who are available for a deeper connection if time and circumstance permits. Even if it's "just" the person bagging my groceries.

> *"I don't want to be anyone's Just, Only or Merely. I'm there to connect. Even if we do it once. Or, once in a while. So I like to think of acquaintances as 'Friendlies.'"*

Small talk fosters trust, creates goodwill and serves as a springboard for at least a surface level relationship. It's also a pleasant way to pass the time and may result in interesting or useful information being exchanged. It's great practice for your social skills and is a building block to future friendships. That makes small talk something of value, a form of social currency. The more goodwill you have in the bank, the richer your social life will be.

So how do these conversations look?

Saying hello, and the person's name (if you know it) is the basic greeting. Asking how they are, or what's up, or anything new, or what's going on – any of those things is an opening bid for small talk.

For example if you ask "how are you" and they say "oh, fine," then the conversation may end right there. Or they could actually begin to answer the question with a statement such as, "Doing great. Planning on knocking off early and grabbing a bite to eat." Or "Pretty good, but looks like we're expecting rain in the afternoon." Or "Stressed out. I've got three tests next week." Or "Saw the doctor this morning and I'm scheduled for a surgery next month."

All of those statements lead the conversation in a particular direction. The questioner may then respond with, "Sounds good," or "Hope I don't get caught in it" or "Too bad," or "Good luck with that." (The surgery definitely calls for either a followup question or at least an expression of sympathy and encouragement!)

I'm not plowing any new ground here, just outlining the obvious. Now, is it necessary that you participate in small talk? At least minimally, yes. If someone directs a small talk question at you, unless your hair is on fire, you're in charge of a toddler, or you're making a beeline for the bathroom, then you need to make some sort of response or you'll be perceived as rude.

Here are some tips to help raise your comfort level when engaging in small talk:

1. Pretend you know the person well. They're a childhood friend! Or, maybe a long lost family member who moved across the country. How do you get your brain to believe that? One way is to picture this person as part of their family unit, where everybody DOES know them well. Now it's your turn to interact with Cousin Janus who'll be thrilled to see your familiar face. Use the same tone you would with a friend or family member.

2. Remember this is a fellow human. You're alive on the planet at the same time in history, perhaps even inhabiting the same country and speaking the same language. That gives you a LOT in common. If you bumped into this same person on another continent they'd be your Instant Best Friend. So conjure up that Instant Magic in the moment.

3. Count on them liking you. It's a technique I mentioned earlier but it's especially important for a small talk situation. Giving off an "excited

to meet you" vibe will turn a conversation from boring to bursting with energy. Where can you get this attitude if you don't already have it, or aren't used to bringing it? Pretend they have secret important information, and it's your job to find out what it is. (Based on the unexpectedly fascinating things I've learned from people, I'm willing to bet they actually HAVE this information.)

4. Be prepared to engage. In other words, don't pretend to be interested. Actually BE interested. Try to have 2-3 shareable thoughts with you. Make it something you'd be reasonably excited to share. Even if it's just an opinion, some personal news, or a weird fact you came across. Find out something about them. "What's the best thing that happened to you today?" "Do you have a nomination for frustration of the week?" etc.

5. Make a (GENUINE) compliment! Take it one step further and tell them why you like whatever-it-is, or how something they've done or said affected others in a positive way. I will even share tardy compliments. (But rather than going stale like bread, they've aged like fine wine!) People are not only surprised that you remembered something that you meant to compliment them on, but they're pleased that you took the trouble to recall the memory and share it. Also most compliments never get old. So don't be afraid to bring them up in new contexts, or if something just reminds you about how great someone is at X, Y or Z.

6. Try to keep a general sense of tossing the conversational ball back and forth. And if you find yourselves on a dud topic, don't be afraid to completely change it up. "Did you hear we're starting to see lizards the size of large squirrels?"

7. Don't be afraid to ask their name again at any point in the conversation. Chances are they may have forgotten yours too.

Small talk is sort of like a starter soil for your conversational plant. You scatter some seeds in there, and you can either nurture them or not. (Oh, WHY did I pick a botanical metaphor for this? The botanists will be self-righteously agreeing that I made a HUGE mistake when I criticized all the emphasis on science in grammar school earlier.)

Small talk keeps the conversation on safe topics that won't require a great deal of concentrated thought. That allows you to just size each other up. We're not consciously thinking this, of course, but as humans we can't help but form an impression when we're engaging in conversation. That's because so much is communicated non-verbally. I don't want to cite research, but the number being used lately is well over 50 percent, edging up into the 75+ percent territory. (Source: AP, i.e. Alliterative Patti)

In a small talk situation you're dealing with low level information. Usually not things of critical importance. You're finding out what the other person is like. How they communicate. Who they are, in a non-verbal sense. What their mood is. And to a certain extent, how they might be feeling about you.

People can't read your mind. But they CAN read your body language. And they DO read it. They sense it, actually. And they will believe your body language over your words. Because your body language, for the most part, is instinctive and subconscious, so it has a tendency to tell the truth. At least more often than our words do. We're always fudging with those words, aren't we?

"Sure, I feel FINE!" (Droopy body language. Half-hearted smile)

Which would YOU believe? So even though there are specific things you can work on, body language-wise, I feel you get more mileage out of actually changing what you feel inside you, and then allowing your body language to reflect that naturally. When it comes to small talk, what you say is actually far less important than how you say it.

Suppose that we all talked with robotic voices, impassive faces, and minimal body movement. How would you feel having that conversation? It would be weird. Probably dull. You'd be creeped out. We're so used to the non-verbal aspect that we don't even realize it's going on most of the time. We just notice if something's missing, or "off," or if it strikes us the wrong way. And we pick up on other people's emotions quite readily. So when engaging in small talk it's helpful to make just about any topic engaging, and treat the conversation as interesting even if it initially isn't.

> *"When it comes to small talk, what you say is actually far less important than how you say it."*

I think one of the best ways to approach small talk is simply to take what's in the immediate vicinity, or grab what people give you, and just run with it with as much happy enthusiasm as you can. Quick example! I was in an elevator last week. I entered first, the guy behind me worked at the place, so he was getting on pushing a work-related cart. I hit the button I wanted and asked him what floor.

He looks at me and says, "Two, but I'd love it if this elevator had a HOME button."

Wow. What a great opening! Naturally, I took it.

"That's a great idea!" I said to him. "We really need an elevator that can take us anywhere. We need a LOT more buttons! Anyplace else you'd like to go?"

He pondered that a moment as the elevator stopped at the next floor. "Maybe shopping," he suggested.

An older gentleman boarded the elevator. He pressed the button for the ground floor. I caught his eye. "We were just talking about having elevator buttons that can take you anywhere," I informed him. "Do you have anyplace you'd rather go?"

Fortunately he looked totally amused by this. It definitely helped that I was using my We're Having Fun Here, Come Join Us tone of voice. It's a playful, happy, somewhat energized tone. It sends the signal that we're kidding around and having a good time. Also it's INCLUSIVE. We're not having an inside joke at his expense; I was inviting him to join in with the "Elevatorevelry." New term I just created.

"Can I pick a vacation?" he asked.

"Definitely," I said. "I was considering that myself, but now I'm thinking maybe I'd like a button to take me right out of 2020!"

They both laughed at that one.

He was still pondering exciting vacation choices as we exited the elevator.

An Elevator to Anywhere! What a fun icebreaker/conversation starter.

But like anything else, you have to "read the elevator." If someone is not responsive to playful fun small talk then you don't keep pushing that at them. And if you live in Manhattan with all those REALLY tall buildings, you might have to be more careful about engaging in elevator conversation.

Small talk can come from anything if you're willing to engage people and have fun with it.

TRICK YOUR BRAIN INTO A BETTER INTERVIEW PERFORMANCE

Many artificial situations ratchet up the stress-meter. Job interviews for one. You have to appear competent, confident, interested in the job and company, knowledgeable about your skills and how they apply to the position. You also have to make a good impression as a team player and someone who would "fit in" with the company culture. Don't forget to ask a few good questions! And be sure to know your "biggest weakness!" (Like, I go off on a lot of tangents...)

An interview requires you to project an emotion you're not necessarily feeling. That's what causes the stress, although that doesn't mean you won't pull it off. If you've experienced the situation before, there's a good chance you'll do fine.

It's also possible an interview will make you incredibly nervous and unnecessarily stressed, and you WON'T do fine. So, what about that? The key is being able to tap into positive emotions and avoid the negative ones.

The importance of the interview scenario may make you nervous, somewhat fearful, imagining bad outcomes. How can we avoid that? Like anything else, practice helps. The dreaded "mock interviews" should be welcomed. If you can get practice from a college career center, or have a family member interview you, or a friend, have someone record you so you can critique yourself. The more mock interviews you do, or real interviews you go on, the more comfortable you'll be. Research and rehearse. There are many books and articles that cover this basic aspect.

But my approach, as always, is going to focus on the attitude, the feeling, the emotion, the VIBE. How do we create some positive emotion in such a stressful scenario? That's where the Mind Magic needs to happen. People often approach an interview with a mindset of not making a mistake. One little thing goes wrong and whoa, you're out of there. You've blown it!

I'll compare it to sports. If you're on the field "trying not to make a mistake," you're not going to perform well. You're going to tense up, you may even "choke." That's when your mind is trying to impose an outcome because it's so important that you not make a mistake. Well, doing it that way is ALREADY a mistake.

Instead of a nervous Don't Make A Mistake Attitude, you need to shift your mindset. You are going to Flip The Script. The new mindset is one of This Job Already Went to Someone Else. I know. That sounds crazy. But stay with me here. They already have someone else for the job. So the pressure is off. But you're going to make them regret their choice. Oh yeah. You're going to make them realize that YOU are even BETTER for the job.

In other words, a crazy sinking line drive has been hit to left field, you're running as hard as you can to get it. No one expects you to catch that ball. It's heading deep. But you give it your all because there's nothing to lose. BAM. You're sliding across the outfield grass with the ball in your glove. How did you do it?

Well I'll tell you how you DIDN'T do it. You didn't do it by measuring the distance the ball was going to fly. You didn't do it by counting the number of steps you'd need to take to get there. You didn't calculate at what angle to dive for the ball. You just put your eye on the ball and gave it everything you had to get there. Because you weren't worried about failure.

"Going into an interview with the idea of not making a mistake is ALREADY a mistake."

That's how the interview needs to go. No worries about mistakes. No concern for failure. Someone else is lined up for this job. But you can still make an impression. You give it your best shot and see how it goes! So you go in there not flat, not nervous, not worried about saying the wrong thing.

You go in there with positive energy and excitement. Because you know you can do this job, and you're excited about the opportunity to work with this company. Ready to ask the interviewer some well researched questions about this job, this company.

Interviewers are not on the lookout for the "one little mistake" that's going to kill the interview for you. Seriously they're not. The reason it feels that way, sometimes, is that you're so nerved up about not making the mistake that you're putting out this tense, non-confident vibe. So when you make a tiny mistake (mispronunciation! Said the wrong thing! Forgot the person's name! Went blank on an answer! Knocked over a water bottle!) that isn't what the interviewer noticed.

The interviewer is picking up on your overly anxious vibe. Not the mistake itself. The interviewer may not even realize that. He or she will just conclude that 'the candidate didn't impress me,' or 'I wasn't feeling it.' In many cases, it was your vibe they were feeling. Just my Opinionated Opinion, from having interviewed people.

Generally they're interviewing people whose qualifications are fairly similar. So, yup, they're looking for someone who has the necessaries AND a vibe they can relate to. A vibe they can work with. A vibe that'll "fit in here." All things being equal, it often comes down to your vibe. It's a lot easier to teach you the definitions of xylem and phloem, if, ahem, you need to know them, than it is to teach you to change your vibe. That's the reason for this book.

Imagine an interviewer going through a stack of resumes and saying, "Oh look, here's someone who seems marginally qualified. I'll bring them in and see if they can persuade me they can do the job even though it seems borderline."

That's ridiculous! They don't do that. They pick out the best resumes of people who they're pretty sure CAN do the job. The interview it isn't about your qualifications, per se (although those will be discussed). It's more about your VIBE. In other words, the very subject of this book. If you do a good job CONNECTING with that interviewer, your chances of landing the job will be much better.

Once you've prepared for an interview, the next best way to increase your odds of actually getting the job would be – to read this book! You need to bring a positive vibe that's ready to CONNECT with the interviewer. That's more important than having a perfect answer for "what's your greatest weakness." (My greatest weakness is making an annoyed face when people ask me trite overused interview questions.)

"If you do a good job of CONNECTING with the interviewer, your chances of landing the job will be much better."

As in social situations, bring 10-20 percent more energy than you would normally give. The interviewer wants to hire someone who is excited about the job, excited about the company, enthusiastic about the interview. Do your research well, and find things to be excited about.

It's difficult to be nervous and enthusiastic at the same time. Banish your worry with enthusiasm. Remember, someone else already got the job, but you have this unique opportunity to make them regret not picking you. So MAKE THEM REGRET IT. And, you just might find yourself with a job!

*

Question: I'm in grad school. I didn't have many childhood friends, and I don't have a lot of people I can talk to. I'm at a new university, so I mostly know people in my department. I also have a girlfriend. I want to connect with people but so far it's been hard. I'm okay with small talk but I can't seem to get past that. No matter how much interest I take in people, they don't feel the same about me.

I recently got picked by NASA to help with research. (I don't need to relocate for the project) I'm totally stoked! I didn't bother telling people in my department. I told a couple of old friends from home, and I mentioned it to my mom. The reaction I got from all of them was 'that's nice,' like it was this routine thing. I'm starting to feel that way myself. My girlfriend was thrilled. She's the only one though. What am I doing wrong?

Answer: Wow! NASA. That sounds totally cool to me! Congrats. If one of my friends told me something like that, we'd find a way to party and celebrate!

There would definitely be a discussion of Space Junk and Black Holes, and possibly we would find some cool interstellar napkins and other paraphernalia at the local party store. We'd have a Lost In Space-themed happy hour or something. To be honest we've celebrated over a lot less than that!

It isn't the accomplishment itself that's important. You have to feel excited for the person, not necessarily the 'thing.' Which you are sensing, I'm sure. So the key is Close Relationships. It seems you don't have a close relationship with your mother, otherwise she'd be 'over the moon' about your NASA news. And the 'old friends' aren't 'close friends,' otherwise their reactions would've been more positive. Sadly I feel I personally just showed more excitement for your cool thing than your family and friends did. That's just frustrating. Let's fix that!

What does it take to form close connections? Caring, Accessibility and Time spent together. You seem to have a number of connections/potential friends that are accessible to you. However you need to take it to the next level by inviting them to do things outside the venue that brings you together. Friendships form over regular time spent together, plus discussions that gradually reveal more of yourself.

Of course friendship isn't just about you, it's about them too. So ask interested questions, and reflect back what they are saying so they know you "got it." (Basically "Active Listening." You reword what they said in a slightly different way, and then check their reaction to that to make sure you got what they're saying correctly.) You should add in your own comments and relate it to your own experience. They will also ask about YOU if they are interested in deepening the relationship.

It's good to have some generic questions ready: 1) Any plans for this weekend? 2) What's the best part of one of your regular days? (To keep this question from seeming out of left field I immediately offer one up, which is, "mine is that first cup of coffee...") 3) Seen any good shows I should put on my Binge List? What kind of stuff do you go for? 4) I've been trying new foods. Do you have any favorite dishes I should try? 5) If you were retired starting right at this minute, what's the first thing you'd do?

Those are some random examples. More often though the conversation flows easily, I ask something about "what's up with you lately," they will give an actual answer, and I simply follow up on that. The key is to be and sound interested. Respond in a "tell me more" voice.

Magically, they will share things that are interesting because I sound interested, and the conversation is actually fun. You're trying to create conversational flow. That's what it means to "click" with someone. You should both be getting something out of the conversation, and by the end you're both thinking to yourselves, "That was fun! We should get together again." That's how friendships are formed.

*

Here's an example of how to turn small talk into a fun conversation. One of our extremely important services to the house was out, and I had to call a customer service rep for a large company. The customer service person named Michael asked me what my name was. I said "Patti."

He paused, then said, "Is it okay if I call you by your first name?" I said, "Sure! 'Cuz that's what I gave you!" He laughed at that, and said, "okay."

So a couple things here. One is they're typically expecting you to give a full name and then they're planning to call you Mr./Ms. Last Name. Since I only gave him my first name that took him a little 'off script.' (Which is where I like to be. Let's interact for real!) Another important thing (and which probably caused him to laugh) was my friendly tone of voice. He could tell I was ready to engage him and kid around.

How did I get this fun and playful tone into my voice? I didn't treat it as this "impersonal phone conversation with a customer service rep." I treated it as a real interaction with a real person, whose job was to help me, but I was going to be a more friendly and interactive customer than he was used to dealing with. So I thought of him NOT as Customer Service Cog In Customer Service Machine, I thought of him as Michael who is probably having a long day and could use a cheerful rather than cranky customer on the other end of the line.

Another thing I did is use body language as if he were in the room with me. Yes, I was smiling on my end, a nice happy smile (not even remotely fake!). I didn't really check, but my body language was probably open and relaxed. Remember, the person on the other end of the line can 'hear' your body language and can sense your smile!

Most importantly, I used a very friendly and engaging tone of voice with him. Sort of difficult to just describe on the page. (That'll be next. I'll be compelled to have some kind of online channel thing where I demonstrate this stuff. My kids will be appalled and will then work very hard to pretend not to be related to me.) The way I'd describe it is a bright and friendly tone.

> ## "The person on the other end of the line can 'hear' your body language and can sense your smile!"

Michael was already mildly amused at my manner. He needed to check a few things on the computer, told me this may take a bit. I'm not on hold, however. We start getting into a silence. Now, in Customer Service World, long silences are standard. No one considers them 'awkward,' it's just part of the experience of Standard Customer Service Silence. But I took the opportunity to engage Michael in conversation.

"What state are you operating out of, Michael?" He said Pennsylvania, the northern part. I said, "So up around the I-80. Closer to Hazleton or Middleport?" He said Middleport and asked why I'm so familiar with

Pennsylvania. (Although I'm from Buffalo, New York, I've blustered around Pennsylvania quite a bit.)

This is why you ask people where they're from, or where they've lived. You might be able to connect to something they say. So I then told the story of how I got my first speeding ticket in Pennsylvania. I lost focus on a looooooong stretch of the I-80. He then described about a recent near-miss traffic ticket, and how grateful he was that the police officer decided to bypass him in favor of faster speeders.

I launched into the tale of how I first became a coffee drinker. I left work one Friday evening from my job at Packard Electric Division in eastern Ohio. My car was packed for a weekend trip to visit a friend in New Jersey. By the time I got to the Clarion I-80 exit in western Pennsylvania, I was already having trouble keeping my eyes open. (Long week!) So out of desperation I pulled off at a fast food drive through and ordered a large coffee. I chugged that coffee between DuBois and Clearfield, and by gosh, I easily sailed all the way to New Jersey without any problem remaining awake!

Somehow the conversation turned toward Florida, air travel, and then Michael shared with me the story of his first ever skydiving experience! We had a very enjoyable time talking together. By the end I had wished him well, and also warned him to take special care with his driving, as it was the last day of the month, and sometimes police officers are extra vigilant about speeders on that day. We ended the call on a very friendly high note and my technical problem on the road to being solved.

It's a judgment call as to whether the person on the other end has time for chitchat. If you offer up some conversation and they sound distracted or hurried, then you're less likely to follow up on that. In this case Michael had to wait for a number of things on his end, and we were able to fill the silence with a fun conversation.

The feedback you're getting from the other person will tell you if you can proceed. Many if not most customer service conversations will not be all that lengthy. However even if it's more routine, I will still push out my friendly tone and I will usually get something positive back from the person, even if it's a comment on how their day is going.

Second thing is, Michael and I had a very fun conversation. If we had more time, or better yet, if it were in person, I would've loved to hear more about the skydiving, and what motivated him to try that experience. This would qualify as a fun conversation that could've gone in a lot of directions if I had met him at a party.

This is definitely something you can do with people in person, or with people who are already acquaintances or friends of yours. Ask a few questions and find something you can comment on or ask about. (I told not one, but TWO playful stories about my travels on the I-80. I actually have another one involving me and a couple of friends and an ice storm.) I got to hear about his near-miss traffic ticket and his skydiving experience and his hopes to visit Florida someday. He was an engaging conversationalist and we could've talked a lot longer had this been a true social situation.

Third, I didn't do this because I needed the practice. Although we can all do things better when it comes to social skills. None of us is perfect in this regard! I did it because I've developed the habit of approaching my interactions with positivity and, where possible, a sense of fun. This means all the interactions. Including the ones with random customer service people.

I didn't do it because I wanted anything special from Michael. Although when you make a connection with a person, they are far more likely to want to help you. So if there is a special tip or coupon I should know about, they will be inclined to help with that.

Life ought to be fair, and all persons treated the same. But if you go out of your way to connect with someone and brighten their day, and have a good conversation (or even something as simple as a fun comment or a genuine compliment), it's just human nature to want to help the person who does that for you a little more than your average customer. Or certainly more than your cranky, demanding, bad mood customer. (Yo! Golf Gal.)

This gives you the appearance of being a 'lucky' person because you are getting the best from people like hot tips, coupons, the name of someone who can help you with something, ideas, etc. But it isn't a matter of being lucky. It's a matter of being friendly. Because I want to help the people I connect with just as much.

If you aren't used to doing that, perhaps it sounds like more 'work.' Well, maybe it feels like work when you don't have that habit and perhaps feel like you're not good at it. I will put a big fat YET at the end of that. This is something you can easily get good at if you just start practicing doing it. Remember, I am the person who was terrified to make phone calls at one time.

You don't have to start with a full-blown conversation like the one I described above. Start small. Start with smiling while you're on the phone. The other person doesn't see it, but you will feel it. Hear your tone change. Start practicing talking to people on the phone simply with a brighter and more interested tone.

If you're not sure what 'friendly' sounds like, then find someone you consider friendly and listen to their tone of voice. That's where most of the friendliness is exhibited. The tone of your voice is actually one of the most important aspects of 'body language.' You can't see someone's tone but you can certainly feel it!

Once you've worked on your tone, then you can practice saying something simple to customer service people, like, "How's your day going?" or "How's the weather where you are?" (if they're not local) Start simple. Practice every chance you get.

Customer service calls are just warm-ups to more important conversations with people you do know. If you can create fun small talk with someone on the phone, you can certainly do it in person. And you can even start transitioning to an interesting conversation, as Michael and I did.

That conversation wasn't just about me. Michael was more than game to hold up his end while doing his work. At one point my fax machine was making weird strangled noises. First I described this to him, then I held the phone to the fax machine so he could hear it. Another amusing moment. (Yes we still have a fax machine. It's a vintage item, like a spinning wheel or a Victrola™ or something.) If however someone's customer service work involves calculus, or squinting at anything, or crossing wires that may shut down service to important parts of the country, then they might not be up for chitchat.

In that case they will sound bored, distracted or not fully present or ready to engage. Remember, it isn't about you. It's about them and their situation. And this really holds for any social interaction. If you try to engage someone and they're not willing or able to, don't make any judgments! Just consider them 'not available' and let it go. Life is all about reaching out. Not everyone will respond, but you can have a fun time with those who do.

I will repeat that because it's so important. Life is all about reaching out. Extend a hand and you may touch a heart. Don't worry about how many people respond. Just have a fun time interacting with those who do.

"Life is all about reaching out. Extend a hand and you may touch a heart."

*

Question: I find it extremely difficult to make new friends. It seems like every time I try to strike up a conversation with someone, it'll go on for a little bit and then other people aren't interested in taking it any further, and a friendship never develops. Any ideas on what I should do?

Answer: It sounds like the conversational part is posing a problem. You need to respond to what they say with a relevant comment, question, observation, or something from your own life. And you need to have a bit of energy when you do it. The key to a great conversation is to have enthusiasm about LIFE, YOURSELF and the OTHER PERSON. (Picture me shouting that. With a big infectious grin on my face!)

It's a bit difficult to connect with someone who has a low-energy self presentation. (Caveat: I didn't say 'impossible.' I said 'a bit difficult.') And please don't confuse enthusiasm with being loud. Enthusiasm means INTEREST. It means a bit of passion. It means a light shining in your eyes. (Not exactly sure how that gets switched to 'on' but I'm 99.5 percent sure it's mental.)

If I made a comment to you and your response was flat, uninterested or simply "meh," then I'd probably think you were terribly uninterested in the topic, so I might switch to another one involving cute animals or exploding whales in the hope of getting a playful or interested response out of you! And if I tried several topics and you were still emotionally flat I might conclude it's ME you're not interested in.

I'd think "WHAT? None of my stories made you crack a smile or seem somewhat interested?" (Sad face. Oh well. Time to find someone else or hit the snack bowl.)

And on your side, you need to inject your topics with a certain amount of passion, interest and/or amusement. If you're not excited about your own topics, you can't really expect that of the other person! Think of topics as ideas in a book or magazine. Do you want to read blah blah blah? Or do you want something that JUMPS off the page with passion and excitement?

That's a rhetorical question but go ahead, shout the answer to yourself! (Note: Please modulate appropriately. The sad tale of me not getting my garbage out in time for the truck does not merit the same level of enthusiasm as me inviting you to a party or describing our recent house fire.)

As I've mentioned in other chapters, Social Energy is an important quality to bring to your interactions. Think of it this way, would you rather be in a PAINTING or a PLAY? Contemplate that for a bit and get back to me!

Question: Every year I get anxious at holiday time because I'm thrown in a room with all these extended family relatives that I hardly ever see and have zero in common with. So we're stuck having this horrible small talk that ends up with long awkward silences that are so stiff that it makes me extremely uncomfortable. I feel like I have nothing to say, and I'm just desperate to not be alone with someone asking about my job. I just can't figure out what to say to people that I see so infrequently.

Answer: If you're human, and they're human, then you've got 90 percent of life in common right off the bat. On top of that you're RELATED to them. So you even have mutual relatives in common and some family history floating around in the Stiff and Awkward Ether. Maybe if you pretended they were total strangers you'd have an easier time of it! Anyway, having common interests is a bonus, but really not necessary for a great conversation.

So you're getting bogged down in boring facts. Guess what. Facts are fine, but FEELINGS are FOREMOST. (I just made that up because your question literally inspired it right out of my skull. And my merry brain cells are just splashing around in the fun alliteration of it too). So the lesson there is: take what you're given and run with it!

Take your job for example. You made it sound like this horrible topic that you want to escape from like it's the Jobtanic, the Wreck of the Employment Fitzgerald or the Loser-tania. (Terribly tasteless and barely buoyant shipwreck puns. Maybe you should avoid me like the relatives!) Instead you could be telling them what you LOVE about your job, or hate about it, or are great at or what you're frustrated by; or funny or heart-warming things, or interesting tidbits or an insider's view on things that have happened on the job. Your hopes and dreams for future jobs. Heck, the very fact that they bothered to ASK about you at all! Remember, you don't even need to answer the specific question they asked. If something is more interesting with your recreational sports team, or your hobby, or your social life or your club, or your significant other, talk about those! Whatever "floats your boat." (Full circle on the shipwreck thing, right there.)

There are no boring topics, only boring ways to approach a topic. A conversation about dog food could be interesting if you have a playful sense of humor! I cannot even describe to you the number of times per week I am compelled to come up with a synonym for cat vomit as I attempt to make such a story entertaining. But I always try!

THE ABSOLUTELY BEST WAY TO WIN AN ARGUMENT

Argumentative conversations are this sense that people have of trying to "win," something, whether it be a debate, an argument, an opinion, a conversation, an interaction. Do you truly want to have a conversation and come away with the sense of: "HA! I really WON that time. I'm the winner! It's only a matter of time before bystanders give me a crown!."

When I put it that way you can see on its face how ridiculous that is. And yet, people are still out there trying to win their conversations. Like someone is going to award them a prize, or put their name on a giant lawn sign, or give them free car washes for life. Seriously! What is the point?

What are the actual odds of changing someone's mind about something by debating them about it? I will just randomly guess they're about zero. If people are open to having their minds changed, they will usually ask for your opinion. i.e. "Hey, I'm trying to decide between a front-load and a top-load washer. What do you think?" or "Gee, I can't decide what elective to take next semester. Have you heard of anything good?" or "I'm thinking my next car needs to be four-wheel drive, do you know anything about that?"

Have you ever heard someone say, "I'm trying to decide whether to register as a Democrat or a Republican..." or "I'm kind of torn between capitalism and communism, can you help me out?" or "I'm switching religions this year –

what should I consider?" For the big stuff people tend to do their own research. On the little stuff they will often reach out for input, and you'll be aware of it when they do.

When it comes to disagreements you don't have to argue. You can just listen and learn something about someone else's point of view. Or ask them questions, either to find out more about their perspective, or to get them thinking of things they may not have considered.

You don't have to be silent. But you also don't have to be confrontational. What do you win when you win an argument? Nothing. Oftentimes less than nothing. You win bad feelings. Or resentment. Maybe a brief flash of satisfaction followed by a Regret Hangover. Which I call a Dang-over. As in "Dang, why did I push so hard on that issue? Now I feel like a jerk!"

I've had to practice not spouting off on anything and everything. I try not to correct people when they say something obviously wrong. I do this a couple of ways. One is, to just Let It Go. Unless it's a directional thing, like someone wants to make a left-hand turn when we clearly need to be going right in order to get to the destination. Or if it's a safety issue. If someone is going to work on an outlet without first throwing a breaker, I will clearly intervene with my opinion before they fry themselves. But anything else, I try to let go.

I probably won't even correct anyone's pronunciation of things, except for my kids, because they're still young enough for me to do that. (Don't want them flouncing into a job interview saying something like 'for all intensive purposes.') Which should be 'for all intents and purposes.' Omigosh. I just corrected it while trying to persuade you to Just Let It Go. See how strong the urge to correct things is? Well my bad.

You can even try this with your spouse. Try not correcting him or her on things that really don't matter. You may even see your popularity soaring within your own household! (I know, I know. Subject matter for another book.)

The purpose of socializing is to have fun, engage people and connect with them. When it comes to people, it's more important to CONNECT than CORRECT. So correcting people is counterproductive to the goal. Which is to have fun, make friends, and connect. Also consider that they might be more inclined to entertain your point of view if they're having fun and connecting with you!

> ## "When it comes to people, it's more important to CONNECT than CORRECT."

There is no prize for being right. There's no award for being the Smartest Person In The Room. There's no bonus for winning someone over to your viewpoint. There's no medal for correcting someone's pronunciation or grammar. There's no trophy for showing someone up. There's no gold star for having a superior point of view. Have I emphasized that in enough different ways?

That isn't to say you can't express your views. Just be careful how you do so. Many people can't get themselves to stop at just a statement, particularly when someone inevitably challenges the statement. So unless you're very sure the person you're talking to is a great candidate for a 'friendly debate,' just let it go.

> ## "You're more likely to change someone's mind if you first win their heart."

The best way to win an argument is to conquer your own need to be right. You're more likely to change someone's mind if you first win their heart.

CHAPTER 7: TAKEAWAYS

1. *When it comes to small talk, what you're saying isn't nearly as important as HOW you're saying it.*

2. *Asking good questions and being interested in the answers creates Conversational Flow.*

3. *In any phone conversation the person on the other end can feel your smile, can sense your body language. You can reach out to them with the tone of your voice.*

4. *Most interviewers already know you can do the job. They are interviewing you to pick up on your VIBE and see if they can picture you fitting in with the company.*

5. *In an interview situation, don't worry about potential mistakes. Instead try to connect with the interviewer.*

6. *Would you rather be in a PAINTING or a PLAY? Brighten your conversations with some enthusiasm and social energy.*

7. *There's nothing to be gained socially by "winning" an argument.*

A TALL GLASS OF CRUSHED ICE-BREAKERS

Conversation Starters. They're like soup starters. They give you a nice basis to develop a full and rich social interaction. There are plenty of things you can add to provide spice or more subtle flavors. You can ruin a soup by adding the wrong thing, too, so you have to watch out for those dreaded Conversation Killers. (Such as taboo topics, deadly dull details or rude remarks.) However even with 'taboo topics' you can use them in the right setting and with likeminded people.

Conversations (unlike soups) can take off in any direction, depending on the participants. The idea is to have a variety of topics for a fun and interesting discussion. This is an area where "know your audience" is important. If you float a topic and it doesn't get any traction, it's probably best to reroute the conversation.

*

Question: Whenever I'm in a large group I'm stumped on how to have an interesting conversation. It'll turn into something like "How do you know someone" or "what do you do for a living," or "where do you live?" After that my mind goes blank and there's an awkward silence.

Answer: One key to this initial phase is to be aware of what could be asked, and then come up with a better than normal answer. So if you're asked how you know a party host, try to add something that will turn it into a conversation starter.

For example, "I know Xerxes from university. We were in the investment club." Or you did theater together. Or he was known as fantasy football expert. Or he got you interested in Habitat for Humanity. Or just add, "Xerxes is a great guy, his parties are always fun and he's the best at barbecuing" (or stock market tips, or home improvement advice, or knowing where to take your car for repairs, etc.)

Be aware of what your friends and acquaintances are known for. Then you can point to their positive qualities and open up other areas of conversation. Complimenting people behind their backs is an utterly charming habit! This is especially useful when you're introducing people. That gives them potential areas to connect.

"Complimenting people behind their backs is an utterly charming habit!

So "what do you DO?" Try to pick out aspects that people might find interesting. Unless they're familiar with your area of work, you don't want to go too deep into technical detail because that could result in Rapid Onset Boredom, which will immediately "ROB" the conversation of all life.

If you're asked where you live, mention some fun things you do locally.

"We have a pretty lake nearby," or "my favorite restaurant is Le Pricey Menu," or "there's a great walking trail." You might even want to research some little-known facts, or historical detail. Nobody wants a lecture, but a fact or two is usually pretty harmless.

For example, Scratch Ankle, Alabama is an actual place that got its name from railroad workers who had to constantly battle mosquitoes. So the name stuck. Or should I say, "the name drew blood?" Your own town or city will have facts or details that could add some color to the conversation.

Another fun one is knowing what the National Day is. Any given day will be National "Something" Day, and usually there's more than one to choose from. For example, on my own birthday there are three separate national celebrations. It is "National Make Your Bed Day," and "National Hot Cross Bun Day," as well as "Patriot Day and National Day of Service and Remembrance."

Many days have half a dozen different designations! That is for the United States, but you can also do it internationally. If I had nothing better to do I'd sit around making up days myself, like "National Off Brand Printer Ink Day," or "National Chore I Keep Neglecting Day," or "National Words of Encouragement Day." This last could be done verbally, by text or with sticky notes! Can you imagine what a FUN day that would be?" And ironically it would technically be WOE day.

You can't just throw out a topic that is too deep or too weird at first. That would feel forced and unnatural. Don't ask someone what their favorite circus character is, or what kind of tree or animal they would be, or what epitaph they want on their gravestone when you first strike up a conversation. That will send someone fleeing straight to the bathroom with a certain sense of urgency.

You can word things to make them more fun. If it's someone you totally don't know you can ask them, "What's on your fun bio instead of your work bio? Wouldn't it be cool to do a resume just based on what we LIKED to do, instead of what we're good at professionally?" I just made that up now, but that sounds so cool to me! Now I want to know what everyone's Fun Resume looks like.

Another good question, standard version, is "tell me about yourself." Honestly, to me this question sounds a little too formal. I'm getting a bit of an Interviewing vibe from it. It feels like there's a lot of pressure! If I were asked this question I'd feel like, "Wow, I guess I'd better hit the most important thing!" But what exactly IS that? I don't even know what kind of answer they'd be expecting.

I'd give it a more fun vibe. "So what's important for me to know about you?" You could argue that it's the same question. But I feel like it takes it away from the Personal Bio aspect and opens it up to any kind of spin you want to give it. So I could answer it with, "I like to cook, so people really need to put up their caloric defenses or I'll slip you some unauthorized cookies," or "my train of thought often jumps the tracks, so look out below!" I just feel that wording opens up a lot more possibilities and there's no wrong answer. Whereas "tell me about yourself" feels like a test that I have to pass.

Another one is, "Anything exciting going on with you or your family lately?" If you get a blank stare, you can encourage them with, "Inside the house? Outside the house? Coming down the road at you?" That can usually break loose an idea or two. (Calving a conversation off a glacier!) That pretty much covers the whole enchilada of life possibilities. Don't say I didn't give you an opening!

If it's the evening you can try, "Anything great happen to you today?"

Other fun starters: Did anything make you laugh today? How did your day go? Do you have anything left to accomplish today? Do you have any plans for this weekend? Is there anything to eat here that I really need to try? Do you know a lot of people here?

"Did you do anything today that can qualify as exercise?" This is a fun one because you might get a straight answer to it, but it practically begs for a creative interpretation or a funny answer. So of course I like it!

Here's one that's a little off the wall, but it will sometimes prompt interesting answers. "What's the best way to help me remember your name?" Because people are obviously used to their own name and its nuances. They probably already know a great way to help you remember it. I once met a woman named Catherine. And she said, "Just think of me as Catherine the Great!" (historical reference) It's impossible for me to forget her name now.

My friend Carol was born on December 25th, so this prompts an obvious connection to a "Christmas Carol." The second time someone forgets my name, I might add something like, "Just think of me as Peppermint Patti, adding a little spicy freshness to the conversation..."

Did you know that peppermint oil dabbed on a cotton ball or sprayed in key places will repel both spiders and mice? True fact. See I'm a walking, talking conversation starter! Don't be afraid to whack that topic with the pinball flippers until you find one that lights up the conversation!

How about, "Have you been anywhere lately? I'm looking for some good vacation ideas." Whether or not they've been someplace recently, they may enjoy launching into one of their favorite vacation trips, which could be interesting to hear about.

If it's the weekend you could ask, "How was your week? The good, the bad, the ugly?" That opens it up to the highs, the lows, the hilarity. If you're going to ask someone if they've read anything lately, be sure to have something similar ready to go. Because they might say no and toss the question right back at you.

You can ask people what they like about living where they are. Even if you live in the same place, they may mention things you're not aware of! I'll put this into a numbered list so you don't have to hunt around in my prose trying to find that darned conversation starter. And I break it up in useful categories:

BASIC ICEBREAKERS

1. What's on your fun resume instead of your work resume?

2. Anything exciting going on with you or your family lately?

3. Anything great happen to you today?

4. Did anything make you laugh today?

5. How did today go for you? If you had to rate it on a scale…

6. Do you have anything left to accomplish today?

7. Do you have any plans for this weekend?

8. Is there anything to eat here that I really need to try?

9. Do you know a lot of people here?

10. Did you do anything today that can qualify as exercise?

11. What's the best way to help me remember your name?

12. Have you been anywhere lately? I'm looking for vacation ideas.

13. How was your week? The good, the bad, the ugly…

14. Have you read anything good lately?

15. Do you live around here? What do you like about it?

16. Do you know any restaurants I should try?

17. Where did you grow up? What's special about it?

18. What kind of pet person are you?

19. What's the first thing you do after work?

20. Do you have a dream job?

21. Have you been out of the country?

22. Do you have anything you like to cook?

23. What's your favorite beverage?

24. Any movies out there that I need to see?

25. What are your recommendations for a binge-watch?

26. Have you been to any concerts lately?

27. Where do you like to hang out around here?

28. That's a great (item of clothing). Where'd you get it?

29. How long have you been at your job?

30. How's today treating you?

31. Did you hear about (news item of that day)?

32. Do you have any kids/how big is your family?

33. Have you met anyone famous? Semi-famous?

34. Have you added anything to your bucket list lately?

35. How well do you know (the person whose party it is)?

36. Have you been here before? (if you're at an atypical location)

37. How did you like (the reason why you're here) "talk" "show" "game" etc.

38. What are the pros and cons of your job?

39. Listening to any good music lately? Can you talk me into another genre?

40. Have you tried any new restaurants lately?

41. What's your favorite conversation starter? (Say it with a smile!)

42. What do you do when you're not working?

43. Have you tried the (food you're eating)? This is crazy good. (if it tastes good!)

44. Are you cold? (Or hot?) How much trouble do you think we'll get into if we start fooling around with the thermostat? (A fun rhetorical question. I don't actually mess with anyone's temperature controls)

45. Did you catch any interesting news today? I missed the headlines.

46. How did traffic treat you today?

47. Did you watch the game last night?

48. I forgot if we've met. I'm Patti... (sometimes I'm just not sure!)

49. Are you ready for (nearest upcoming holiday)?

50. You look fun. What's happening here? (this is sort of bold and playful in case you feel like throwing caution to the wind)

51. I heard you know something about (or are an expert on) X. I need details.

52. How long have you lived here? What do you like about it?

53. What's your number one favorite restaurant around here?

54. Pop phone quiz—is the last pic on your phone something you can show?

55. What was the best part of your day so far?

56. Anything exciting on the line for tomorrow?

57. I might want to change streaming services. What do you use?

58. Are there any podcasts I should be listening to?

59. Do you have any go-to apps that I should have on my phone?

60. Are you working on anything right now?

*

That's a lot of ice breakers. The key is to use it as a jumping off point. I try to ask something STICKY. That's something people can latch onto so they can relate it to themselves, their lives, their ideas. A sticky question will resonate with people, will give them an opportunity to talk about something that they'll likely have an answer for, and it'll allow them to follow up or even steer the conversation in a related but different direction. Most of these are really designed to invite the person to give a more free form answer.

A conversation isn't like a quiz show. It isn't question/answer, question/answer, question/answer. It's more like, question/explanation/oh really, tell me more/additional info/that's cool, what about…/clarification more info, then throw a question back to you/answer. In other words, there's conversational FLOW. So what keeps it flowing is starting with a sticky question that they can latch onto, then you coming back with an interested comment or follow-up question.

You want to link to what they're saying, whether it's something you know, something you've heard of or something you've experienced. If you have none of these, then simply ask a related question, or rephrase what they've said (active listening) so they know you understood correctly. You can always add, "That sounds cool, can you tell me more about that?" or "sounds like you know a lot about it, I'd love to know the details."

*

I'm going to provide other icebreaker lists for more specific purposes, but let's go to a question:

Question: I don't like dealing with silences in conversation, especially with people I've just met. I feel pressure to bring up another topic. That makes me feel stressed, and the silence feels even more awkward! I feel like most of the time I'm pretty boring. What makes someone fun to be around?

Answer: It isn't necessarily the topics themselves that are boring. It might be that you're bringing a lack of social energy to them. I try to have a playful frame of mind, even when I'm by myself. That keeps me on the lookout for interesting ideas and tidbits during my day that amuse me. It's an attitude thing. A VIBE thing.

Bringing a fun vibe is not something I do only when I'm going to be with other people. I want to cultivate that as a habit so I'm fun and entertaining in my own company! Self-entertainment is a great skill to have. You can get serious things done while still having a fun vibe. I would define a Fun Vibe as a sense of playfulness and energy.

So how do you bring a Fun Vibe to your conversations? Well, if you're lacking social energy, it might leave you unsure what you want to get out of a conversation, other than not wanting to mess it up or having it end prematurely. Even I feel pressured by that! The conversation may FAIL. It might be epically boring!

So let's Flip That Script!

Instead of treating the conversation like a delicate china plate that you're holding onto, trying not to break it, and hoping desperately that your conversational partner will like whatever small talk entrée you've delicately placed at the center of your dinnerware, let's do something different. Let's pretend it's an UNBREAKABLE LIGHTWEIGHT PLATTER OF MANY COLORS that you can flip into the air, juggle, catch, toss or spin in any direction. Whatever topic you place on the plate gets stuck to the energy and flies around with it!

It's your enthusiasm for the person and (Whatever The Topic May Happen To Be) that will inject a Fun Energy into the proceedings. How do you communicate enthusiasm? An open, interested smile (authentic, using your eyes), good eye contact, an animated tone of voice.

So if someone says they work in real estate, you ask something like, "Wow. I hope I can get some good tips for when I'm ready to buy a house. What are some of the worst mistakes first time buyers make?" or "I'll bet you get all kinds of clients. What are some of your best and worst ones like?" Etc. You can apply this type of questioning to lots of things. It is a playful and interested energy that makes an interaction fun. And I think it's key to actually BE interested in the person and what they're telling you, not to fake that.

I think a lot of Awkward Moments come about when your Insides don't match your Outsides. So pretending to be interested in a conversation when you're really not creates awkwardness that people can feel externally and YOU can feel inwardly. You don't line up, you don't match. So, AWKWARD.

That's why I say don't fake this stuff. You need to CREATE joy in your heart. You need to BECOME interested in others. You need to FEEL some enthusiasm in order to be able to express it well.

Suppose someone is telling you something that is excruciatingly boring. Don't just stand there blankly and try to keep a half-hearted smile plastered onto your face. DO something about it! Rescue the conversation. Help redirect so it acquires more energy, more fun, more interest.

"Hey I'm just the general public here. Tell me your best inside info about your company. I don't need to know about your accounting techniques. There's a risk I'd just blab it to a competitor or something…" Or, "Who's the craziest character that you work with? What are they like?"

In other words, it's okay to nudge the conversation into a more interesting area while still keeping to that topic. Or change it up entirely.

> *"It's your enthusiasm for the person and the topic that will inject a fun energy into any conversation."*

In addition to asking good sticky questions as conversation starters, you also have to be prepared with information of your own! If you ask someone what they've been up to, you should also have an answer to that very question. Now one thing I do NOT do is give someone a version of my latest 'to do' list, or just run-down of my day.

I try to say things that others might find interesting, or funny, or worth commenting on. And things that might prompt something similar from them. Like if I'm battling a particular household pest, I'll tell them about the successes, the failures. I'll inject any appropriate drama: "Then the ants re-appeared at the WORST possible moment," or "We thought we had won the battle, until the next day when I started hearing more suspicious squirrel noises," or "I swear the spider was the size of a PASTA BOWL, and the only way we were going to defeat it is with a broom and a shoe," or "so then the wasps became super ANGRY, and I fled into the house," or "After I killed the FIFTH fly I knew we had a bigger problem," or, "Then we saw the cat scamper to the other side of the house with a squirming LIZARD in its jaws," or "Finally we commenced a truly epic battle with the FLEAS…" We have had a lot of pest drama over the years. Fortunately not all at the same time.

Any time something amusing or weird happens during my day, I will save the incident for future telling as quick entertainment. Because stuff like that happens to me on a daily basis, (sometimes even on an HOURLY basis), I feel 100 percent sure that crazy/funny stuff is also happening to you at least as frequently.

If you're not accustomed to noticing and/or remembering these things, make that a new habit. Anything that happens that is: funny, weird, unusual, entertaining, heart-warming, worth noticing, etc. It's all conversational fodder. If you're not used to noticing, you should carry around a small pad of paper, or add notes in your phone.

The icebreaker questions above are all-purpose conversation starters. What if you're with a group of people you otherwise know pretty well? Here are questions for a deeper and more thought-provoking conversation.

DEEPER ICEBREAKERS

1. If each day was four hours longer, what would you do with the extra time?
2. What was your worst cooking disaster?
3. If you could be a Star Wars character, which one would you be and why?
4. What people are most important to you apart from family members?
5. If you could live anywhere in the world, where would you pick?
6. What is your dream vacation if money were no object?
7. What's your favorite childhood movie and what do you love about it?
8. What's the best gift you've ever received? Most unusual?
9. What are your favorite ways to relax?
10. If you had a free round-trip plane ticket, where would you go?
11. If you didn't have your current job, what would the next runner up be?
12. Do you have a secret project you're working on, or hope to have in the future?

13. What's the worst advice you've ever gotten? (or just garden variety awful)

14. Do you have a favorite quotation?

15. What three words would best describe you?

16. If you could only keep one of your current possessions, what would you pick and why?

17. If you could have a miracle occur in your life, what would you ask for?

18. If there was a movie of your life, who would play you in the lead role?

19. What are your hidden talents?

20. What is something your friends probably wouldn't guess about you?

21. If you could meet anyone from history, who would it be?

22. If you were giving a TED talk, what would your topic be?

23. What would your dream job look like?

24. Being totally objective, (wink) what is the best part of your personality?

25. What's the craziest thing you've ever done? (that you're willing to admit)

26. What things do you value most in a friend?

27. What have you binge-watched that's totally worth it?

28. What's one of your most embarrassing moments?

29. What advice would you give to your younger self?

30. Finish the sentence, "Never have I ever…"

31. What's your favorite article of clothing right now? Or in your past?

32. What's the worst injury you've ever had?

33. Tell me about a pivotal moment in your life.

34. What are you grateful for?

35. What are you proud of?

36. Which is your favorite season and why?

37. If you were stuck on a deserted island, what three things would you bring?

38. What are you looking forward to?

39. What's the most important thing for me to know about you?

40. What do you want to be when you grow up even more? (super fun!)

41. What inspired you to be in your job/industry?

42. What motivates you?

43. What did you want to be when you were a kid?

44. Would you like to start a new hobby?

45. Where's the last place you traveled? How was it?

46. What's your biggest pet peeve?

47. Have you ever had an experience where you might have died? What was it?

48. What hobby would you do if time and money weren't a consideration?

49. What is the best thing you've ever made?

50. What question are you sick of answering?

51. Do you have any repetitive dreams? How does it go?

52. Do you own anything that you don't like to share?

53. What is your best physical quality? Keep it PG rated.

54. What would you do with a million tax-free dollars?

55. What would you choose as a superpower?

56. If you had a theme song playing every time you entered a room, what would it be?

57. If you named yourself instead of your parents, what name would you pick?

58. What makes you laugh the most?

59. If you could be in any decade, which one would you want to be living in?

60. Who's your role model?

Wow. Sixty icebreakers. And sixty deeper questions. Why is there any awkward silence at all when there is so much to talk about? This doesn't even count the more standard questions like how's your mom doing, what do you have going on today and what's that you're eating? Plus, there's a 50 percent chance that the other person might ask YOU something, so technically you only have to think of half the conversation.

There are no wrong answers, so you can't be penalized. It feels correct to say that, even though I realize that there are several horrible dictators who would clearly be bad role models, and thus a 'wrong answer.'

*

Question: I have a circle of close friends that I've known since high school. (I'm mid-twenties) I'm fine having a convo with them, but I'm never comfortable when I'm alone with one of them. When there's three or more people I take a big part in the conversation and it feels great. But if it's just two of us it's awkward and there are uncomfortable silences. I have the same problem with new people or acquaintances. Can you help?

Answer: First off, it isn't all on you. They're responsible for their half of the conversation! So take some of the pressure off yourself. Even if they're keeping up their end, it sounds like you're having trouble responding in a way that keeps things flowing smoothly.

It's helpful to have a couple opening comments or questions. I try to have at least one brief anecdote in my hip pocket. Something small that made me smile. Some little disaster or near-disaster. Traffic issues. Pet issues. The weather. Whatever. You can ask what's going on with them: family, job ('for money!'), fun, future. I've seen this labeled on the internet as FORD: Family, Occupation, Recreation, Dreams. Not sure who made it up, but it isn't mine. Borrowed! I'll be returning it next week…

After that it's all LINKING. You link your comment or question to what they've said. Or you might take a small piece and link it to another related topic. Be happy. Be interested. Be excited. Encourage them with a smile. Use active listening. "Wow that sounds like you had a bummer of a day at work. I hope you rewarded yourself for surviving..." etc. Then...link, link, link.

That's how a good free-flowing conversation is constructed. There's also nothing wrong with a topic being finished and asking a completely unrelated question. You indicate that with a transitional tone of voice. "So...what are your plans for next week?" Or "Do you have anything interesting happening?" or "What's going on with the family?" or "What are you doing for exercise lately?" or "Do you know anything I can binge watch?" or "What's the latest at work?" or "Have you been anywhere to eat that I should try?"

You don't ask a question like you've handed off a football or a relay baton, and you're done with it. You need to take a true interest in the person's response, to encourage them with your comments and questions, and to be interested in engaging them, whatever the topic may be. It's possible you may need to be more energetic about that.

There's no quicker way to kill a conversation than to ask a question and not appear interested in the answer! Smile. Good eye contact. Interested tone of voice. Link, link, link. Have fun with it! I always find out interesting things from people and I love being informed and entertained by them.

> ## *"There's no quicker way to kill a conversation than to ask a question and not appear interested in the answer."*

So did you think I've run out of questions, at 120 of them? Ha! No way. My family is famous for interrogations. When we were living at home, my siblings and I would walk in the door from someplace, and if both parents were in the vicinity, suddenly we found ourselves in the middle of a barrage of questions. Oftentimes coming from left and right. Or one parent was sitting and one was standing as they fired questions at us.

"Who was there, what did you do, what street did you take, what did you eat, how long did you stay, where did you park, did you run into any construction, who went with you, did you take them home, did you see anyone's parents, I hope you thanked them, did you go anyplace else, were any of the kids drinking, are you SURE, how many people were there, isn't that what's-his-name's daughter, what does she look like now, do they still live there…"

I mean, it was incredible. Oftentimes we would flee to the bathroom just to get some respite, although that didn't keep them from asking questions from outside the bathroom door. It was impossible to bore my father. He was a never-ending bottomless well of questions. Sometimes we'd have to distract him with a statement that would throw him off, such as, "I think I saw the dog outside in the front." (which meant the family dog escaped the fenced backyard). Or, "There was some mail in the box, but I forgot to bring it in." (dad had a mail obsession), or (my favorite), "I think I smell something WEIRD!" (This would set my father off on a wild goose chase until he assured himself there was nothing dangerous going on anywhere in the house. I think he was primarily concerned about gas leaks.)

Okay, on to more great questions. This one is for teenagers, high school age kids, up through college age.

SCHOOL AGE ICEBREAKERS

1. What's your favorite class? Why do you like it?
2. What's your favorite food?
3. What's your favorite restaurant?
4. What clubs are you in at school?
5. Who's your best friend?
6. What shows are you watching?
7. Are there any podcasts I should listen to?

8. What games are on your phone right now?

9. Where would you go if you had a time machine?

10. Have you seen any good movies lately?

11. Do you play any sports?

12. What's the first house or neighborhood that you remember living in?

13. Do you have any superpowers that people don't know about?

14. What do you look for in a friend?

15. What do you look for in a girlfriend or boyfriend?

16. Do you have a pet?

17. Do you have a stronger relationship with one of your siblings? Or one of your parents?

18. What was your most embarrassing moment in school?

19. What's your biggest pet peeve about school?

20. Do you have a favorite teacher or professor?

21. What do you do for exercise?

22. Do you think you could've handled living before this period of time?

23. How many decades back do you think you'd try?

24. Would you change anything about your childhood?

25. Are you going to have a pet when you're older?

26. How old do you want to be if you get married?

27. What makes you happy?

28. Who's your favorite music artist?

29. Who used to be your favorite music artist when you were younger?

30. What was your favorite kids' TV show?

31. What do you watch now?

32. What's the biggest thing going on in your life right now?

33. What kind of car do you want when you're older?

34. Do you have all your grandparents? What are they like?

35. Show me your best selfie.

36. If you had a podcast, what would it be about?

37. Have you been out of the country? Where?

38. What was your best Halloween costume?

39. What was your best vacation?

40. What's your favorite article of clothing?

41. What did you used to wear as a kid that was HORRIBLE?

42. Do you have any fun activities or hobbies?

43. What have you been doing recently?

44. What's the last thing you bought online?

45. What are your plans for (high school, college, grad school) etc.

46. What foreign language would you like to speak?

47. Which social media do you spend the most time on?

48. Have you ever had to go to the hospital?

49. Who's your favorite actor?

50. What three things can't you live without?

51. Do you have any recurring dreams or nightmares?

52. If you could go on a cross-country road trip with any historical person, who would you pick?

53. What are you obsessed with?

54. What would your perfect day look like?

55. Who has influenced you the most in your life so far?

56. If you could make up a school subject or college major, what would it be?

57. What would be the best punishment for annoying people?

58. Would you rather lose all your possessions, or all your photos?

[SPOILER ALERT]

59. How did you find out that Santa isn't real?

60. What is the craziest thing you've done?

*

So do you think I'm out of questions NOW? Or, do you smell something WEIRD? (haha) Of course I'm not out of them. But let's go to a question.

Question: I can't get people to vibe with me. It seems they like the idea of me more than the actual me. I'm horrible at small talk because it all feels generic. It's just this lame formula of asking the same types of questions over and over, and I really don't care about the answers. I'm the odd man out in most conversations. Is there any way for me to fit in better?

Answer: I don't think small talk is as boring as you make it sound. The problem could be your energy level. Also, you have some control over the small talk. You don't have to ask a question whose answer you don't care about. That seems like a losing strategy. Ask a question you ARE interested in knowing the answer to!

I noticed in your question the word 'vibe.' It's worth asking what that means, what causes that magical moment to happen when you are vibing with someone. Usually it's because you're talking about something that you both are passionate about, so extra energy gets into the air as you enjoy exchanging ideas. With ENTHUSIASM.

There are two things that need to happen: 1) You need to find topics that you can have enthusiasm for. It needs to be enough of a general interest that others would enjoy it too. E.g. talking sports with a fellow fan; games with a gamer; movies with someone who likes the particular genre/actors that you do. Or something of general interest to anyone. Second is you need to communicate that enthusiasm for the topic. The more topics you care about and have a strong opinion on, the more areas of conversation there will be.

For example, suppose you asked me about my favorite food. Well, my eyes are going to light up because I LOVE talking about food. Will I limit myself to just one food? Of course not! The next thing you know, you'll be hearing about the joys of pasta, my cravings for chocolate, what I would love to do to an avocado, how I like my steak cooked, why the pizza in Buffalo is better than anywhere else in the country, my method of cooking chicken wings, and what's so special about my lasagna. I'll either have bored you to death or invited you to dinner.

But I would also ask about your favorite food, and I'd expect you to vigorously defend your choice. (Notice I haven't even picked a favorite. I'm too busy creating an extensive menu of options.) A lot of topics can set me off on a whirligig of enthusiasm, and food certainly is one. You have to decide what topics work that way for you, and also which of them might have a broader appeal. See, I even managed to get excited about this imaginary conversation!

CREATIVE ICEBREAKERS

Okay, so here's a list of questions for people who like something a little deeper or out of the ordinary:

1. Has your life turned out the way you expected?
2. What gives you the greatest joy in life?
3. Do you have any big regrets?
4. What's your take on aliens?
5. What fictional character would you love to hang out with?
6. Who's your candidate for least talented famous person?
7. Do you have any guilty pleasure TV shows?
8. What makes you irrationally angry?
9. What word did someone have to correct your pronunciation of?
10. What's an unusual flavor combo that you like?
11. If you had a reality TV series, what would it consist of?
12. What's the strangest gift you've ever gotten?
13. What is the purpose of dreams?
14. What nickname would you pick for yourself?
15. If you got to make up a holiday, what would it be? When would we celebrate it?
16. Did you have any unusual childhood habits or interests?

17. Have you made any decisions that changed your life in a major way? How?

18. What's an example of you behaving badly?

19. Which animals do you think belong in heaven?

20. If you could give your younger self some advice, what would it be?

21. Have you ever convinced someone something was true that wasn't?

22. If you could make up a profession for yourself, what would it be?

23. What country do you know the least about?

24. What do people assume about you that isn't true?

25. What do you still want to accomplish?

26. What living person do you admire?

27. Would you want to keep living without electricity?

28. What random skill would you love to have?

29. What modern thing are you completely sick of?

30. What are the top three things on your bucket list?

31. What do you think is the perfect age?

32. If money were no object, what would your dream house look like?

33. Have you seen any movies more than three times? Which ones?

34. If you were able to get rid of one animal from the planet, which one would go?

35. What superpower would you like?

36. Would you switch lives with anyone?

37. Can you remember your best meal?

38. What was your favorite childhood game?

39. If you could see the future, what is one thing you'd want to know?

40. What is one of your earliest memories?

41. What will people be having nostalgia over 25 years from now?

42. Do you have any embarrassing clothing fail stories?

43. If you had a Life Apprentice, what would you teach that person?

44. If you had a boat, what would you name it?

45. What was the hardest job you've worked?

46. What were you obsessed with as a kid?

47. What is your favorite word or phrase from a bygone era?

48. What's the best way to measure success?

49. Has anything ever happened to you that's unexplainable?

50. What are you known for in your group of friends? Your family?

51. What was your best decade of life?

52. What do you do to improve your mood?

53. Do you have any irrational fears?

54. What's your favorite room in your house?

55. If you could take anything from earth and make it disappear into a black hole, what would you send?

56. Do you have any useless talents?

57. What famous person would you NOT want to be stuck on an elevator with?

58. What was your most ridiculous injury?

59. If you had only one month to live, how would you spend that time?

60. What would you like people to say about you after you die?

*

One reason for so many questions in this chapter is that they are merely ideas. Questions can be about anything. Variations are endless. Add to that things currently going on in your life, others' lives, your town, your local area. And things you find interesting. And things you read or hear about that are interesting. It's all a matter of what lifts your luggage, what blows your hair back, what moves your needle, what bakes your cake. It's your job to figure out what other people are interested in talking about too.

When in doubt, talk about PETS! Pets are endlessly fun. Anyone can entertain me with a good pet story. Even historical pet stories. Remember, pets are as interesting and entertaining as family members, but they cannot be embarrassed by stories pertaining to them. That's why pet stories are the best. No one can be upset that you've told the story. There are no secrets about pets. (Watch. The minute I make a claim like that, someone will come up with a reason why their pet details need to be a federal secret. That's always the way.)

Just in case I haven't given you enough conversation starters, I will offer a final set.

BONUS ICE BREAKERS

1. How do you want your life to be different a year from now?
2. What mistake did you learn the most from?
3. What's your biggest procrastination item that you wish was already done?
4. What should you really make more time for in your life?
5. Do you think you can make your dreams come true? What would it take?
6. Who or what can you count on most in life?
7. What's something that you've changed your mind about?
8. If you could magically add something to your life, what would it be?
9. Have you tried anything new that you wish you'd done sooner?
10. Do you have any big unanswered questions about life?
11. What's your favorite way to reward yourself for something?
12. What's your most ridiculous irrational fear?
13. Name someone you find to be inspirational, whether famous or not.
14. Which do you like better: change or stability? Why?
15. What would be your perfect breakfast if there were no health considerations?

16. If you had to share your most important life lesson, what would it be?
17. What's some great advice you've gotten from someone else?
18. What's your favorite kind of store to shop in? (Top three for more fun!)
19. If you had a totally free day to yourself, what would you do with it?
20. What mindset or way of thinking have you been able to overcome?
21. How good are you at keeping secrets?
22. What's your favorite place to hang out?
23. What's the best thing about you right now?
24. What do you have a love/hate relationship with?
25. What's on your Wish List?
26. What's something that you think is a waste of money?
27. What would most improve the world right now?
28. Does anything make you feel homesick?
29. What do you love to do with a group of people?
30. To what extent do you think people can change?
31. What have you done that's totally out of your comfort zone?
32. Name something you're looking forward to.
33. Are you usually early, late or on time?
34. What's your best healthy habit at the moment?
35. How do you influence those around you? (intentionally or not)
36. Name something very popular that you can't stand.
37. Are you an indoor person or an outdoor person? Why?
38. What's something you should do for yourself that you don't get around to?
39. Name your favorite charity. (or if you could create one, what would it be?)
40. Name something you take for granted.
41. What's a great compliment that you've received?
42. What do you like to waste money on?

43. How complicated is your life?

44. What stresses you out?

45. If you could be someone else, who would you choose?

46. If this turned out to be your last day on earth, what would you regret not having done?

47. Name something that was a wake-up call for you.

48. Have you learned anything about yourself lately?

49. Do you have something that you won't compromise on?

50. Name one Red Flag and one Dealbreaker in a relationship. (romantic or otherwise)

51. Name something you like to do spontaneously.

52. What's something you're still not good at but you keep trying?

53. How have you changed in the last five years?

54. What's something about you that's impossible to hide?

55. What kind of decisions do you spend too much time on?

56. Have you taken any risks lately?

57. What's your favorite Urban Legend?

58. What's something that went better than you thought it would?

59. How would a friend describe you? How would an enemy describe you?

60. Large or small, have you ever solved a mystery?

*

Although I've called these lists "ice breakers" obviously there are some that wouldn't be the first thing you'd ask someone. There is a definite mix of "ice breakers" and "conversation extenders." But after tossing off 300+ in this chapter alone, you shouldn't be at a loss for something to discuss! If you find this massive list overwhelming, then write out some fun ones, put them in a jar, and pick out the "question of the day." See if you can work it into that day's conversations! My idea for randomizing it a bit, but you can use your own.

This chapter would not be complete unless I came up with the perfect bookend. We opened the chapter with Conversation Starters. We'll close it with Conversation Enders.

How do we know when a conversation is over? Sometimes we can just feel it winding down to a natural end. But, what if you're done and you want to gracefully exit?

CONVERSATION ENDERS

Here are some standard conversation-enders:

"It was great talking with you. I've gotta run." Or reverse it. "Well I've gotta run! It was great having a chance to catch up." You don't have to be specific on what you're doing next unless you want to share that. Often people will waste excess mental energy on what people will think of their "reason" and if it's "legit" or not. Life is too short for over-thinking! If you want to share the reason, go ahead. Otherwise just keep it generic and move on.

If you're at an event where food is present, a natural conversation ender comes with your empty cup. "I'm headed for a refill. Nice talking to you."

If you're someplace where you know plenty of people: "I need to catch up with someone, but it was great meeting you! (or talking with you)."

"Thanks for all the great info, let's talk again soon."

"I need to make a phone call (shoot off a text), but this was fun."

"I really enjoyed talking with you. I'm headed for more snacks."

At a networking event: "Thanks for sharing some great tips. Is there anyone else here you think I should meet?"

At a party: "I'm going to say hello to the host. It was nice to meet you."

At a party or a networking event: "There's someone I'd like you to meet."

(Target person should be nearby) "Zeus, I'd like you to meet Apollo…" (give a few details about each person)

"I need to do some mingling, but thanks for the interesting conversation."

"I'm going to hit the restroom, catch up with you later."

"I've had a nice time talking with you, enjoy the rest of the party."

"I'm glad we had a chance to catch up, let's do it again."

"I have to get going – nice chatting with you."

"Just saw a friend come in, so I'm going to say hello."

"Thanks for all the great news. Keep me in the loop."

"Gotta be heading out, but it's been great!"

CHAPTER 8: TAKEAWAYS

1. *You're only responsible for half the conversation, so don't stress about shouldering all the burden.*

2. *Try to ask "sticky" questions that people can latch onto and have fun with.*

3. *A conversation is not a fragile thing. Don't treat it like something you will accidentally break if you don't say "just the right thing."*

4. *If you ask a question, make sure you're interested in the answer.*

5. *The feeling in your heart should match what you're trying to express externally. So don't 'pretend' to be interested in other people, BE interested in them!*

6. *Icebreakers are just starting points. Conversations can go in any direction as long as you LINK, LINK, LINK.*

DOING THE DEEP DIVE TO FIND YOUR VIBE

This key chapter is about attitude. It's about mindset. It's about VIBE. It's this thing that exists that most people take for granted. We often don't even think about it. Because it's always with us. It seems (and is) part of, "who we are." That's unchangeable, right?

I think our essence, the Deep Down Real You, the person of value, is unchangeable. But, how we think about ourselves, and others, and life in general, IS very much within our control. How we express ourselves to others is also within our control.

The Deep Down Real You can look very different to people depending on our communication skills and habits. Even people who are great at communicating about themselves still do it imperfectly. Just like we can't instantly teleport anywhere except in science fiction, we can't instantly understand each other perfectly except in MindMeld Fiction. Now there's a genre with all kinds of weird future potential!

A very large part of your capacity to have a great interaction with someone is your ability to enjoy their company. And that is so hard to do when you're feeling uncomfortable. (Just sort of summed it up in a nutshell right there. But, that's the essential problem people tend to have.) Then here is the other problem. MOST of the world is STRANGERS. Yep. True fact. So we're kind of stuck with this Mostly Awkward Situation right off the bat!

What to do, what to do?

Well the idea is to turn the strangers into acquaintances, thus increasing the comfort level. And then the goal after that is to become friends with at least some of them, so that way you can have a fun and happy social life. Sounds so simple when I say it that way!

In all honesty it IS that simple. It's just that many people perceive a lot of obstacles between Point A (Acquaintances) and Point B (Buddies). Most of those obstacles are internal, and you can readily overcome them with practice, determination, and most of all, the sure belief that it can be done!

Coming back to your mindset for a bit. You not only need to train yourself in some of the skills. (basics like eye contact, energetic greeting, smile, active listening, open body posture, etc.) You will need to retrain your MIND into an attitude that reaches out to people and invites them into your life.

See, people will not be comfortable coming into your life unless they feel welcome. And getting them to feel welcome requires more than just you existing in the same space with them. Aren't there those people you've worked with forever and they're not your friend? How about the person at the next desk over? What about that guy across the hall? The neighbor you never talk to? The woman you always see at the gym? I'm not suggesting that you befriend all those people. There may be reasons why that makes no sense for you. But you should have that ability, if needed.

So how do we create this sense of comfort? It all starts in your mind. Before you put the smile on your face, you need to put the smile in your BRAIN. Of course you don't have to do that, and there are many times that you don't. That is called the insincere smile, or the forced smile, the fake, the perfunctory smile

– see! The thing even has multiple names for its existence. That's why there are a lot of fake smiles at work. It's actually the perfect place for them. They're an accepted social currency there. But for people you want to really connect with, you're going to have to come with the Real Thing. A genuine smile.

> *Before you put a smile on your face, you need to put a smile in your BRAIN."*

In order to produce the real smile your brain is going to have to smile internally first. Which means your attitude is going to have to smile.

Also I want to acknowledge that there are many, many reasons why your attitude might not be smiling. One of the biggest is: it hasn't developed the habit. Another is that you haven't gotten much positive feedback. Yet another is just plain bad stuff is going on in your life. But when it comes to socializing it's important to put that in the background at least for a while.

In order to make people comfortable you have to be in a happy place in your brain. If your brain isn't already there you need to create that happy place for yourself. Because a good interaction requires both people to be comfortable. So start with yourself, and then you can invite the other person into that space.

Where does this happy comfortable attitude come from? For one, you will have worked on the basic social skills. They are extremely important but still basic enough that anyone can master them. I'm not asking you to give a speech in front of thousands. I'm not asking you to give a terminal diagnosis to a dying relative. I'm not asking you to calm down someone's road rage. I'm not asking you to give a wedding toast. I'm not asking you to solve a situation involving hostages. I'm just asking you to practice some simple things. Smile. Energy. Speak. Comment. Compliment. Question. Show enthusiasm. Initiate. Check in with people. Don't give up.

Your first area of comfort is that you've worked on these skills, not a few times, but lots of times, like, every time you interact with a stranger. You've done it repeatedly until you KNOW you can get a smile out of them. You're SURE you can deliver a comment, question or compliment that will brighten their day. You're certain that your energy and vibe will carry the day.

Being able to do all that (which you can practice EVERY DAY if you so much as go out for a cup of coffee or buy a pack of gum at the grocery store) is a huge reason to feel comfortable in your mind. It should give you a feeling of confidence that you can interact with anyone and bring something positive to that.

The other part though is your literal attitude toward other people. And your own general VIBE that you want to bring to them. If you just bring the social skills you can have a fine interaction. But if you bring more than that, an attitude of positivity, friendliness, openness, that is where you edge into territory where you can start making friends.

Having this sort of Social Psyche will result in you looking at people with positivity. You will give them the benefit of the doubt. You will assume they are probably a great person, you just need to get to know them. You will be curious about them and want to know some details about them. You will be willing to share a few details about yourself because that will increase their comfort level with you.

Like anything else, you have to train your brain to think that way if it doesn't come naturally to you. A bonus aspect of this is that if you start using your social skills more effectively, people will act in a more friendly manner toward you, too. That will make it easier to switch on your Social Psyche.

If you're not used to being this sort of person, I can understand finding it difficult to start. If the motor on your Internal Enthusiasm Engine has never been cranked up or turned on, then hesitation is natural. This is where you start seeing internet advice like "Fake It Until You Make It." I understand the intent behind that, but I'm not crazy about the characterization of "faking" anything.

Although I definitely agree that getting out of your comfort zone will feel unnatural at first. But I like to describe it this way. If you've been living in a manner where you're on the periphery of life, in a social sense, and not contributing much, then you're mostly a non-participant. You're there, but not really THERE. You're waiting for life to come to you so you can react to it. Like any good rock, statue or landmark, you're waiting for something to happen.

At some point you have to step over that hard, bright line of waiting and reacting, and you have to start GIVING and LIVING. Instead of waiting for the world to interact with you, you need to bring TO THE WORLD the best you have to offer in terms of positivity, interest in other people, joy and enthusiasm. You can't sit around hoping something fun happens. You get to literally BE the fun!

Even if you're not used to doing that today, you can cultivate those basic social skills and then start bring JOY to people. That's the whole point of social interactions. Sharing joy with each other! Giving them something in terms of attitude, interest and positivity that will increase the overall happiness of the interaction, of the moment, of the world. Your attitude should not be one of taking, faking or waiting. It should be one of giving, living and winning. So don't 'fake it until you make it.' Instead, GIVE IT until you LIVE IT.

Most people will react positively toward your friendly overtures. People tend to respond in kind. There will always be a few people who won't. Let's make two important decisions on that.

One is, it has nothing to do with you. The other is, we have no idea what's going on with them, so we're not going to make any judgments about it. They could have anything from a toothache to a horrible problem. It could be distraction, it could be lack of social confidence.

If people aren't in the mood to talk to you or smile at you, Do Not Judge. Just be grateful that you are in the mood to smile even if they are not. Be ready to engage people. Those who are open to it will respond. Those who are busy or less inclined will be less open. Follow your cues from that.

"Don't 'fake it until you make it.' Instead, GIVE IT until you LIVE IT."

A smile is a direct way to communicate your internal state. That's why the fake smiles leave us feeling more like somebody gave us a curt nod or a brief glance, which is to say they've acknowledged you but haven't exactly welcomed you.

A fake smile is not a social sin, and I'm not trying to suggest that it is one by calling it fake. All I'm saying is that it's communicating something different than a real smile. It basically acknowledges you and indicates that the person you're dealing with is trying to be pleasant.

Pleasant is better than indifferent or, of course, hostile. But it's also a far cry from warm, open, accepting, friendly, engaging or interested. Who do you want to hang out with – someone who's pleasant? Or someone who really wants to get to know you? And they're excited about that fact?

There's plenty of room for Pleasant in life. But I didn't write this book just so you could learn how to be pleasant. Pretty much if you stop scowling you can be pleasant. I wrote it so you can have the ability and MINDSET to take it much further than that if you want to. (Notice I said 'if you want to.' You don't have to befriend the entire neighborhood, the entire apartment complex, the entire office or the entire softball team. Although you could.)

I want you to have the ability to make good connections with whomever you meet. And in my personal sphere even though many people are acquaintances, I still like to go beyond Pleasant, and make things Fun and Friendly if I can. That's just how I roll.

*

Question: People I've known from the past somehow don't remember who I am. I have a great memory so I know who these people are right away. I'm not sure if they really don't remember, or they're just pretending not to remember.

So every time I have an interaction like that I can't help but feel insecure. Either they think I'm boring, or they just want to avoid me. What can I do?

Answer: You may have a better memory than most. You could check with your siblings and see if they have similar memories of these people. But, if you're feeling that some of these people definitely should remember you, and now they don't, that's a problem. I agree that it could be either thing—you made so little of an impression that they don't remember you. Or, they simply don't care to acknowledge you now.

Reminding them is one option. But that isn't really the point, is it? The point is, why did you fade from their memory to begin with? Or what was it about you that they don't really care to acknowledge you now, even if they do recall you?

Take this scenario for what it is. It's a symptom of a problem. It's a problem that can be fixed. So be glad that you've gotten this feedback. Also be grateful that it's made you uncomfortable. That's a great motivation to change! Which is what this book is all about. Notice the first word in the title. CHANGE.

Instead of dwelling on the past, make a change to your present. That change is to become the sort of person people remember. Sometimes people allow themselves to fade into the background, and they literally become "scenery" in other people's lives, rather than a main character in the "movie" that should be your own life. What makes people remember you? In a word: ENERGY. Enthusiasm. Without that, you risk being overlooked. That's the quickest and most effective way to become memorable.

Don't make it a misguided energy. The sort of thing that results in the class clown or the class troublemaker. Yes, those are both attention-getting types. But you don't want to be remembered solely for causing trouble or being the loudest person in the vicinity. (although if the jokes are really good I may stick around for that!)

You want to be remembered for connecting with people, having a good time with them, and generating rapport. That has nothing to do with being annoying, excessively loud, or even overly entertaining. Although if you're good at being entertaining, go for it, but it still isn't a substitute for actually connecting with people.

What's the difference between annoying energy and positive energy? Annoying Energy seeks to glorify itself, or draw attention for the purpose of being noticed. That's only appreciated if you have substantial talents as an entertainer, which most of us don't have. If you're a celebrity or an otherwise talented type, people will be fine with you dominating a gathering. However if you're a regular person, no one really appreciates someone who 1) hogs the conversation, 2) makes a scene, or 3) is loud for the sake of being loud.

What if you're just naturally loud? There are definitely people who fall into that category. Like natural entertainers. If it's part of your inborn disposition, and you get good results with it, let it be. If however you find yourself left out of things, or you get the impression you're annoying people, or just otherwise question if that aspect is a help or hindrance, it might be worth thinking about toning it down. Otherwise you're good to carry on with the entertainment.

It's difficult to communicate enthusiasm without confidence. Beyond changing your mindset, you have to first work on practicing the basic social skills so you can get very confident in that aspect. Then when you communicate your enthusiasm for people it will flow easily.

When I think of people I've met in who have had an Enthusiastic Vibe, they are almost impossible for me to forget. I can remember them like they're right in the room with me. Some of them are people who were pretty peripheral to my life, yet there they are, prominent in my memory! And also think about how true that is, if you review such people in your own mind.

What is the difference between you and them? Perhaps a few social skills that you need to practice to perfection, and then added to that, your VIBE. That is what you need to change. Then you'll be memorable not only to the people you meet from here on out, but you may even be able to establish a connection with those people from long ago.

It's fortunate that this specific series of incidents brought to the forefront a problem. And the problem bugged you enough to want to do something about it. And now you've discovered that the solution isn't that difficult. It'll just take some practice and a mindset shift. It's a good day, baby! I've just handed you the relay baton. It's your turn to run with it!

WHAT IS VIBE?

There's an aspect to this that's hard to quantify. I call this mindset thing your Vibe. We can't measure it, unless we use the measure of other people's opinions. But it isn't anything scientific. Vibe is a mind thing, but more importantly it's a HEART thing. In order to get my mind to feel what I want it to feel, I really have to feel it in my heart first. And if the feeling I need isn't already there, then I work on my thoughts and feelings until I get the heart feeling, the VIBE, that I want.

What does it mean to 'work on' that? I imagine it's different for everybody. For me it could be prayer, meditating on certain types of thoughts, focusing on gratitude, looking on the bright side, finding the good in others, making deliberate efforts to improve my own mood and outlook.

In spite of the problems and challenges that life throws at us, I think we can train our brains to be happier. Even though we might not be able to fix those problems and challenges, we don't have to let that dictate our thoughts or mood. There's no benefit to remaining stuck in an awful place when you can think your way to a better one.

"We can train our brains to be happier."

I'm not suggesting everybody have the same vibe. We're all individuals! Everyone should bring the thing that is unique to them. But for many people what is unique to them is buried deep down, not communicated all that well, or just settled into a less vibrant spot that doesn't allow people to see it. That doesn't make it any less valuable, but it does make it more difficult to discern.

When I say to bring up your social energy level, it will be up to you to determine what that will look like. For some people it may mean a lot of energy. For others, maybe not so much. They're humming along at a quieter level of energy. That's still okay! But if you aren't making the social connections you want to make, you may need to amp that up just a bit so people can get a good look at the real you, and have access to enough energy to want to connect with you.

That may be a warm, quiet energy. But it STILL has to reach out in the direction of other people. Otherwise you just remain behind your force field, unintentionally keeping people out. You need to give off enough energy so people know someone's home, socially speaking. Nobody comes knocking at the door of a dark house.

> ## "You need to give off enough energy so people know someone's home, socially speaking. Nobody comes knocking at the door of a dark house."

I guess I'm speaking non-scientifically when I refer to Vibe. At the same time, it's something that I can feel within myself, and that I can feel coming from other people. So, does a thing exist if you can't measure it, but you know it's there? I've based a whole book on something I can't prove exists, yet I know is there. I know it's in my heart, and it's amplified by my mind, and I'm pushing it out there at some certain distance for other people to feel. What distance? I'm not sure. All I know is I take it into the room with me. And so can you.

Imagine it as a heartbeat. Everyone's got one. But in a social sense I'll call it your Vibe-Line. Picture it going up and down like it would on a heart monitor.

Except, it's your VIBE Monitor. Your Vibe goes everywhere with you, and it's either strong, positive and electric, or maybe weaker than that. It's your job to amp up your Vibe-Line enough so people can feel your happy, positive energy.

You can't possibly communicate that if you remain encased in carbonite, frozen inside a statue or safely tucked away behind your force field. Yes, all of those things are SAFE. But you're living on a very challenging planet! You're not here to 'play it safe.' (Keep in mind someone with a literal Safety Obsession is telling you this!)

You're here to make the most of your brief life because let me assure you right now even if you live to 100 your life is still BRIEF in the grand scheme. So take your normal precautions, but seriously, get out there and start giving it away! Or to put it in athletic terminology, leave everything on the field. That is to say you're not holding something back in the locker room or on the bench, or 'saving it for later.'

There's no point in going to your grave with your greetings ungiven. Your compliments unsaid. Your stories untold. Your happiness unshared. So you must practice those basic social skills daily until you know you can deliver those greetings, say those compliments, tell those stories and share your happiness.

"There's no benefit to remaining stuck in an awful place if you can think your way to a better one."

*

Question: I find it difficult to connect with anyone new. I have some long-term friends, but when it comes to new people it's hard for me to go beyond the superficial stage with them. A friend told me she thinks I'm fine when I need to talk to people at work, but that I seem shy when meeting new people otherwise. I know technically there's nothing to fear, but I can't seem to click with new people. What's my problem?

Answer: Plenty of people find it difficult to meet a stranger. Worrying about what they're thinking, what their impression is of you, and whether or not you'll click is a lot to worry about. If there's anything to leave at home when you're going out to socialize, I'd say "worry" is probably the Number One thing on the list.

Here's a weird way to put that worry to rest. You say you're having the worst time connecting with strangers, and that you never get past the superficial, and that you don't seem to click with them. So, that technically is NOT a worry. This is known as Using Failure To Your Advantage. Don't spend any amount of time worrying about something that you've done nothing but FAIL at. So! Moving on.

Where does that leave you? Basically with a situation which you can treat as a social experiment. You've lowered your expectations to zero. Maybe even zero degrees KELVIN! So, super low.

One way to get past the superficial is having a one-on-one conversation in a relaxed state. Like getting a coffee together. Or grabbing lunch. Or going out for a drink. Or taking a walk. Or going to the gym together. It's difficult to have a meaningful conversation in short bursts! So getting out with someone gives you an opportunity to go deeper.

As an aside, maybe I should develop something like the 60-Second Capsule Convo where you get to learn something deep about someone in a minute or less. "If you had to come up with a dying wish in under a minute, what would it be?" Or I could call it the Two-Minute Drill Dialogue: "Name five things that are most important to you in life, they don't have to be in order." I probably wouldn't try that on an acquaintance though. Maybe with a close friend, just for fun. An Experimental Capsule Convo!

The advice above is predicated on the assumption that you simply haven't had enough time to go deeper with people, and those are ways to create that time and space. Since this is not a new problem, and a friend describes you as situationally shy, then likely you're not going deeper with people because you're not clicking with them. So the self that shows up in these interactions is a guarded self that's overly cautious and not comfortable letting people in.

Your mindset is one of concern. Maybe even 'performance anxiety' to an extent. More worried about how you will appear to them than who they actually are. Even if you give the outward appearance of bringing your defenses down, if your mind and heart are filled with caution, that's the vibe they'll get. And it will prevent you from clicking with that person. I know I told you to leave your worries at home. But if you've been doing this for years, obviously if you leave home the full-sized suitcase of worries, you will still pack a carry-on duffle bag of worries and bring it 'just in case.'

So the conversation is getting sidetracked because you're giving off the Uncomfortable Vibe. Even though you quite possibly already have decent social skills in a general sense. I'm going to suggest you go back to the beginning 'as if' you didn't have those skills. Go back to the part where you need to practice saying hello to total strangers. (like at the grocery store, the bank, the dry cleaners) You need to not treat these people as random ciphers who fill parts of your day.

You need to treat them as if you live in Small Town America, or Hale and Hearty Village UK, and these people are IMPORTANT. Whoa. Did I just suggest a random stranger might be important? Huh. How did I just let out that vital secret? Yes, people are important. Even random strangers.

However we live in a modern fast-paced society that is disconnected from the type of lives people lived, say, 75 years ago. When you were supposed to know who your neighbors were, and you said hello to Mrs. Smith, and you asked after the family of your mail carrier or the milkman. Then you wouldn't think of treating these people like strangers because, basically, they weren't. And now that most people seem to be interchangeable cogs in a giant Indifferent Daily Life Network, we tend to treat them in a pretty perfunctory manner.

So yes, I'm going to create work for you here. You need to start treating each and every one of those workers as a PERSON. A person that you are happy to see, delighted to have a few moments to chat with, and that you care enough about to make a comment, or a compliment, or ask a question of. Once you start doing this on a regular basis you will notice several things. One, it is a skill, that you can get good at as you practice it. Each and every time you go out. Do you want to be lazy, or do you want to have a good social life?

"Do you want to be lazy, or do you want to have a good social life?"

Answer that question for yourself before continuing further. Next, you will find it personally rewarding, as these people are PEOPLE, and it is always nice to have a good interaction with someone that makes both people's day better. Third, the very act of initiating regular Stranger Conversations will serve to reduce your fears and make you very comfortable approaching other strangers in the form of people who might potentially inhabit your social life. That may not sound true to you, but it IS.

That is your homework, as assigned by me. When you've done that for at least several weeks, more probably months, I think you'll start noticing a change in your attitude. Then when you want to approach strangers with joy and enthusiasm, you'll be able to do it. And then you'll have conversations that click.

WHAT IS A GREAT VIBE?

This Vibe I'm talking about. What does it consist of? And why is it important? Well let's dive into it.

Having some vibe means having energy. What makes life different than a picture, a snapshot? Vibe is short for 'vibration' which translates into movement, or, energy. We are creatures of emotion. Your vibe and your energy allows you to communicate that emotion to others. For me that is a positive emotion, so I'm communicating positivity and joy. That's what I want with me in a social situation.

What if you're not a positive person? What if you're not feeling any joy? Well, no one is feeling joy all of the time. But for your social interactions you should at least be able to summon up some positivity and joy for that. If for no other reason than you're happy to see people and be able to hang out with them! Isn't that reason enough to feel positivity and joy? For me it is.

Socializing is about good feelings, good conversations, exchange of information, good times, enjoying each other's company. I associate all that with positivity.

Another aspect of a great social Vibe is thinking out loud. Now, be careful with this one. Say what you're thinking, but try to at least filter it in terms of who you're with and what their concerns might be. In general as long as you have the goal of being respectful of people's feelings first and foremost, it's helpful to censor yourself less. Share what's going through your head as long as it isn't something that will hurt or embarrass anyone.

Another aspect of a Great Vibe: Act Boldly & Hesitate Less. I'm talking primarily about harmless social things. I am NOT advocating risk-taking behavior. So don't throw caution to the wind with your personal safety. However you SHOULD approach that person who looks like they're lost if you can help them (and it seems safe to do so). Or you SHOULD ask the coffee server what they would recommend for breakfast because another opinion would be welcome. Or you SHOULD ask the management to turn the music down if you need to hear yourself think. Or you SHOULD ask for a favor or a freebie, because you never know unless you ask. You SHOULD make that remark to a stranger because you caught their eye and they smiled.

A Great Vibe says hello. You don't just talk to your friends, you say hello to everyone. You greet the strangers! You include everyone where possible. You let the restaurant servers in on the action! They're now part of your gang. It's a vibe of inclusiveness.

A Great Vibe is Decisive. (I have trouble with this one because I like to weigh options!) So I will solve this by either being the one to offer options: "Here's three choices of where we can eat!" or, I don't mind being the one to choose from among options. But don't hem and haw forever. Pick something!

A Great Vibe listens really well. That means listening because you care about the answer. Listening because you care about the person. Following up with good questions because you really want to know. Not listening just so you can hear for when they're done so you can say your thing. A good listener is a treasure.

A Great Vibe likes to interact. Don't eliminate yourself from this possibility if you're not enjoying your interactions currently. That often happens if you're not great at it. If you're on the quieter side, you should still enjoy those interactions that you DO have. Even if they're quieter and more often one-on-one. A quiet positive vibe is still a Great Vibe!

A Great Vibe usually exudes positive body language. This is of the open, welcoming type, with good eye contact, turned toward the person. Not with arms crossed (Unless you're cold). If you're communicating with enthusiasm and positivity, your body language will do this naturally, you really won't have to think about it. So I would focus more on the mindset that causes that, rather than on the body language itself.

A Great Vibe has little fear. This was sort of a huge one for me, thinking back to my fearful school days. I had a lot of fear back then, and was much more comfortable just watching life more so than participating in it. But overcoming that turned out to be a matter of repeated exposure to that which I was fearful of.

That's why I assign you the homework that I do. Repeated exposures. Just like driving a car was scary the first few times you tried it. Then, repeated exposure got you to the point where you can literally have your mind wander to zillions of other things while you're driving, because driving has become automatic. Social fears can be banished in the same way. But it takes lots of daily intentional efforts. Just like driving does. By the time you're done with my homework I'll have you driving the social equivalent of a stick shift!

"By the time you're done with my homework I'll have you driving the social equivalent of a stick shift."

So where does the fear go? Well, it's still worth being concerned what people will think of you. I am to a certain extent, anyway. That's normal. But the key is that even if some individual decides they really don't like me, or we have a terrible interaction, it isn't going to ruin my life (or theirs).

It's just a one-off. My Vibe is still intact. I'm personally going to be fine. You don't have to be liked by everyone. Nobody is liked by everyone. So just get over that idea, and realize everything is going to be fine, even if you run across someone who really, really dislikes you. That's okay. That's what makes the Globe Spin.

*

Question: What do I do when I walk up to a group and it's just silent with everyone on their phones. How do I break the ice?

Answer: Try this: "Hey, who can show me the LAST picture they took on their phone?" Energetic tone. Big smile. It beats standing there quietly waiting for someone to look at you! Don't be a spectator. Life is a full participation sport.

Question: What are your most effective tips on how to socialize, have good conversations and make friends?

Answer: Well that's pretty much this whole book, but I'll try to sum it up. 1) Don't worry about what other people think about you, focus on what YOU think of THEM. 2) Add energy to your interactions. Low Energy = Low Sociability. 3) Bring The Fun.

HOW TO "BRING THE FUN"

I know #3 bears explanation. People ask this all the time. How, how, HOW do I "bring the fun?" Bringing The Fun simply means having a playful, happy vibe, along with an inclusive, energetic outlook. You're not part of the scenery. And you're not excluding anyone. The more people you can bring in, the merrier. You know you're having a good time if the waiter or waitress magically feels like they're part of the party! That's inclusive. That's a Fun Vibe. (That's also "good service," and ultimately a "nice tip!")

You're there to say hello to people. Use their name at least once. Don't overuse it, though, or they will start worrying that you have something to sell them. Bring an enthusiastic energy to what you're saying. Enthusiasm and joy are contagious. As are apathy and gloom. Which are to be avoided for a fun social occasion.

To get in this sort of mood I play fun music before I go out to see people. I focus on what I'm grateful for. And even if I don't know the people, I IMAGINE in my head they're a friend, and treat them that way. That breaks down barriers really quickly! And because I'm pushing this fun attitude out toward them, I'm not worried at all about what they may be thinking of me. I'm lighting up their smiles with my smile. Ignition!

And here's another weird tip. What if you're in a situation that is more intimidating than normal? For example, you're facing an entire roomful of people where you don't know anyone. Or you're seated at a table for a dinner where you absolutely don't know anybody, and they're all with people they know. Or you're the Solo Lone Person at Summer Camp. Or you're starting out at a new school. Or you're lost in a city by yourself. Or your significant other just introduced you to his or her family for the first time and then suddenly had to go out on an errand or make an emergency trip to the bathroom?

In oddball intimidating cases like this, I try to create a mindset where I'm a celebrity. (I know. Weird!) That gives me an extra dose of confidence that I don't normally have. It's like Green Lantern's ring, or Popeye's can of spinach. Or I have more of 'The Force' than Yoda does. So once I tell my brain that I'm a celebrity at least for the next 10 minutes, I can get into a mood where of COURSE everyone will like me and want to talk to me and have fun with me. Because I'm a freaking CELEBRITY.

So I head out there with my Super Famous Celebrity Attitude, and, whaddaya know, people DO like me and want to talk to me. And we have a lot of fun. I really don't need to remain a celebrity any longer than the first few minutes, because by then I'm having a good conversation and I can just be my normal social self. Another important note about the Celebrity Trick—you have to be a nice and approachable celebrity. Obviously being haughty and stuck-up is NOT the vibe you want there. Yeah it's a super odd trick and I only use it occasionally when I feel the situation has the potential to overwhelm me in the sense that I will be affected by the mood of the room instead of vice versa.

*

Question: I think I've developed a bad habit. When I go out in public I'm never sure what to do with my hands. Because of this I end up pulling out my phone so I've got something to hold and look at. The problem is even though it makes me less anxious to do this, I feel like it's keeping me from making connections around me. I'm not sure how to stop myself from doing this. Can you help?

Answer: I have no idea what I do with my hands when I'm socializing. I've never even thought about it. I'll try to notice the next time I'm out!

You know what's funny is that back in my grandparents' generation they used to use cigarettes for the same thing! It was like this whole ritual, with exciting accessories like lighters, matchbooks and ashtrays. And look how that ended up. Lung cancer! Not that a phone will give you a health issue like that, but when you're with people (as opposed to using your phone to touch base with people or connect with them), then the phone is an obstacle that will keep you from connecting with the people right in front of you!

The good news is you're aware of the problem. You can also use it to your advantage, and this is how. There are things that you should be reminding yourself to do socially if you want to make better connections and expand your social circle. So each time you feel that overwhelming temptation to pull out your phone, instead do one of the positive things that will help propel you forward socially.

Examples of those things: go up to someone that you don't know, say, "Hey, I didn't catch your name, I'm Poseidon..." and start a conversation. Or, speak to someone that you do know who's present and pay them a SINCERE compliment. "Vesta, I like that necklace. Do you remember where you got it?" or toss out a fun conversation starter, "I'm taking a mini survey. Have you ever done karaoke? Would you rather be a performer or a spectator?" (I just used this one recently, and there were a lot of fun answers!) Or whatever you can come up with. There are lots of internet ideas for fun conversation starters. There are plenty of ideas right in this book!

Question: It seems nobody really cares about me, and they just take me for granted. When I ask, they say they like me, but I end up resenting them because they won't even acknowledge that I'm not as important to them as other people. I feel they're being dishonest about it. I feel like I'm a nice person and always putting more effort in than they do, and if I just disappeared no one would care. It's just depressing.

Answer: What I'm hearing is that no one in your life openly rejects you, but their words and actions otherwise indicate they don't care, or at least are somewhat indifferent to you. I feel ya—we humans want to feel important to SOMEBODY. It doesn't have to be a huge crowd. But feeling like you're important to no one is a huge bummer.

But here's the thing about that. You can't force people to feel a certain way. The only person you have control over is yourself. If any change is going to happen, that's where it has to begin. So let's flip the game board on them and start over!

You have expectations of others and they aren't meeting them. That approach is doomed to failure because you can't insist that any individual loves you, likes you, or even treats you politely. You CAN change yourself, and how you project that self to others.

You can also be more focused on what you bring to others rather than the other way around. What kind of energy are YOU pumping out there? Are you friendly and positive to: relatives, friends, acquaintances, strangers, social outcasts, pets? Who YOU are should be consistent. If you're putting positivity out there, then you don't need to worry about what you're getting back.

"What kind of energy are YOU pumping out there?"

Now what I suspect you'll say (and I could be wrong), is that yes, yes, I do all these nice things for people and those people still don't care about me.

Well, okay. But WHY are you doing the nice things? Is it to get them to notice you, like you, love you? If you approach life in a transactional way, people sort of sense that and don't like the feeling it gives them. In fact they may take it a step further and accept your (whatever: favors, gifts, attention, money, compliments, you name it) and not give you what you want because they didn't agree to that bargain.

I'm riding a subtle point here, but people want to be valued for who they are, not what they can give you. And likewise, they are inclined to like you (or not) for the same reason. So if your motivation is 'getting' something from them (even if that 'something' is a legitimate human need like love, friendship or a pat on the back), by gosh, their Inner Skeptic will find a way to not give you what you want. Why? Because you need to like them for who they are, and they need to like YOU for who you are. I feel like I'm talking in this maddening circle, so hopefully my meaning is flying out there at you due to the centrifugal force of me slinging it around.

So the point is, just giving people stuff, whatever it is, will not gain you love, friends, respect or even a stick of gum, necessarily.

What's the solution to this impossible conundrum? Well it's this. The goal is becoming the legit person that you aim to be. You need to offer the world your best and truest self with no expectation of a return on investment. Then you swim through the Sea of Humanity until you find your School of Friends.

> *"You need to offer the world your best and truest self with no expectation of a return on investment. Then you swim through the Sea of Humanity until you find your School of Friends."*

I'm not saying to withhold any of that stuff I mentioned earlier (favors, compliments, attention, love, offers of baby-sitting, whatever). But what I AM saying is to put that out to the world because you like and respect people and want to make them happy. Not because you expect something in return from them.

I'll give you an example from my own life. I make food a lot. Sometimes I have extra. (a dozen cookies! Stuffed shells! Blueberry coffeecake! Spaghetti and meatballs! Key lime pie! Pasta salad!) Sometimes I even make extra on purpose. Maybe I perceive that someone needs it. Maybe I just want to share it. Maybe I want someone to TRY it.

But whatever the reason is, it is not because I expect them to march back to my house with food of their own. And I don't give them food so that they're nice to me. I really don't have any expectation at all, other than that they smile at me when I give it to them. That's it! If they thought I had some sort of ulterior motive, that just wouldn't feel right. I've made the claim in the past that Food should be a Love Dialect, haha.

So my motive in any food giveaway is pure joy and altruism. And hopefully I didn't botch the dish and leave them merely with a "thought that counted" and a "container that's dirty." (And as a quick aside there are a lot of other ways of saying "I care." It could be a bunch of flowers, a basket of fruit, an offer to do an errand, a quick text or phone call, a card in the mail not attached to a holiday, send them that picture from your phone that you know they'd appreciate, etc.)

That's how your motives should run as you do things for people. Now the other end of the equation is yourself and how hopeless it feels to not be valued. This is where you need to start making friends, one at a time.

Because friends WILL value you, and they will be happy to accept whatever you're bringing, and they will do things for you in return because they like and respect you, not because you've given them anything. They want to give to YOU, not to a sense of obligation that you've created. Again, here I go with the subtle distinctions, but I swear to you it's a distinction that matters. People don't want transactions, they want FRIENDS.

CHAPTER 9: TAKEAWAYS

1. *Vibe comes from feelings, emotions and beliefs held deep inside you.*

2. *You need to smile with your BRAIN, not just your face.*

3. *Instead of being part of the scenery in other people's lives, become the main character in the movie that is your own life.*

4. *Use Failure to your advantage. If you've persistently failed at something, lower your expectations to zero. Now there's nowhere to go but up.*

5. *Bringing The Fun = having a playful, happy vibe.*

6. *People don't want transactions. They want friends.*

READY, SET, FLOW

I'd like to wrap things up by not only re-emphasizing my most important points and takeaways, but also by very specifically stating what I am NOT saying.

If you skim quickly you might get the impression we all need to be the same happy, joyful, energetic person and that will somehow transform you into a person with good social skills who can make friends and create good connections with people. And you may conclude, "that's not me," so therefore give up before even trying.

Well stop right there. You didn't read closely enough.

We are NOT all the same person. We aren't anything close to being the same person. We share a common humanity that allows us to connect when we approach each other in positive ways. But we are all unique people with an individual story. There is no way anyone should be trying to change themselves into anyone other than who they are. I feel deeply about the sanctity of the individual. We shouldn't attempt to smother our uniqueness under the cover of a Fake Anything. So that is NOT what I'm advocating.

At the risk of repeating myself like the parent that I am, and at the risk of you ignoring me like a tuned-out teenager, we all need to be true to who we are deep down. At the same time, "who we are deep down" can be difficult for people to see if we don't present ourselves in a way that is accessible. And you aren't accessible until you can engage people in a friendly manner, with a certain amount of social energy, and in a way that allows you to (gradually) tell them about yourself as you find out more about them. It sounds so simple, yet it's difficult for so many!

Although I recommend bringing a lot of positivity to the social equation, I absolutely acknowledge the presence of negativity in our lives. Close friends play a key role in helping us deal with that negativity. But even in our worst moments, spewing negativity indiscriminately doesn't do anyone much good. Think of it more as a timed release instead of a septic tank explosion.

I do emphasize bringing more social energy than you're used to doing. Hanging back and waiting for the world to tap you on the shoulder is no way to engage people and make them a part of your life.

I'm not trying to turn us all into loud extroverts. In fact, I'm not trying to turn *anyone* into a loud extrovert. (Although if that's who you are, you keep doing you!)

I know people who are quiet introverts. But the reason I KNOW them is because they absolutely will engage one-on-one or in small group situations. They may not be the last one to leave a party. They may not be telling lengthy jokes. But they will absolutely have a warm and engaging conversation with all the attributes needed to make a friend.

Positivity, Interest in others and Enthusiasm (PIE). Any quiet introvert can have all three of these things. Enthusiastic does not necessarily mean LOUD. People who participate in conversations with a quiet enthusiasm are just as fun and engaging as louder folks who are always talking over you.

You can see the enthusiasm of introverts in the brightness of their eyes, the warmth of their smile, the energy in their tone, the quality of their questions, the thoughtfulness of their answers.

Not only is there room on this planet for quiet introverts, there is an absolute necessity that we have them! There are so many jobs that introverts do better than the rest of us that our modern civilization would probably self-destruct without them. Introverts can be a joy to talk to, especially when you've spent too much time networking in a room with loud extroverts, or people pretending to be such. Give me an introvert and a cup of coffee. We're going to have a great conversation, probably about something deep!

"You can see the enthusiasm of introverts in the brightness of their eyes, the warmth of their smile, the energy in their tone, the quality of their questions, the thoughtfulness of their answers."

Loud extroverts have things to learn too. Like taking time to draw others into the conversation. Adjusting your tone based on whom you're with. Picking up on people's moods, and noticing things about them. Directing the conversation to someone who hasn't had a chance to speak.

Memo to the world: Don't tell people that they need to smile, or that "you're so quiet." Nobody wants to hear that. It just embarrasses the person it's directed at. If you want someone to smile, try "how's your day, what's going on with you?" with a smile on your own face. If you want a quiet person to speak up, say something like, "how about you, Hercules, do you have any ideas on the Global Slinky Shortage?"

Or say, "Hey, Hercules, what was the craziest part of your day so far?" or "So, Aphrodite, what have you been working on in secret? If it's classified, then I'll settle for your most interesting pet story." Those are just my examples, but you can be creative when it comes to questions. The idea is to be open in your questioning. Do it with a tone that sounds like you're interested and BE interested.

The key is not to change who you are, but to change how you PRESENT who you are. Communicating with a lot of negativity is a bad habit. We all have negativity in our lives, annoying things, tragic things, awful things, things that just can't be solved overnight. And everyone has health stuff to one degree or another. That's unfortunately the nature of the planet.

Think of it as a reminder that we're all commuters who don't exactly know where the end of the line is. Yes, we're all literally riding on a Commuter Planet! So we all have things to be negative about. But you don't have to communicate primarily with negativity. And you don't have to think that way, either.

You may find yourself responding in the same old negative pattern. Upon realizing that, notice it, then make yourself rephrase it right away. "Hey, I didn't like how that sounded, I meant to say XYZ." Or "I'm sorry that came out that way. How about ABC."

This can become a game as you retrain yourself into more positive speaking patterns. Give yourself a point for every time you correct yourself aloud. After a certain number of points reward yourself. Eventually you'll recognize how much negativity you've inadvertently allowed into your life, and how much fun you can have while extinguishing this habit. And, it's a GAME. With PRIZES. I'm in!

It would surely be nice if I could just explain in this book how to do things, and simply by reading and understanding, voilà! You could do the things. (Actually for some things that's actually true. Like fixing your smile, or the general look on your face. You can do that right this second. DO IT. Do it NOW!)

But for many things practice is needed. Picture Hall of Fame shortstop Derek Jeter. Did he learn to field a ground ball on the first try? Definitely not! Even if someone told him exactly how to do it, and showed him too, it took many hours of practice before he got competent, and years after that until he got really good, and honestly a few decades more until he became the MVP shortstop who is enshrined in the Major League Baseball Hall of Fame.

Or picture world class ice skaters. Do they know how to do an arabesque, an axel or a spin just by hearing about it or watching someone do it? Same thing with dancers, golfers, pianists, artists, you-name-its.

Now I know what you're thinking. You're complaining in your head that many people get good at socializing without seemingly having to do a bunch of hard work. And it's true that they 'get it' early, and then they build confidence and work on their social skills naturally.

That's the easy way. Although there are plenty of people who have acquired social skills easily and naturally, they could also work to be better and get rid of some bad habits. In other words, we can all improve!

But maybe you're not one of those people and you just feel stuck in the "I'm not good at: Socializing, Making Friends, Talking In Groups, Getting To Know People, Establishing A Friend Group, Expressing Myself Well, etc." Any or all of those things.

So you're Derek Jeter at the age of five with his first glove and baseball. And you're going to have to figure it out and work at it.

The good news is it isn't going to take you decades to get good at socializing. It won't even take you years (although maybe it'll take you years to get GREAT at it). But it probably will take you months of consistent work. I don't think that's too high a price to pay for the ability to connect with people, make friends and HAVE FUN. In fact, how much fun is FUN, really, if you have no one to share it with? Not so much!

If ice skaters can awaken at 5:30 a.m. each morning to hit the rink for a few hours before school, or dancers and athletes can spend a couple hours each day practicing their craft, or artists can keep at the canvas for long hours into the night, then I think you can do the little I ask of you. Which is to take your brief interactions each day, and start turning them into fun 2-3 minute opportunities to practice your social skills.

That's important whether you succeed, fail or are not sure what the heck you did. You keep at it until you start seeing small results. And then bigger results. And then more confident results. And then you keep working at it, and improving on different aspects that you didn't work on before. And yes at first it's work, but as you start getting good at it, suddenly it doesn't feel like work at all. It feels like FUN. Because you can brighten someone else's day. You can brighten your own day. You can take your superpower with you everywhere you go because you KNOW 90 percent of people will respond positively to your attempts to interact in a fun, positive way. (That's a low estimate)

FORGET ABOUT PERFECTION

You don't have to be perfect. You just have to be a little better than you were yesterday.

By gaining these small skills in a gradual way, and repeating them over and over consistently, you will gain confidence that you can do this anytime, anywhere. And then when you're out with people, you don't have to worry about this skill, that skill or the other skill. You won't be thinking about that at all. You can instead focus on the essential point of this book. You can focus on your VIBE, and what you're bringing to the person you're with.

When you're out interacting with people, I don't care where it is, whether it's a social event, a professional event, a public event, a family event, a fund-raiser…doesn't matter. The VIBE you're going for is not "let's just mark time because we happen to be in the same space together." Look at watch. Look at phone. Look at weather. Look at door. Look for the bathroom. No, no, no! That isn't why you're there.

The vibe you want is, "Come HITHER, into my world!" (not meaning it to sound like a Victorian pickup line, but, nice use of a vintage word right there.) Anyway, that's the attitude you should be going for. "I'm excited to be here. I'm ready to meet people, or re-connect with people, or have a great conversation with people"—whatever is available in the moment.

So I'll open up my brain a little and tell you what I'm thinking when I meet up with people. (My brain is like a pinball machine, so I apologize for any lights, buzzers and strange noises you may encounter as I use the flippers to bat the ideas around.) First I'll tell you what I'm NOT thinking about.

I am NOT thinking about any of the social skills that we all use when socializing. Not thinking about my smile, my eye contact, my body language, what I'm wearing, what I'm going to say…NONE of that. I'm also not thinking about what they're going to think 'of me.' Sure, they'll think something. But so what. Not my concern. I'm not worried about whether the interaction is going to succeed or fail.

They could meet me and quickly decide I'm not their type. They may think, in fact, that I'm incredibly annoying. You never know what someone is going to find off-putting. But the point about all of that is to say, if the interaction goes badly I'm not going to take it personally.

"Maybe some other time!" (if it's their mood.) "Maybe some other lifetime!" (if I'm not their cup of tea) Whatever. Life goes on.

So what AM I thinking about? If it's a friend, I'm thinking, "oh wow, here's Minerva, we're going to have a great time talking!" If it's an acquaintance or maybe some casual friends, I'm thinking, "Hey, here's Zeus and Hera, I haven't seen them in a while. Wonder what's new with them? We're going to have fun getting caught up." If it's a stranger I'm thinking, "Well here's a Random Ancient Goddess to hang out with, I hope she has a fun vibe, let's check it out, I'll approach her like we're already friends!" So I'm bringing a Bring the Fun, Bring the Joy, Bring the Happy type of vibe with me. It's a playful frame of mind. Let's have some fun together as we exchange information.

I don't think it's my job (or anyone's job) to "be entertaining," but I DO make an effort to entertain at least *myself* with my vibe, attitude and approach to life. In doing that inevitably I end up sharing that vibe with whomever I'm with. Therefore I'm sharing some playful energy in a "ready to engage, ready to exchange (info), and ready to enjoy" our time together.

Doesn't have to be loud. Doesn't have to be overtly entertaining. I may not have anything to offer other than my opinion of the weather, the fact that my shoes feel too tight or which of our cats did something ridiculous that morning. But armed with ONLY THAT, I think any interaction can be fun if you're willing inject a playful energy into your observations, and to take what people give you, follow up on it with interest and a certain amount of receptive enthusiasm. Not an excess amount of enthusiasm, but instead I'd term it a "Happy To Be On Planet Earth With You Today" type of enthusiasm.

If the event is more serious, like a networking thing, or something involving bankers and lawyers, or just a meeting at which regular serious topics are discussed, well guess what, I still bring the playful vibe, but I try to tone it down so it's more bubbling under the surface, not calling attention to itself, but still ready to inject some playfulness if the discussion permits it.

This is admittedly a bit of a nuance, so it's always better to underplay this than overplay it until you get the hang of what you can get away with. Unless you're at a wake or funeral, or something serious of that nature, you can bring along a playful attitude to just about anything as long as you don't go over the top with it. You don't want to distract from the purpose of The Whatever, or draw excess attention to yourself unnecessarily. As always, "your mileage may vary."

Socializing should not feel like work. It should be fun! And playful! Not something you dread, avoid or fear.

Once you've worked on developing the basic social skills that you can (and must!) practice at every opportunity, it then becomes a lot easier to rescue yourself from that ocean of self-consciousness people can sometimes drown in.

Don't put too much pressure on yourself. If you're just getting the hang of things, head out to socialize with the INTENTION of racking up a few Fails, just to get them out of the way. That really lowers the stakes, and makes everything a whole lot easier!

Then you will find that the successes are happening too, and then they will start outnumbering the fails. Then you will start getting an occasional failure, and it won't matter so much. Because most of your interactions will go well, and you'll be enjoying them.

Your Vibe isn't so much about the Outer You as it is about the Inner You. Your inner self should be ready to get out there and engage with people, and it's your attitude toward others that's going to help you actually connect with them.

THE KEYS TO CONFIDENCE

What about this elusive quality called Confidence? Where does that come from? How does one get it? To an extent, confidence comes from developing certain specific social skills that you can get better at with practice, and knowing that those will work for you when you need them to. The more success you have with it, the easier it becomes and the more confidence you'll develop.

But even more important than that, I think, is the idea that in any given social interaction, if you approach it with the right attitude and use your social skills to the best of your ability, you can have confidence that the outcome will be OKAY, no matter the result. YOU will be okay, no matter what the outcome is.

Say for example, you're asking someone out on a date. The person may say thanks but no thanks. Thanks but I'm busy. Thanks but you're not my type. Thanks, but I'm already dating someone. Those are all a form of NO. Well, so what? You asked, they answered. You used your social skills to make it a fun interaction, even though you didn't get what you wanted out of it. If you played your social skills correctly, they may even regret having to turn you down. But either way, YOU'RE OKAY.

That's confidence.

In part, that comes from having done your homework, having practiced so much that you know if you don't have a perfect outcome now, you'll get a better outcome down the road. It also comes from not everything riding on the response of one single person, whether it be one potential date, one potential friend, one potential business deal, one potential interview.

Because the idea in expanding your social skills is expanding your social LIFE to the point where you have a lot of different possibilities going on. So you don't have 'everything' riding on one particular person, one particular answer, one particular outcome. Instead you have LOTS of possibilities, so you know that if one thing doesn't work out, something else will.

That generates confidence.

So don't beat yourself up over any failure, even if (more like, WHEN) it comes even though you feel like you've gotten good at things. Your feeling of confidence may ebb and flow depending on how your day is going or what your mood is like. That's okay too. That's human. We're all like that. But keep coming back to your center, to your core goodness, your sense that you've practiced these skills, you can do these things, and whatever comes, YOU WILL BE OKAY.

Because if you take the time to develop your basic skills, and then put a positive effort and a happy energy into your interactions, well, that's more than a lot of people are doing. It may even be more than most. You will attract goodness into your life by interacting on that level.

Anytime you socialize with people, embarrassing stuff happens! Goofy stuff. Silly stuff. You have to realize it's funny, not something you have to overly focus on. Just laugh at yourself and move on. Don't worry about your insecurities. Everyone's got some. I don't care if you're senator or a celebrity; a student or a CEO. Insecurities, when used for good, keep us honest, keep us laughing at ourselves. Don't use them for gloom and doom, use them for humor and a healthy dose of humility.

One day many years ago I went to the mall by myself for some shopping.

It wasn't until the end of this shopping trip that some merciful fellow shopper mentioned to me that I had a sock stuck to the back of my sweater in a perfect example of static cling. (Moral of THAT story: always shop with a friend! Or look behind yourself in the mirror before venturing outside.)

So you can sit around and worry about how awful that experience was. Or you can just really get a big laugh out of it. I come from a family where everyone is always in stitches. Personally I do probably at least one ridiculous thing per week, so what story you get depends on when you ask.

Also, when entering social situations have no specific expectations on what the outcome of the interaction will be. Just let the conversation flow and see where it goes. The idea is to have some fun, share ideas and information. Maybe you'll even learn something. You're not putting on a performance, you're Creating A Connection.

"You're not putting on a performance – you're Creating A Connection."

*

Question: How can I get rid of these thoughts that go, I'd try that BUT. Like, 'I'd wear that jacket, but it might look stupid," or "I'd try that joke but it probably would fall flat," or "I'd like to ask that person to hang out, but they probably have too many friends already", etc. How can I change this attitude?

Answer: People are FAR more concerned with themselves than with you. Listening to your doubts is no way to live life to the fullest. Pack your "Buts" and your "What Ifs" into your ugliest mental suitcase. Maybe one with a weird design, a gacky color or a scratchy fabric. Something that has a busted zipper, a wonky wheel and a torn handle. Pack it all up in there, rip off the tags and LOSE THAT LUGGAGE.

Don't get to the end of your life without having taken some risks and LIVED. People from 100 years ago may have had social fears that kept them from doing things they wanted to do. What a shame if they didn't, because 100 years later no one cares, and few people probably did at the time either.

Think about what you'd want it to say on your gravestone (other than the usual stuff like date/name). Do you want it to say, "He never bothered anyone." Or "She never said anything ridiculous." Or "He never embarrassed himself except for that one time and we all remember it." Is THAT what you want it to say? Of course not. You want it to say something like, "He was a great friend," or "She always brightened up our time together," or "He was always willing to try again," or something like that.

I think I might want mine to say, "She made things interesting," or "She brought The Fun," or "She regrets forgetting to unplug the toaster." (joke, that last one) Think about that look on your face. Do you want people to remember you with a smile on your face? Or a bored look? Or Resting you-know-what Face? I can picture people in my head right now and can tell you what their usual look is. You don't even need to be dead and gone! So that's something to think about changing depending on what's staring back at you when you look in the mirror.

I've frequently advocated how you should use your brief transactions as opportunities to develop and practice your social skills. I saw an example of that recently that was not initiated by me that I'd love to describe for you.

I was doing late-night grocery shopping. I greeted the cashier in a friendly manner. She asked if I found everything I was looking for.

"Yup, sure did!"

Notice I could've just said 'yes' or 'yeah' or 'uh-huh' and left it at that. My answer instead sort of implied I was in a good mood and ready to engage.

Which, suddenly, the guy that was bagging the groceries suddenly did! The store had a Whitney Houston song playing ("How Will I Know" if you really want to know), so he said, "Do you like Whitney Houston? Are you a fan?"

This question almost threw me off my game, because 1) I wasn't expecting that in the way of small talk, and 2) He was a high school or college age kid. How did he even know who Whitney Houston WAS? On top of that, even though Whitney was pretty big back in the day, somehow I had gotten this far in life without ever being asked my opinion of her. I literally had to decide right then, on the spot, what my Official Opinion on Whitney Houston was, even though I had never given it any thought!

Also I have this annoying habit of being painstakingly honest. So even though this was an innocent mini-convo at the grocery checkout, I wanted to give him my true nuanced answer. And of course all this contemplation needed to take place in the space of two seconds in my brain because now the cashier was looking at me, wondering how I was going to deal with the Whitney Houston Dilemma.

"Well," I said slowly, trying to give myself enough time to formulate an opinion, "I enjoy her stuff when I hear it, although I don't go out of my way to play it either." (Whew! Honest, but not overly critical or effusive.)

Then the cashier said, "I don't really listen to her."

Okay this cashier also appeared to be late teens/early twenties. WHY does everyone know enough about Whitney Houston that I felt I had been teleported back into the 1980s except for the fact that no one had permed hair or pegged jeans?

The bagger then chimed in with, "She's extremely talented. She has an awesome voice!"

Then the cashier added, "She isn't my style, but she's okay."

At that point I went on to say, "Well I do like that one song she did from The Bodyguard…"

Then the bagger said, "What was that called, something like—"

The next thing you know the guy in the line behind me suddenly shouts, "I will always love YOU." (Thus identifying the song title)

The three of us sort of stared at him for a moment, almost disbelieving what we had just heard. This stranger had just declared his love for us in the checkout lane. That's what it sounded like anyway. And then he laughed, and said, "I love Whitney Houston. She's great."

This guy is maybe in his forties or fifties, so by rights he ought to know who Whitney Houston is. Then, the cashier starts singing the song! Don't worry, she was continuing to ring up my groceries while all this was transpiring. These grocery personnel are clearly multi-talented.

So what WAS that? It's an example of four people who would be having a great time together if we were out at a party. Instead it was a brief grocery store vignette. But the point is every one of us decided to socially engage with each other in a fun conversation, even though it wasn't required. It was initiated by the bagger, who merely picked up on the fact that I was a 'ready to engage' customer, and he decided to run with what was in the immediate surroundings, which was a Whitney Houston song.

Immediate surroundings/situation is always good fodder for a statement to a stranger, or a comment of any type. Both I and the cashier joined in on the banter and participated, and with a fun enough vibe that the guy behind me felt welcome to join in. It almost felt like we were starting to film the beginning of a musical. It was mildly surreal, for a grocery store encounter!

No matter which of the people you are (customer, bagger, cashier, random person overhearing it all), you can choose to participate or not. Now I could also have ignored the bagger's question, or given him a curt yes or no answer and seemed disinclined to talk further.

If you're willing to engage, you won't always get people who will flow with you, but oftentimes you will, and then you can really have some fun! So I usually try to keep myself in that mode, and I end up with a lot of fun interactions from it.

Also I hope you noticed what we created. It was a Circle of Warmth! A pretty big one, actually, we were having so much fun with it that it extended into the checkout lane behind me.

What can we learn from this minor incident? A number of things:

1. Commenting on your surroundings and what's going on in your immediate vicinity is a great way to engage total strangers in a casual conversation (i.e. "small talk.")

2. If you engage in a friendly, open manner, you have a pretty good chance of getting a positive response.

3. Whatever your goal is in participating, whether you're practicing your social skills or just want to improve your mood through a little light-hearted conversation, the encounter can be fun for all.

4. If you are on the lookout for opportunities to interact, you'll find more than you think.

Whitney Houston is clearly a superstar. Even the "Zoom Generation" knows her, for Post Malone's sake! Definitely there are fans who will always love her. (*Note. I only know who Post Malone is due to one of my sons being a fan.)

MOTIVATIONAL MUSINGS

My goals in writing this book were several. One was to give people hope that they can change for the better. Another is to give people reasons why they should. If you'd like different results than you've been getting in your life, why not make the effort? Also I wanted to really make things as simple as possible. So much self-help stuff seems impossible to retain in your brain.

No wonder people are awkward trying to remember and incorporate the specifics! Keep it simple, take it slow, build one social skill at a time, and PERSIST. Persist as if you were training for the Olympics. There is no such thing as 'one and done.' Part of acquiring new skills is developing new habits. It's easier to not make the effort. It's also easier to not speak up. To not reach out. To not bother. To not initiate. To not follow up. To not care.

Do you really want your life defined by all the things you're NOT doing? I don't!

One of my goals is to be your personal cheerleader. I think that everyone can make improvements in how they socialize. Most of you can make huge improvements in a shorter amount of time than you might be imagining. The process and the path are there in front of you. It does require some "work" and "effort." And persistence. And an unwillingness to allow yourself to be discouraged.

Keep a list or a special calendar and make notes about habits that you're trying to develop and mark it down. Or color code it. But keep track. If you do the things you will get the results. If your calendar starts with some activity and then tapers off and goes blank, then you'll know why you're not making progress. So don't let your calendar falter. Fill it up! And celebrate your successes. Soon those successes will be their own reward.

One of the biggest problems people have in terms of improving their ability to socialize is the tendency to want immediate results. Which I totally get! We all want that. We want to be 20 pounds lighter next week. We want that promotion tomorrow. We want to stop procrastinating yesterday. (haha.)

Like any worthwhile goal, success doesn't occur overnight. And if you're hoping for instant success, well that's about as easy as becoming a virtuoso pianist or superstar athlete or computer coding expert overnight. Sure, some people have a natural gift, but most develop their skills through much trial and error, along with persistent practice.

Unfortunately what happens is you try some technique like, "I'm gonna smile more," or "I'll ask better questions," or "I'll invite someone to do something with me," and if it doesn't work out, you give up on it and say, "SEE! I'll never change. I'll always be anxious, awkward and introverted." Instead of being the smooth, social and self-assured person you'd like to be.

But you can get there if you put the work in. It takes one interaction at a time. Maybe a few failures along the way, but those will be steppingstones, not roadblocks. You will get the hang of it. You will do better. You will gain confidence.

You will realize that the party does not start outside you. It starts WITHIN you. You can take it wherever you want to go. The room doesn't have to affect you. Instead, YOU can affect the room. You don't have to sit there and wait for people to judge you. Instead YOU can bring a fun, social vibe and not worry about what they're thinking.

The less you're worried about what they're thinking, the more fun you're probably bringing. Both for you and them. Eventually you'll realize that your ability to be social, to be fun, to connect with people, really doesn't depend on them much at all. It's an ability you carry within yourself, and to the extent that they feel receptive, they will respond to you, and probably in a positive way. Yes of course their response is important, and it matters, but that doesn't affect your innate ability to connect.

A Missed Connection can be for any number of reasons, and most of them have nothing to do with you. So don't worry about those, and don't let them get you down. Because you are equipped to connect. Once you have that skill no one can take it away from you. It won't be on your resume because it won't need to be. Ironically this skill will be almost as important as most of what IS on your resume.

That's why it's worth taking the time and putting in the effort to develop it. Social skills and a Changed Vibe can take your average life and turn it into an extraordinary life. Both in terms of how much you enjoy what's going on around you, and how much joy you can bring to other people. The more selflessness you can imbue into your spirit, the greater positive results you'll have. In my opinionated opinion.

> *"A Changed Vibe can take your average*
> *life and turn it into an extraordinary life."*

So having said the above, do you think that puts me in the camp of 'not caring' what people think? Because I'm Not Worried? Ironically, no, it doesn't mean that. Of course I care what people think. Particularly my relatives and friends. And even the cashiers, bank tellers and dry cleaners, to some extent. Why wouldn't I?

Of course I make an effort to be pleasant, friendly, dressed for the occasion, and have conversations that are reasonably appealing and make sense. (I mean, I at least cared a LITTLE that I was entertaining an entire mall-ful of people with my Static Cling Sock Display.) Caring what your friends think is a key part of friendship.

At the same time I'm not WORRIED about what they think. I'm not worried because my self-esteem is not on the line. My self-worth is not at risk. They are not going to hit at my heart with stabby tools because they're friends. And if a misunderstanding occurs, or they're going through something I don't understand, or I'm going through something they didn't realize, and we hurt each other, then we'll stop and assess the moment, and ask each other, "hey, what's THAT about. That hurt!"

Misunderstandings happen. But that should not rock your self-image. That's contained within you. You can have care. And you can have concern. But you need not have WORRY. That's the point you need to get to on this self-esteem thing. It needs to come from inside you, not from other people. Not sure if that's a social concept or a self-development concept, but, whatever. Bonus!

So I promised I wouldn't leave you with a gazillion numbered concepts stuck in your head by the time you leave this book. I will take the broth and boil it down to the bone. I call it Ready, Set, Flow.

1. **Ready**: You're going to approach that person for a great social interaction. Whether it's a cashier, a clerk, an acquaintance, a stranger, a co-worker or even a friend. Doesn't matter. You should be READY with your genuine smile. You're not just smiling with your mouth, you're smiling with your whole ATTITUDE, and you should feel it particularly in your eyes.

2. **Set**: You've determined you're going to engage, and you're ready with a friendly greeting, a followup comment or question, and even a spare anecdote or observation in case one is needed. You'll KNOW what a friendly tone of voice sounds like. You must reach out with that warm and welcoming voice that automatically breaks down the barrier between you and the other person, and invites them into your world. Give them that Vocal Hug and create that Circle of Warmth.

3. **Flow**: You've got your MINDSET of positivity, openness and INTEREST in the other person. Take that mindset and let the conversation FLOW wherever it goes. Share the joy. Let the other person feel Your Vibe and welcome theirs.

Ready, Set, Flow = Smile, Tone, Mindset.

HOMEWORK

I'm assigning you some homework. I don't want this book to be a case of you got a few tips, thought they were interesting ideas, and then forgot about them. The point is to make a life change for the better. Whether you're starting at the beginning or whether you're great at socializing already.

We can ALL improve. Thus, the need for homework. That's how we're going to develop new habits. I promised you I wasn't going to lecture you or pontificate from on high. So I'm going to JOIN you in doing this homework. If I'm doing it, you can do it too!

I'm calling it the 10-Week Vibe-Boosting Challenge. Why 10 weeks? Research shows that on average we need about 66 days to create a habit that will stick. And 10 weeks is about two months. So I've got something for us to do every single day of that two months! Here are the things. There is one for each day of the week:

1. Greet someone new with a full sentence and a full smile. Not just "Hi," but "Hey, how's it going?" or "Hi, how are you?" or "Sure is nice out today, isn't it?" (Those are samples)

2. Issue an invitation. It doesn't have to be big. It can be an invitation to a meal, a coffee, a drink, to do an errand, to go for a walk or a run or a drive, to a specific event or activity. It can be an invitation to study, to hang out, to watch TV, to play a videogame. BUT! It needs to be someone you wouldn't invite ordinarily.

3. Compliment Someone. If you know their name, use their name when you do it. I want this to be a full sentence. So, "Nice SOCKS!" isn't good enough. A better example would be, "That jacket looks great on you," or "You have a wonderful way with animals," or "You have a great sense of humor," or "You really made a difference on this project."

4. Strike up a Conversation. This needs to be with someone you wouldn't normally talk with. If it's a complete stranger it's okay if it's brief. But go out of your way to engage.

5. Send a connecting text. Again, not someone you would normally text. I decided to tie this in with that old wedding tradition where you have : Something Old, Something New, Something Borrowed, Something Blue. (Don't ask me to explain that. I completely ignored it when I got married.) Anyway, you could pick someone OLD (i.e. someone you haven't texted in a long time, or maybe an older relative if they text), someone NEW (you have their number but haven't had occasion to text them yet. So, create a reason!), someone BORROWED (friend of a friend!), and someone BLUE (someone who's having a rough time and could use some cheering up.) That would take care of four weeks of habit-forming connecting texts.

6. Make a phone call. NOT to someone you normally call. This is one I've been bad at. Every time I call an old friend we have a GREAT conversation, and I think, "Gee, I should've done that sooner!" You could call an out-of-town friend. A grandparent. A relative you haven't seen in a while. An old boss or colleague. A former teacher, coach, neighbor or teammate. What if you feel like you don't have a great REASON to make the call? Try "Hey, something reminded me of you, and I just got the urge to get in touch." We'll have plenty of time to NOT make phone calls once we're dead, right? (Another of my weird Brain Hacks!)

7. Ask a favor. Not a HUGE favor. But sometimes we're reluctant to bother people and we do things ourselves that we could really use help with. And it's a great chance to connect! If you don't have a favor to ask, then find someone who might be busy, or has a lot on their plate, or who doesn't get a lot of help, and OFFER a favor. Still a great chance to connect either way! But get out there and ask or offer.

I don't care which day of the week you do which thing on, but I'd like you to do one each day. That way you're pushing yourself out of your comfort zone on a daily basis. I'd like you to keep track of what you did. You need to do these things while using your awesome social skills that allow you to connect with people. If you need to work on that first, do the practicing with the various clerks, cashiers and baristas around town so you can get the proper VIBE going. Then, bring that VIBE to your 10-week homework assignment. By the end of all this vibing and connecting you should be a better person with a better life. Myself included!

If you hit a speedbump in the form of a cranky person, or someone who's rude, or shuts you down, or scowls at you instead of smiles, or ignores your invitations or refuses to do you a favor, well, remember failure is a steppingstone to success. You have to endure a few failures before achieving anything great.

By the end of this exercise you should recognize that you're developing a

Superpower. One that allows you to connect with people with ease, and have fun doing it. So do your homework and build that awesome Vibe!

*

A final question I want to address:

Question: How can I be someone others love being around? I want to be someone that people like no matter where I go.

Answer: Oh wow. If we were in person I'd be staring at you in slack-jawed amazement. Because, what a question. Doesn't the whole world want to know how? And I'm not confident I have an answer to that. If I did, then this book would be like a mega-bestseller! Haha. Kidding. Well, not being an academic expert hasn't stopped me from giving an opinion up to this point, so I'll give it my best shot!

First off, most of us never reach that rarefied status. We're too busy making sure our opinions are heard, our insecurities are soothed, our accomplishments are admired. In other words, we're too self-involved! It's a matter of degree of course. We're all capable of being unselfish, and oftentimes we do a halfway decent job of reaching out to others. That's why we're able to make friends. But universally loved? Oh my. Let me tell you the story of my Historical Nemesis! Never mind. I don't want to put myself in a mood.

But I'll try to answer the question! Because I've observed life, and obviously I've written a book about improving your ability to socialize, so to a certain extent I've covered at least some of this.

You need to give off positive energy, a welcoming attitude, spread a contagion of enthusiasm and good vibes. It helps to have a sense of humor and an interest in others. You have to really come almost completely "out of" yourself and be focused on the people around you and what's special about them.

So you joke with them, make up a nickname for them, remember their stuff. You accept them for who they are. You're comfortable in your own skin, happy

240

to reveal "a bit" about yourself, but definitely not an excessive amount unless of course it's one-on-one. Your expression is playful, approachable, ready to engage. You make people feel special. You're not afraid to tease (nicely!), you're not afraid to introduce yourself, to welcome someone to the group, to include those who hang back.

You come up with ideas. You compliment others IF you have something sincere to say. You joke with people about their STRENGTHS, not their weaknesses. You turn up the temperature of the room both with social energy and personal warmth. You are fully present, not distracted. You fear nothing. Because there is nothing to fear.

At its essence you have to love people, love being with people, and care even about those you have minimal interaction with, or in all likelihood will never see again. Yes, even those people! Because that type of acceptance of and interest in others is a Universal Vibe that people will pick up on. Most people won't bother putting out that kind of vibe to people they don't see much, or will never see again. But if it's innate in you to be that way, it will come out and it will touch those in your vicinity, even people you don't know well or even at all.

These are the sort of people that others remember from having met them once. They make that much of an impression. I don't know many people with that kind of vibe, but I have met a few. They are extraordinary and most of them don't even know it. So I stand back in awe of such consummate socializers, while I clutch my insecurities to my heart. Sure maybe we all wish we could be that way. But it's really a fearless place to be. Where you have no worries about what people think because you're too busy giving it all away.

Most importantly their goal is not to be loved by you. Their goal is to connect with you. Simple as that. It's funny how chasing love makes it flee from us like a beautiful butterfly that's impossible to catch with our outstretched, grasping hands. But if you relax and make an effort to not only hear what people say, but to see what's deep inside them and feel what's in their hearts, then, sometimes, that pretty butterfly manages to gently land on your head or your shoulder or your knee.

So a lot of that is attitude and life outlook and an almost incomprehensible confidence. But at the same time it assumes a command of the basic social skills as a foundation, which is what I've tried to address in this book. Is that type of Vibe something you can achieve with the goal of becoming that way? I honestly don't know. It's really something I'd call a Fearless Agape Lifestyle, exhibiting a sort of love and connectedness that not many achieve.

I really didn't want to answer that tough question, but now I guess I'm glad I did. It gives us all something to shoot for!

WRAPPING UP

To hit some other final thoughts, I hope you're not thinking "Wow, this is all too much, I don't want or need a life overhaul. I'm comfortable in my small space." Well maybe you are, and I don't necessarily take issue with people who feel like they don't need a change.

Change is hard, and maybe for some it isn't necessary or worth the effort. But if you want something DIFFERENT, if you think you have room for improvement, or just would like to see what happens if you try out something new, well now you've got a place to begin. And a reason to start. It doesn't have to be an overwhelming overhaul. It could just be a tiny tweak.

Maybe we can make life better one interaction at a time. Many of us go around safely ensconced in our self-protective bubbles. Wouldn't it be nice if we could reach out more often, even if we need to vanquish our reluctance to do so. Wouldn't it be nice if we could connect instead of just safely keeping to ourselves. Wouldn't it be nice if the world became a better place because more people took time to care, to listen, to share, to say hey I understand.

We could make an effort to dissolve those invisible force fields that stand between us and another person. Between us and the world.

When you're out there meeting another person (whether you know them or not), the primary thing you're trying to communicate is not words, or an idea, or anything other than an EMOTION. And that emotion is one of joy and happiness to meet them, with a hint of associated confidence that this is going to be a great interaction. You're not worried about what they'll think of you. You're focused on what you will bring to them. Period. End of story. Don't worry about what you did with your hands. (Still don't know what I do with my hands.)

If you can keep focused on that ONE THING, instead of the myriad other things that will just weigh you down and confuse your brain, you will do fine. The goal is to release yourself out of your judgy, self-critical brain, and into the flow of positive emotion that you are TRULY capable of bringing to other people when you give yourself permission to do so. All it takes is some focused, persistent practice and a personal pep talk.

I want to thank with anyone who has stuck with me this long in the book. I'm honored if you read this far. I hope after all this you will consider me a friend. I've just poured my heart out to you so there ya go. And I hope some of us get to meet someday. I have some cloud formations I'd like to describe to you. Maybe a recipe to share. And a cat tale or two.

I want to close this book with a prayer I'd like to offer for all of us. It is an Old Irish Prayer.

May God give you...
For every storm, a rainbow,
For every tear, a smile,
For every care, a promise,
And a blessing in each trial.
For every problem life sends,
A faithful friend to share,
For every sigh, a sweet song,
And an answer for each prayer.

Amen baby! Thanks for hanging out with me, I definitely enjoyed it.

ABOUT THE AUTHOR

Patti Panara lives in Lakeland, Florida with her husband, two college-aged sons and four cats. She is a graduate of Mount Mercy Academy, Lehigh University, Clarion University and the University at Buffalo. Former career amusements include public relations, advertising and marketing for Packard Electric Division of General Motors, Brand Names Sales and the Niagara Frontier Transportation Authority.

By the same author: novels *Buffalo Winged* and *Sisterly Advice*, available on Amazon

Learn more at PATTIPANARA.COM

9 780972 601597